KINGS OF THE ROAD

A Journey into the Heart of British Cycling

By Robert Dineen

Aurum
Press

First published 2015 by
Aurum Press Ltd
74-77 White Lion Street
London N1 9PF
www.aurumpress.co.uk

A catalogue record for this book is
available from the British Library.

ISBN 978 1 78131 354 1
eISBN 978 1 78131 476 0

Typeset in ITC New Baskerville by SX Composing DTP, Rayleigh, Essex
Printed and bound in Great Britain by CPI Group (UK) Ltd, Croydon, CR0 4YY

CONTENTS

PROLOGUE

For anyone familiar with the history of British cycling, the scene emerging on Blubberhouses Moor is an unlikely one. On a sunlit July morning, there are several thousand of us awaiting the Tour de France peloton; men and women, young and old, many in Lycra, some in their club's gear, a few phoning home to ask if the TV helicopters overhead have caught them on camera. Racing bikes are strewn across the turf, Mexican waves have flowed through the crowd and a bagpipes player, also in Lycra, is belting out his third song since I arrived, yet the Tour de France peloton is not expected here for at least another hour.

'It's incredible, all of it,' says Michael Breckon, my companion and a stalwart of the sport, who has arranged for a group of us to take part in this magical weekend. The scene is especially moving for him because he grew up in nearby Harrogate, where today's historic stage will finish, with Princes Harry and William watching among other luminaries. Michael has been involved in every age of cycling, golden or otherwise, in Britain since the 1950s. As a shop errand boy who ran deliveries on his bike, he defied his middle-class mum to take up what was strictly a working-class pursuit. As a superb time-trialist, he competed in the sport when it was still recovering from the 'civil war' that tore it part. As a national team manager, he held a key role when cycling's popularity sank into a depressing decline, becoming, as another cycling old-timer put it, a refuge for 'loners, eccentrics and the occasional lifelong enthusiast'.

'If you'd told me that the Tour would come to the roads I cycled on as a kid, that I still ride on, and that there would be this amount of people . . .' Michael says, his voice trailing off.

The numbers that have turned out for the spectacle in Yorkshire are certainly impressive. Police will estimate that five million people lined the streets to watch the Grand Départ of the 2014 Tour de France, with three million of them travelling in from beyond the county borders. Christian Prudhomme, the Frenchman who is director of the Tour, has been so moved by the scenes that he will declare it the most successful Grand Départ of all.

Nowhere has the sport's recent resurgence in popularity in Britain been more memorably expressed. Presumably the spectacle will help to ensure that the renaissance continues, adding yet more recruits to the three million of us who cycle in Britain now at least once a week, filling the urban bike lanes and drawing thousands to sportives, and encouraging governments to invest hundreds of millions of pounds in making roads better suited to the pursuit. Presumably it will also help the already burgeoning cycling industry, with its equipment and clothing and touring holidays, its increasing numbers of magazines and websites (and, yes, books). We live in straitened times, but cycling is booming.

Just consider the group of friends that Michael has gathered.

They include a retired Army officer who runs cycling holidays across old battlefields, several senior executives who would rather network in the saddle than on the golf course, a middle-aged woman who trains almost as hard as any leisure cyclist I have met, and a geologist who chooses his work according to the quality of cycling country close to the dig site. Another is father to a recently retired British world champion – Katie Colclough. Perhaps Britain has produced so many world champions in recent years that it is hard to organise a cycling trip without bumping into somebody with a connection to one.

From Sir Bradley Wiggins, Mark Cavendish and others who have ridden on the road for Team Sky, to Sir Chris Hoy and Britain's all-conquering track team, the success of Britain's professional cyclists in the twenty-first century has, of course, been crucial to the sport's resurgence. They have helped to inspire millions of people to take up cycling or to pursue it more seriously than they previously had, or, in some cases, to embark on a career in the sport.

As a result, the cyclists and their stories are deservedly well known. We have read about Wiggo's mod music collection and his absent father. We have marvelled at the story of how Chris Froome learnt to ride on African plains. We know how hard Victoria Pendleton's father pushed her when she was growing up. They all rode at a time when cycling was in the mainstream, so they were all asked to tell their tale.

But what about the heroes who competed before cycling's renaissance? Have all their stories been properly told? Aside from a few notable exceptions – Tom Simpson and Brian Robinson, for example – I think not because I have spent the past year interviewing a selection of the most compelling and found that most of them had rarely, if ever, been asked to tell their tale in any depth. Though this seemed an oversight, I was glad to be given the opportunity to correct it because their stories were often fascinating. To me, their achievements were especially inspiring because they lacked the support provided to the modern cyclist, forcing them to make even greater sacrifices than their successors have done and to overcome even longer odds.

In an attempt to write a character-based and unashamedly idiosyncratic history of the sport until the turn of the new century, I spoke not necessarily to the most successful cyclists of the past, but to those whose careers I found the most interesting. Often they were individuals whose name cropped up the most frequently while I was riding with my club, delighting in cycling's rich but often untapped oral history. Always I chose only those subjects whom I could meet, picking interviewees from successive generations, in the hope of demonstrating to the many new cyclists in Britain what the sport used to be like and how far it has progressed. This meant speaking to people at different levels of the sport, too – at the grass-roots and the elite. It felt appropriate because, historically, the connection between the different levels of cycling seemed unusually strong, at least compared to more popular sports. I have also taken the liberty of writing about my consequent journey from being an outsider to the very heart of the sport. I was inspired by what Michael said to me once: 'I think it was Cicero who said that, without an understanding of the past, the present is of little interest. You have all these new cyclists and there is so much history for them to discover. You could fill several books with the stories still waiting to be told.'

CHAPTER ONE

A rebel recalls the 'war' that tore his sport apart

In a dining room above a pub in Covent Garden, the great and the good of British cycling's past are swapping mildly inebriated insults across the floor and, frankly, I am concerned. If the men of the Pedal Club – and it is only men, unfortunately – are in the mood for making affectionate fun of one another this afternoon then I fear that, as the post-lunch speaker, I am about to feel the sting of their sarcasm.

I shouldn't have been surprised. For the cycling writer, the Pedal Club is potentially the most difficult audience of all, given that it grants membership only to those men who have made some 'significant contribution' to British cycling. Already this afternoon, for example, I have spotted Steve Heffernan, Commonwealth champion on the track in 1974, Jim Love, a veteran of the 1948 Olympics track squad, and Keith Bingham, the recently retired doyen of cycling writers, among many other illustrious figures I have not recognised. If you do not know your subject these men will find you out.

My brief is to discuss the biography I have recently had published of Reg Harris, the great post-war sprinter who conquered track cycling like no Briton before him. Writing it, naturally, was a labour of love, requiring eighteen months of detailed research and a lot of burnt midnight oil, so I am confident of holding my own when talking about him. I am just worried that my limited background in cycling is about to be exposed.

For until I stumbled upon Reg's story while researching the 1948 Olympics in my job as a sports journalist, I was no more interested in cycling than any other sport. I rode to work, occasionally ventured out on the bike into the Essex countryside near my home in east London and took a keen interest in the Grand Tours but that was about it. I have nothing like the experience of any of the men in here and I am concerned that will upset them. What right did I, an interloper, have trying to chronicle the life of a man who would have been a hero to a good number of them? None, really, other than that I was fascinated by him.

I decide, then, that my best hope is to stick closely to the facts of Reg's life rather than try to engage in broad cycling comment that might reveal my technical shortcomings. I tell them how Reg, an illegitimate child, was raised by a single mum in a Bury tenement and how he climbed the ranks of the domestic amateur scene, winning all manner of prizes – silver cutlery, pocket watches, china sets – which he traded in at the local pawn shop.

I earn nods of recognition from the older members of the club as I describe the professional scene that Reg encountered on the Continent in the late 1940s, one that he embraced whole-heartedly, thrilling huge crowds wherever he went. He also inspired thousands of kids back home in Britain at a time when many working-class and lower middle-class people cycled because to them it was the only affordable means of transport.

Turning to his unlikely comeback in the 1970s, I wonder just how much of it I should discuss. Reg paid off his rivals to allow him to win the national title at the age of fifty-four, but I am worried that the club might fear my exposure of it represents spitting in the soup. 'Oh, don't worry, we all know what happened,' says one diner, spotting my hesitancy. 'We all know what he was like, too. Quite the cocky sod, to be honest.'

Laughter ensues and I feel an overwhelming sense of relief. I have reached the end of the speech and not raised a single heckle. To judge by the respectful silence, I think they might even have been engaged. I never hoped to reach the standards set by the Olympic and world champions who have addressed them over the years, but I might just have held my own.

The Q&A begins. 'So, what did you think of our sport?' one diner says.

Sorry, *your* sport?

'Well yes, I mean, presumably you're not a cyclist.'

Rumbled. In my language alone, my shortcomings had been revealed. I confess that I have come fairly recently to the sport and attempt to placate him with an honest account of how much I enjoyed being immersed in it. I trawled archives dating back to the 1930s and was intrigued by the subculture I discovered. I spoke to stalwarts of the sport about Reg, learnt about their lives and wondered why their stories had similarly not been told.

'Perhaps you could write about them in another book, then,' he says.

'It is funny you should say that', I reply, 'because negotiations on one have already begun.' But while I write this one, I will also fulfil a recently acquired ambition to learn how to become a proper cyclist, too.

To begin, a little background, starting with a bike race in the late Victorian era. This was 1894, shortly after the introduction of the safety bicycle that has been the prototypical design for all bicycles, with its diamond-shaped frame and identically-sized wheels. At the time cycling was popular mostly among middle and upper-class gentlemen, who were the only ones who could afford a bike, but it was unpopular among many other road users.

The event was important for what happened when two cyclists from the North Road Club in Hertfordshire accelerated past a woman driving a horse-drawn carriage, prompting her animal to rear and her briefly to lose control, which in turn caused the riders to crash. No one was hurt but the woman was appalled and complained to police who, in turn, threatened to ban cycling from the roads within their jurisdiction. The threat was not carried out but it sparked fierce debate among the British cycling community at large, many of whom could still recall the attempt sixteen years earlier to have their pastime banned from the roads – an attempt that failed only when an amendment to the Highways Act did not make it through Parliament. Quite how the argument escalated to the extent that it did is uncertain but escalate it did, eventually prompting the National Cyclists' Union (NCU) to ban road racing altogether, rather than risk cycling itself being outlawed.

This was draconian, a form of 'voluntary apartheid', as the cycling historian Tony Hewson called it. It was also desperately sad for anyone with an interest in a sport in which Britons had excelled ever since James Moore, the Suffolk-born veterinary surgeon who moved to France in his youth, won the first recorded bike race, around Parc St Cloud in Paris, as well as triumphing in what for a long time was claimed to have been the first organised road race, from Paris to Rouen, in 1869. Its status has since been downgraded, after evidence emerged of other, lower-profile races preceding it, but its significance is undoubted and, at the time of writing, you can see the 'boneshaker' bicycle on which Moore won the race, with its differently sized wheels and two-tubed frame, at Ely Museum in Cambridgeshire.

British riders still enjoyed international success in the 1890s, too. Perhaps most famously Jimmy Michael, the five-foot one-inch Welshman, won the world one hundred kilometre title in Cologne in 1895, and his great rival, Arthur Linton, who like Michael was raised in the Rhondda mining village of Aberaman, broke the world hour record and won the prestigious 350-mile race from Bordeaux to Paris in 1896. Many believe that Linton's death two months after that second, formidably demanding achievement was the first in cycling connected to doping.

The NCU's ban, however, meant that Britain's road-racing pedigree fell into rapid decline, just as the sport was about to take on a higher profile abroad, with the inaugural editions of the Tour de France and Giro d'Italia staged in the first decade of the new century.

Not that British cyclists allowed their competitive spirit to be entirely quelled. The renowned Frederick Thomas Bidlake emerged to take a prominent role. In time he would lend his name to the annual award – the Bidlake Prize – given to the British cyclist thought to have made the most significant contribution to the sport over the previous year (the list of past winners reads like a who's who of British cycling greats – Cavendish,

Wiggins, Burton, Simpson, Harris, among many lesser-known administrators, too) and he was an outstanding cyclist in his own right in the late nineteenth century, but it was as president of North Road CC that he made his own most significant contribution. Bidlake and North Road decided that the best response to the ban on road racing was to organise time-trials instead. They were not the first instances of that type of racing but the North Road events were pivotal for they led to time-trials emerging across the country in lieu of massed-start road racing, which had ceased altogether until the occasional closed-circuit event was allowed at motor racing venues, a poor substitute for the real thing.

To ensure that time-trials remained low-profile, and thus did not upset the NCU and the police, they took place in covert circumstances: at dawn, on courses with code names – a letter-number configuration used to this day – and with entrants required to wear black. Known as 'private and confidentials', they spawned their own ruling body as well, the Road Time Trials Council (RTTC). Time-trials (known as TTs) proved so successful, and so acceptable to other road users, that the NCU came to recognise them on condition that the surreptitious circumstances in which they took place remained.

For the next four decades, the road-racing scene in Britain comprised TTs. At the peak of their popularity, in the 1940s, they had become so widespread that it was estimated there were 150,000 active time-trialists in Britain. At the same time there was growing opposition to the ban on massed-start road racing, fuelled by news from the Continent of the epic races that were taking place. As Tony Hewson, who raced successfully in the 1950s, put it, road racing in Europe seemed 'magical', especially to young men frustrated by the resistance to change that the NCU and RTTC – the two of which comprised many of the same officials – continued to exhibit.

As a result, on 7 June, 1942, with roads near deserted because of the war effort and municipal authorities concerned with more pressing problems than the potential safety issues that a cycle race might spark, Percy Stallard took it upon himself to make a little piece of history. The former British squad cyclist organised the first massed-start road race in Britain in the twentieth century, from Llangollen, in north-east Wales, to his home town of Wolverhampton.

It was an epochal event. The NCU banned the twenty-nine 'rebels' who started the race and the officials, such as Stallard, who organised it, preventing them from entering other cycling events across the country. The sport's one dedicated magazine, *Cycling*, lambasted them. So, too, did officials in clubs across the country, yet Stallard and his colleagues cared not. In running the event with the co-operation of the police and in attracting a reported 2,000 spectators to watch it, they had proven that road racing could take place successfully in Britain.

A few months later they organised a second race, the Circuit of the Wrekin, which circumnavigated the 400m hill in Shropshire after which it was named. Stallard set up his own ruling body, the Midland League of Racing Cyclists, which inspired affiliate branches in London and the north of England, and 'illegitimate' races began to take place elsewhere. In November 1942, and at Stallard's instigation, the regions merged to form the British League of Racing Cyclists (BLRC). By the next year, the number of 'leaguers' had reached 450, which was far fewer than the 60,000 cyclists who were signed up to the NCU, but it was enough to represent an insurrection.

Cycling in Britain was in crisis, one that serves as the starting point for the history that this book will attempt to trace. If British cycling can be said to have a 'modern' era then it began not after the Second World War – as is the case for other fields of study – but during it, with Stallard's seminal event. This era is worth examining because the 'civil war', as it was known, that followed those rebellious road races has shaped the sport. Some would even argue that British road racing would look very different now were it not for what happened then.

In a book that will link generations together with profiles of seminal or simply interesting individuals, the first interviewee I have chosen is Dave Orford, a former racing cyclist, prominent official and still an outspoken presence within the cycling community. I have heard about him anecdotally but also read a few of the many letters that he has submitted to *Cycling Weekly* over the years, usually correcting a historical point or contributing to a debate about the sport's past. Previously one of the most active 'rebels' who dared to race on British roads, he appears to be more engaged on the subject of what exactly happened then and what was the civil war's legacy. As I arrive at the train station close to his home in the small Derbyshire town of Belper, I am hopeful that an enlightening afternoon lies ahead.

Belper is a pretty place, with quaint shops and long rows of old, low stone walls. Dave lives on a street of terraced houses on a hill that rises sharply as it leaves the town for the countryside to the north. Though not all the houses on his street are numbered, it is easy to spot Dave's home for his is the only one with an illustration of a cyclist in a yellow jersey in its front window. This is not the first time I've seen this image adorning a cyclist's home, showing the owner's allegiance to the sport, but I've never seen an interior like the one I discover behind Dave's front door. 'This is like a museum,' I say, aghast at the amount of cycling memorabilia on display. Posters and photographs cover the walls from ceiling to floor, depicting everything from old cycling heroes to Dave himself, in competition and receiving awards. There is much promotional literature for long-forgotten races. Sideboards and cabinets house trophies and certificates from Dave's career, from his younger days as a semi-professional – which meant he was provided with a bike and a jersey – to his latter years as a veteran world champion. I could spend a good hour happily studying this material, but it is, well, a little unusual. I mean, if cycling was indeed once a refuge for eccentrics, my host must have been chief among them. 'Hmm, live alone then?' I venture.

'Oh yes. I decided after my second relationship fell apart that I would never live with a woman again,' he says, without any apparent hint of regret. He explains how he was once tempted by a beautiful neighbour to leave his wife of twenty-five years only to discover that the neighbour would not accept Dave's first love.

'I was a prat really,' he says as we sit down to a bottle of red wine and a box of cakes that he bought especially for my visit. 'This woman had eyes like Sophia Loren's and she spirited me away, but there were rules, you see, and it didn't work out. Her final words to me as I left her home were, "I am not prepared to play second fiddle to a bike." But she knew I'd been a bike rider. What was I supposed to do?'

If cycling is an unforgiving mistress, Dave submitted to it wholeheartedly from the moment he first began riding as a teenager, shortly after his mother died, because it provided an emotional release for him. By that stage his dad had died, too.

Dave suspects that his parents both succumbed to asbestos poisoning; his father worked in a factory and his mother would wash his work clothes. This left Dave to be brought up by an uncaring stepfather, with cycling being an escape from his home life. 'It was loneliness really,' he explains. 'Being at home was a pain in the arse. I wasn't wanted there, so I was going out on these rides. It's calming when you're with nature, riding along. I tell you what, though. I never used to go past the infirmary where she died. Never wanted to.'

In search of the company of other cyclists, he joined his local branch of the Cyclists' Touring Club, but this liaison didn't work out either because the CTC members were mostly averse to the road racing that had quickly begun to stir Dave's imagination, especially the continental version of it that he would see in imported French magazines. He couldn't read French but he could still look admiringly at the photographs of iconic cyclists such as Fausto Coppi, Gino Bartali and Rik van Steenbergen, to name only the three men that he identifies. They were sufficient to excite the imagination of a boy growing up in far away Derby. 'We would ride across to Wolverhampton every Saturday afternoon – we had to work in the mornings – to look in the window of this shop that sold French magazines. I can even remember its address – 30 Broad Street. Just to be able to see pictures of these men was wonderful,' he says, having thought nothing of making the forty-mile trip as a teenager to earn such a privilege.

By the time Dave started racing, shortly after the Second World War, the number of leaguers had trebled to more than 1,000, and continued to grow as soldiers returned home. Soon, the division between union members and leaguers was evident at every level of the sport. Roger St Pierre, the cycling historian, recalled how the two groups frequented different cafes, used different bike shops and swapped insults when they encountered one another on the road. This rivalry even descended into violence. 'Oh, it was bad enough that there were several occasions where there were major fights,' St Pierre said. 'You're in a league club and there's a union club coming towards you: it's pumps off and whack them as you go by.'

For all that the rift was unwelcome and damaging to the sport's reputation, the thrill of the battle was often exhilarating for the leaguers. 'The civil war was awful and it set the sport back dramatically in Britain, but being a rebel is appealing when you're young,' Dave admits, with a smile.

They distinguished themselves from the old guard by their cultural tastes, too. Leaguers staged events such as the Charlie Parker and Lester Young Memorial Races, named after prominent musicians in the bebop jazz scene that was considered the rebels' music in 1950s America. Dave himself played double bass in a jazz band, and indeed jazz music is playing in his home as we speak.

Partly because of their shared opposition to the BLRC, the NCU and RTTC were by now closely aligned and remained determined to quell the rise of what they regarded as an unruly, suspiciously foreign pursuit. In official meetings and in their declarations to the press, they accused the BLRC of being uncivilised, and even politically dangerous, at one point claiming that they were a front for the Communist Party. Not that the leaguers would have been overly insulted by this as they had established connections with the FSGT, the French communist cycling body, and the Republican sports movement in Ireland. As St Pierre said: 'They were young and radical. Of course they were left wing.'

At the time, *Cycling*, the predecessor to *Cycling Weekly*, was the only publication serving the sport and was fiercely supportive of the NCU. It offered only limited coverage of continental racing, almost none about its nascent domestic cousin, and frequently published editorials critical of the league. It was through frustration with this political stance that cyclists gave it what remains its nickname: the Comic.

To fill the void that *Cycling*'s editorial stance created, the league established its own publication, *The Leaguer*, which it posted to members in return for a subscription. Copies of it are scarce. You will not, for example, find it in the archives of the British Library even though it is designed to store every publication in the English-speaking world. Nor does *The Leaguer* turn up online.

Until today, I have never actually seen one, but Dave has unearthed a copy for my visit and placed it among the pile of literature relating to the British League of Racing Cyclists on his coffee table.

As I carefully turn its yellowing pages, I feel like a historian of modern Russia would on discovering an early copy of *Pravda*. Subtitled the 'premier paper for racing folk', it combines race reports from home and abroad with evocative photographs. One depicts Dave Bedwell, described by *The Leaguer* as the 'Iron Man of Romford', as he prepares to launch his celebrated sprint on a quiet village road. Beneath it are advertisements for Viking and Hercules bikes, while the news page details the latest developments in the battle with the NCU and includes an editorial that Stallard has written.

Dave knew Stallard well. In Dave's role as road race secretary for the East Midlands branch of the league, he ranked among Stallard's chief lieutenants. What was the great man like? 'He was like the Führer!' he says, laughing. 'He'd fall out with everybody, including me. It was his way or the highway, but we owed him so much that we didn't take any notice [of his temper].'

Dave's job required him to consult with the police and design race courses across the region. More often than not he would compete in them too, and invariably fared pretty well, eventually reaching 'independent' status, as semi-professionalism was known then. He competed in some of the league's biggest races, including their blue riband event, Brighton to Glasgow, which by the end of the decade covered 793 miles over seven days and attracted crowds estimated to be 20,000 at both the start and finish alone.

Though it was some spectacle, circumstances for the riders were formidably difficult. In an age of austerity, many lacked the money to pay for accommodation and instead slept rough overnight between stages, after stealing into a farm outhouse, say, or taking shelter in a hedgerow.

The cost of staging the events was also prohibitive and, by 1950, the BLRC had begun to incur crippling debts. The civil war had cost the NCU, too, both in lost membership fees and the damage done to its reputation, but still they refused Stallard's repeated attempts to reach some form of truce.

The NCU argued that it still feared that the safety problems inherent in road-racing threatened the legality of the sport, but the police's silence on the subject undermined that. Having managed to arrange talks with representatives of the Department of Transport in 1945, in which the league put forward the case for its legitimacy, it had not suffered a word of official complaint since.

Finding veterans of the civil war who were sympathetic to

the union is difficult, making it hard to present a balanced account of what happened. Even so, there seems no reason to doubt Dave's view on why the union was so reluctant to engage with the BLRC. 'The old officials in clubs just wanted to run things as they had been for years,' he says. 'The NCU and the RTTC were the same people, they had all the power and they desperately did not want to lose it. At an official level, the whole thing got quite nasty.'

To illustrate his point, Dave directs me to a photograph beside his front door of a cyclist called George Lander, winner of the 1950 Brighton–Glasgow when he was only nineteen. Short and raven-haired, he is sucking in lungfuls of air while demonstrating the climbing ability for which he was renowned. Many considered Lander to be the outstanding talent of his generation and the British cyclist of that era who was most likely to make an impression on the professional scene on the Continent. The Italian team Frejus thought likewise and, shortly after his win in Scotland, offered him a contract. To accept it, Lander needed to relinquish his BLRC membership and join the NCU as the union was the only British authority that the UCI, the sport's global ruling body, recognised and therefore only the NCU had the power to issue an international racing licence.

Rather than immediately accede to Lander's request to join, the union waited until he had relinquished his affiliation to the league and then declared that he was banned for life from joining them. With his hopes of making it as a professional crushed, Lander tried to return to the league in the hope that he could at least continue to compete in Britain, only for the league to bar him too as punishment for his defection. When he committed suicide about a decade later, his widow linked his prolonged psychological decline to what he had gone through as the victim of the sport's political impasse. 'She said it was all to do with that,' Dave says. 'The whole thing was a disgrace, unbelievable. They played him like a football.'

For the league, official recognition from the NCU was crucial, partly because, without it, the UCI would not grant it the power to administer an international racing licence. This, in turn, meant that the increasing number of racing cyclists in Britain had nothing to aspire to beyond domestic competition.

With the NCU apparently unprepared to soften its stance, Stallard appeared to realise that the BLRC was more likely to achieve its aims by convincing the UCI of its legitimacy instead. Partly for this reason, in 1952, he assembled a team to represent Britain in the Peace Race in Eastern Europe, which was open only to amateurs and therefore did not require an international licence.

His motivation was not purely political, for the Peace Race was the toughest amateur cycling event in the world at the time and would represent an enormous challenge, both for riders and for Stallard in his role as team manager. Running from Warsaw to Prague via Berlin, it took seven days and crossed some formidable terrain, including the mountains of East Germany, roads that had been destroyed in the Second World War and were still unrepaired, and huge cobbled sections. For the host communist nations, it was an important propagandist opportunity and their cyclists were given whatever support they needed.

Certainly nobody expected the racing ingénues from Britain to make much of an impression, yet that is just what they did, with the Scotsman Ian Steel winning the race and Stallard's squad winning the team award. 'It was after the Peace Race that things began to change,' Dave says. 'The UCI realised that we had riders of ability.'

To reward the achievement, the UCI agreed to give the BLRC official recognition on the condition that it sorted out the mess with the NCU within three months. The union, in turn, understood that it had to ensure this ultimatum was met or else it would risk seriously upsetting the UCI. Thus, finally, in April 1953, eleven years after local lad Albert Price had sprinted down Wolverhampton Park Road to win the first 'illegal' road race in Britain, the NCU agreed to lift its ban on the sport.

The terms of the agreement meant that it was an uneasy truce, with hardcore leaguers unhappy that the union would get to organise its own road races alongside the league's because they suspected the union wanted eventually to run road racing, too. Stallard was especially upset that his colleagues had voted to accept the union's condition that it would retain control of the international racing licence, a compromise agreed to in the belief that the NCU would now be permitted to grant the licence to whoever qualified for one. But, as Dave says, it was nonetheless 'the beginning of the end of all the silliness', and was the first step towards the two bodies eventually amalgamating six years later, when they formed the British Cycling Federation (BCF).

One is tempted to wonder how different the history of cycle racing in Britain might have been had Stallard not organised that first illegal race or had Dave and the rest of the leaguers not been prepared to continue in defiance of the NCU for so long. Certainly there are some experts who insist that the complexion of the sport today would be very different. They argue that it would have taken Britain's best road men and women even longer than the five decades they needed to rank consistently alongside the best in the world. As the journalist Herbie Sykes wrote: 'All of you riding and racing on this sceptred isle owe a debt of gratitude to Percy Stallard.'

Crucial to this argument is the belief that the NCU would never have rescinded the ban without being forced to. 'No, I don't think they ever would have done,' Dave says. 'They had fought us so desperately that they were just not prepared to do it by then. They were happy with the status quo.'

The collection of photographs that Dave has produced for my visit includes one of Stallard on his bike. He looks short, compact, with the hair around his temples shaved, military-style, and his slightly protruding teeth clenched in determination. He is wearing laced shoes and white socks and a white, striped jersey. Black clothing was anathema to the racing cyclist because of its connection to the dowdy, time-trial scene.

In 1992, Dave was given an old pair of Stallard's cycling shoes at a dinner to celebrate the BLRC's fiftieth anniversary. The gift was a symbolic one. With Stallard having recently taken up residence in a retirement home, veterans of the league wanted Dave to fill Stallard's shoes as their figurehead in negotiations with the union. For even half a century after the civil war, such talks continued intermittently in the hope that the old rebels would finally be granted official recognition for their pivotal role in the sport's development. They had never received it, they assumed, because the BCF would risk offending the reactionary old union members who were still active in the sport.

This recognition was granted, sixteen years later, in a statement from Brian Cookson, the president of what is now

British Cycling. Cookson also sent a letter to Dave in which he acknowledged the role the league 'played in re-introducing road-racing and pushing the sport dramatically forward'.

Cookson notes that Dave had inundated him with letters urging him to make this statement, which coincided with the fiftieth anniversary of the amalgamation between the union and the league. Why did it matter so much to him? 'It's because we had to fight for so long,' Dave says. 'It was a labour of love. That's all it was, mate. You don't work like that for nothing without wanting some kind of comeback, and we got it. My only regret now is that Stallard never got to see Wiggins win the Tour. It wouldn't have happened without him.'

CHAPTER TWO

Tracking down the trailblazer who rescued British road racing

I would like here to be able to recall my idyllic youth in the saddle, the rural time-trials and carefree family touring holidays, of regular visits to the local grass-track meeting or weekend tandem adventures – just the kind of formative experiences that shaped so many cyclists' childhoods.

But I cannot. I grew up in suburban Hertfordshire in the 1980s, a time when cycling was taking place so far into the fringes of popular culture that I scarcely knew it existed, not as a pastime anyway. I'm discounting the mountain bike craze of that period because it was an imported American phenomenon, and proved transitory anyway. Instead, I am undergoing my cycling education just as I'm supposedly passing my physical prime (such as it was). At least I know I am not alone. Thousands, perhaps millions, of middle-aged (or thereabouts) British men of my generation are doing exactly the same.

It has been an expensive apprenticeship. I have graduated from aluminium commuting bike to entry-level carbon racer and overhauled my cycling gear at a cost of several hundred pounds. To find the strength to complete both my eleven-mile commute to work, as well as the extended rides I often take before my evening shifts in central London, I have consumed more white (energy) powder than Tony Montana ever did and spent more time riding in circles around Regent's Park than I could justify to anyone with a rewarding social life. I have explored the Essex lanes near my home, too, either alone or with one of several friends who have taken up the sport.

The Reg Harris Cyclosportive, on the August Bank Holiday weekend, is to be my first proper, organised event, and I'm a little apprehensive. I shouldn't be. I am reasonably fit, and it is not as though this is a competitive event, not officially anyway. Sportives are designed especially for cyclists like me and my friend Ronan. Both of us are newcomers to cycling. We lack the fitness to race properly and never seriously considered taking part in time-trials, not when most take place in the middle of nowhere, still at around dawn and seem like an odd, lonely thing to do.

It is thought that the first sportive was La Marmotte, the fearsomely difficult Alpine event launched in 1982. In Britain, though, they have really taken off with cycling's 'revolution' this century. Over the past three years alone, British Cycling has reported a 200 per cent increase in the number of people participating in them. This, however, is the inaugural year of the Reg Harris sportive. It was inspired, apparently, by the increased interest in Reg that my book about his life sparked, although that seems a bit odd given how few people bought it!

The route is not too demanding, fifty miles, albeit with a few sharp Lancashire hills. A few hundred entrants have signed up and more are expected to turn up today. The signing-in time is between seven thirty and eight thirty a.m. but, given that it is a Sunday, we assume the organisers will be relaxed about this.

At around eight forty-five, we pull into the primary school car park that is serving as the starting point for the event and meet the last wave of cyclists rolling away. Several of them point at their watches and laugh as they spot our dismantled bikes in the back.

While arguing over whether to blame my leisurely breakfast or Ronan's frankly excessive ablutions, our panicked attempts to reassemble the bikes are sufficiently entertaining to draw a small crowd. Ronan fails to work out how to use the pedal spanner; I struggle with the pump. A helpful car-park attendant suggests that, rather than take the bikes apart, we should have tied them to car racks like everybody else did. Ronan takes a moment to wonder what Reg, the arch perfectionist, would have thought of having his life documented by a man involved in such a scene.

By the time we finally make it to the start line, organisers outnumber us by about four to one. The official starter set us off via his horn speaker. 'Careful!' he bellows as I turn quickly out of the car park, determined to make up for lost time but failing to spot a car emerging from behind another, parked, one. I pull on the brakes quickly enough to avoid a collision, but for a split second forget how to unclip from my pedal cleats – possibly because I tried them on for the first time in our hotel room – and tip slowly to the concrete.

Trapped beneath the frame, I am wriggling like a beached seal to free myself from the pedals when I hear: 'Isn't that the guy who wrote the book?' A boy aged no more than seven then walks towards me, looking bemused. 'Now that's not a very good start, is it?' he says.

No it is not, I agree, but at least it is a start.

I had thought that I would not get to meet Ian Steel. I emailed my first two interview requests to him and did not get a response. I wrote a letter, only for him to turn me down, apologetically, explaining that he had been struggling with his health since suffering a stroke a few months earlier and, anyway, he felt that the one extended magazine article devoted to his triumph at the Peace Race was sufficient coverage for his achievement.

Given that the victory had changed the course of British cycling I begged to differ and petitioned him again several months later, albeit more in hope than expectation. 'Your letter arrived at an opportune time,' his emailed reply said. 'I will be in London this weekend to celebrate my diamond wedding anniversary with my wife Peggy and my sister Margaret. We wish to take in some shows, shop for the ladies, and take in the Christmas atmosphere.'

It might possibly be the most formal personal email that I have ever received but then it was typical of the graceful and charming man whom I find waiting in the reception of his Kensington hotel. Aged eighty-five, Ian is still climber-slim and light on his feet, bouncing up to offer a warm handshake and big smile. 'I didn't want to miss you so I thought I'd wait right by the door,' he explains. To speak, he must press the voice box in his throat that he had fitted to tackle throat cancer sixteen years ago. 'I hardly even notice it now,' he says. 'Only in photographs when I have to take my hand away from my throat.'

For some quiet we decide to go to his room, but get lost in

the maze of corridors. It is a surreal moment, being unable to find our way out of the ground floor of a small building with a man celebrated for the speed with which he crossed Eastern Europe. He takes it well, though, rolling his eyes upwards at his confusion, laughing his endearing, barely audible laugh, until eventually we reach our destination, three single beds still unmade. With the women shopping, we pull up two wooden chairs and rewind five decades.

You will not find much written about Ian online, just a brief Wikipedia entry and a handful of interviews on cycling websites. The politics of *Cycling* magazine meant that it hardly covered his career. The one interview that does justice to his victory is the (excellent) one that Herbie Sykes wrote for *Rouleur* magazine and which almost scuppered my interview with Ian. Sykes described him as British cycling's 'stage-racing messiah, a man who won the biggest race in the world and the biggest sporting event in the world, bar none'. I am not certain that is quite true – the Tour de France was twice the distance of the Peace Race – but winning the latter did represent a formidable achievement given Ian's humble background.

Like many men of his generation, whose families struggled to afford a bike for their children, Ian first rode one running errands as a message boy, in his case as a teenager in Dunoon, the town on the Firth of Clyde to which he had been moved from Glasgow during the War.

He barely stopped turning pedals as an adolescent, first as a schoolboy and then as an apprentice pattern-maker back in the city of his birth. As an eighteen year old, he joined his local cycling club, Glasgow United, and, like several generations of British cyclists, was introduced to competition through time-trials, winning over distances of twenty-five, fifty and one hundred miles, as well as a twelve-hour time-trial, in his first year with the club. 'I had tunnel vision,' he says. 'I never had anything to do with girls, drinking, smoking, nothing like that. Just cycling.'

Like Dave Orford, he spent part of every Saturday in a newsagent that sold French newspapers, drawing him into the world of road-racing. 'Robic, Coppi, Bartali; illicit, guilty pleasures,' he told Sykes, listing perhaps the three greatest cyclists of that era. 'I became desperate to race.'

Glasgow United were affiliated to the NCU, forcing Ian to switch to the rebel club Glasgow Wheelers in 1949. As adept at massed-start racing as he was competing against the clock, within a year he was crowned Scottish champion. 'I was just a natural,' he says.

That success earned him a place on the Scottish team heading to Paris-Lens, the prestigious race for amateurs. He looked poised for victory while in a two-man break with a Belgian rider, only for his opponent to double-cross Ian, exploiting his naivety by pretending that he would allow the British ingénue to take overall victory in return for the sprint primes. Instead, after sitting on Ian's wheel, he bagged the lot. It was an important lesson. 'He said it was just habit,' Ian says. 'It was my turning point. I thought, "Never again will I trust anyone to say the race is yours".'

The performance earned him another promotion, to the Viking team competing in the first Tour of Britain, in 1951. Competing as an independent, which meant he was now allowed to win prize money, Ian stunned the field by winning three of the twelve stages and claiming overall victory by more than six minutes at the climax on Hampstead Heath. His most decisive effort came in the longest stage, the gruelling 160-mile trek from Morecambe to his home city of Glasgow, in which he held off a series of sustained attacks to finish first and surge into the overall lead.

The £120 first prize was equivalent to about three months' wages for Ian. 'Before the Tour of Britain few people outside of Scotland had heard of him,' *Sporting Cyclist* magazine wrote. 'Now he was Britain's best roadman. Within a year he would become one of the most promising in the world.'

The race had covered 1,403 miles – almost twice the distance of its 2014 edition – yet unlike his modern counterparts Ian worked full-time, as a carpenter for his brother-in-law Bob Thom, no mean 'independent' cyclist himself, at his soon-to-be-opened bike shop in Glasgow.

How did he train? 'Well, it was twenty-two and a half miles each way to the bike shop and I used to ride every day. My brother-in-law joined me but struggled to keep up. Did me the world of good. I'm not sure you could say the same for him.'

By now Ian knew that he had a special talent for climbing, his gift having first emerged when he rode away from the pack on a hill twenty miles from the finish of the Scottish road race championship. 'I loved the climbing, loved the mountains. There were races where I would be in a small group and I would think to myself, "Go!".' He cuts a hand through the air. 'And I would hurtle up the road and I would look around to see how many I'd dropped, and then the others would straggle up. So I'd do the same again and look around and feel quite chuffed at all these bikes behind.'

He received his invitation to the Peace Race the next season. Though only four years old, the race had a formidable reputation for the demands it placed on riders. Comprising twelve stages over 1,326 miles through Poland, East Germany and the Czech Republic, it crossed long sections of pavé, 'with cobbles as big as footballs', as the late cycling historian and administrator Chas Messenger described them. It crossed the Ore Mountains and covered broken roads and long dirt tracks. With good reason was it known as the Tour de France of the East.

Communist newspapers in the three host countries had conceived the race to try to improve the increasingly tense political relations between the nations. Though East European riders dominated the field, foreign teams were invited to take part to strengthen it. The organisers also wanted to showcase their athletes and their societies to the West. Only once had a non-East European cyclist won it and that was considered a mistake that was not to be repeated.

Ian did not appreciate the political importance of the race but he knew how demanding it was. And he had prepared for it, in his own way. 'I would find all the cobbled roads in Glasgow,' he said. That was it? 'Oh, I felt that I mastered them: don't hold the bars tight. Just let things rattle away but keep the revs up.'

The British team that flew from London to Copenhagen and on to Warsaw also included Frank Seel, a Mancunian plumber; the Yorkshireman Ken Jowett, another strong climber; Les Scales, a cockney toolmaker; Bev Wood, who could also climb well, from Manchester; and Ian Greenfield, a Scot who Ian recalled as 'a tough cookie'. As manager, Percy Stallard took with him a masseur, Charles Fearnley, and Ian's brother-in-law Bob Thom as a mechanic.

On signing off their visa applications, the British Consul made it clear that the team were travelling beyond its jurisdiction in going behind the Iron Curtain and that therefore it could not be responsible for them. That left the British-Polish Friendship Society to arrange a modest send-off party in London, while Polish authorities arranged for a group of locally based Britons to look after the squad in Warsaw.

Once there, the significance of the event quickly dawned on the team. They were presented with flowers at the airport and given an armoured escort through the city to a civic reception in a plush hotel, where they joined the other teams being introduced to Marshal Konstantin Rokossovsky, the Polish defence minister and commander of the Soviet forces in the country. 'The others were in suits, national flag on the pockets,' Ian says. The Britons were in their civvies. Realising that Rokossovsky could not speak English, they greeted him with a collective 'Bollocks!'. As a group, their personalities had gelled, crucially.

The opening ceremony in Warsaw's national stadium was, in Ian's words, 'the most incredible experience'. The venue was sold out, filled to its 100,000 capacity. As well as all those cheering spectators, it had marching bands, thousands of flags and huge, imposing images of Stalin. At the climax of the ceremony, a thousand white doves were released into the sky as symbols of peace.

Outside, the streets were lined with more people than Ian had ever seen. Though he did not realise it, schoolchildren had spent weeks preparing banners to display and workers were released from their factories to create the image of a happy and open society. Three years later, Ian would ride the Tour de France, but even the French did not embrace their event quite as enthusiastically as the Poles did the Peace Race. 'Oh, there were millions,' Ian says. 'More than you could imagine.'

The highlights reel of the race on YouTube shows riders passing pavements full of people, apartment blocks with packed terraces, and suspiciously well-organised children, all sporting a bicycle and a broad smile. To a soundtrack of buoyant folk music, the footage also briefly depicts Jan Vesely, the brilliant blond-haired Czech rider and favourite to win, and Jean Stablinksi, the French future world road-race champion with the receding hairline, and Steel himself, tall, lanky with a mop of black hair.

Stallard prepared the British team well. He studied the route of each stage and identified the decisive segments, such as the worst climbs and points where the wind was likely to change direction. He also picked out the most dangerous opponents and pinned their numbers on to his riders' handlebars so that they could watch out for them. 'He was cantankerous,' Ian says, 'but he was good.'

Stallard identified Ian as his best hope of success but was fearful of the youthful Scot's natural exuberance. Stallard warned him against attacking too early, insisting that he kept his gunpowder for the mountains, where the race was likely to be decided.

However, after the euphoria of the start, Ian could not help but follow an early break. He was promptly dropped, a novel experience for him. 'I got a real telling off from Percy. He wanted us to stick together and I had disappeared from the others. I learnt my lesson, though.' Riding prudently for the next five days, he edged up the general classification, while managing to avoid the crashes and punctures that were befalling his rivals. The Belgian team ran out of frames within the first week. 'There were flat roads, cobbled roads, dusty roads, but we held it together. The team's spirit was superb.'

Ian knew that Vesely was the danger man – he had won the race in 1949 after all. When the Czech rider moved into yellow after the seventh stage into Chemnitz, Ian decided that he would take the race to him the next day in the mountains, regardless of the blazing heat and the prospect of a thirteen per cent cobbled climb known as the Steel Wall. 'The race had been so flat until then so I just glorified it,' Ian says, describing the freedom with which he cut loose, combining with Greenfield and Jowett to put nine minutes into Vesely and take the overall lead. 'It felt unbelievable.'

The Britons' effort moved them to the top of the team classification too, turning the race on its head for the remaining four days. While before they had operated stealthily, keeping Ian in contention without exposing him, now they were marked men. Every team was watching them.

In rapidly deteriorating weather, the attacks came again and again, with Vesely and Stablinski leading them. Ian, though, still using the tubular tyres on which he started the race, would not be broken and he led heading into the final stage. To win overall, all he needed to do was sit on Vesely's wheel, just like the Belgian rider in Paris-Lens had done. Ian claimed victory in front of 220,000 devastated fans at Prague's Strahov Stadium.

Vesely embraced Ian at the finish, admitting that this 'skinny' Scot was a deserved winner, but the organisers were not quite so gracious. Just as they had refused the Britons clean jerseys to wear on the podium after each stage, so they denied them a lap of honour. Ian never received the new car that was supposedly reserved for the winner, either. The British squad won the team prize as well, but they too were denied the motorbikes that were due to them. Instead, their prize haul included crystal, a camera, a radio and a watch. Ian was given a new bike too, but he left that with a Scotsman who had covered the race for the *Daily Worker*, a newspaper for communists in Britain.

Elsewhere the British press effectively ignored the achievement. Reuters ran a few paragraphs on its news wire. *Cycling* magazine published a twelve-word report. 'Other than that, nothing,' Ian says. 'I've got a couple of books that were written, but all in German.'

Perhaps Ian's greatest reward was the job offer he received from Viking, to work in their factory in Wolverhampton. Bob Thom would be his immediate boss and the company would allow him time off from the production line to ride, a perfect arrangement for the glittering career that was apparently ahead of him.

He went with another Stallard-led team to the Tour of Mexico and looked poised to win that before he crashed on a descent. He entered the Tour of Belgium and twice started the Vuelta a España, only to withdraw on both occasions, once with stomach trouble, the other time because all his team-mates had withdrawn, leaving him with a hopeless task. This was a familiar experience, the result of Ian being much stronger in mountainous races than most of his compatriots. 'It would whittle down and down and I'd be left on my own with two officials and a mechanic, so I just said, "Ah fuck it, there's no use". I had no incentive to really race; I had no team.'

He went to the Tour de France in 1955 as part of the first British team to take part in the race, and was riding well in the mountains when he was asked to serve as a domestique for a less talented team-mate, Stan Jones, possibly the result of Ian not being part of the Hercules team that dominated the squad. Infuriated, Ian's patience snapped the next day after he had refused to drink the contents of a suspicious bottle and the soigneur involved lost his temper with him. 'He said, "Did the little pot help you?" and I said, "No, I just poured it out". He said, "I am finished with you!" And that was it, I went home.' He was aware of the amount of doping among the professionals abroad and was already disillusioned with it.

He raced for another year, joining a British team-mate from the Tour, Tony Hoar, on the Cilo-St Raphaël team led by the great Hugo Koblet, but the Swiss rider was a shadow of the man who won the Tour in 1951, and Ian had lost his love for the sport. Fed up with the politics, drug-taking and ruined opportunities, he quit cycling, aged only twenty-seven. He had not added a major victory to the one he scored four years earlier, despite never feeling out of his depth among the greatest of riders. Within months he had left the sport altogether after the Scottish Cycling Union refused to allow him to take up a position as national road race secretary, the job that would have allowed him to pass on his knowledge to the next generation of road racers. They reasoned that, as a former professional, he was banned from returning to the amateur ranks.

'I said to Peggy, "That's me finished with cycling".' Did he ever regret the decision? 'No. I look on my career only with pride. I was very fortunate that I was able to make the decision when I did because I was competing with all these people who were druggies.' Besides, he had scored the pivotal victory needed to transform road cycling in Britain. 'Yes, it was the turning point. It needed something like my win to make it happen.'

Ian and Peggy live in the town of Largs on the Firth of Clyde. Since his retirement they have enjoyed some adventures. Keen sailors, they have travelled half the world in a boat, visiting Europe and North America, with Margaret, a widow, often joining them. They have overcome obstacles, too, teaching them to enjoy life when they can. Peggy recovered from cancer of the oesophagus; Ian has had two replacement hips, as well as having had throat cancer.

The surgery did not prevent him cycling. Until he suffered the stroke, he would ride into town, pick up the shopping and complete three circuits of his 'course' before returning home, completing an invigorating thirty-mile trip. Though he has designs on riding on a static bike at home, his connection to cycling now is restricted mostly to the functions he attends. He is an honorary member of the Pedal Club.

Living in good cycling country, he sometimes encounters groups of cyclists and will occasionally engage them in conversation. He does not say directly that he was the last Briton before Sir Bradley Wiggins to win a major stage race abroad, but he prompts them to find out.

'We'll go into a little café and the bikes will be lying outside. I am not big-headed but I look at the bikes and I think, "Should I?". Yep, I'm going to have a word with them. I say, "Like the bikes, they're beautiful. I used to be a bike rider, you know. Many years ago. I've had success. If you go on to Google and type 'Ian Steel cyclist', you'll get a string [of results]." They'll be, "Oh, we'll remember that. We'll do that." And I say, "Oh, one of them's the Peace Race", and they go, "Oh, we're not in your class!" which is quite nice really.'

It would have been nice for them, too. They were lucky to meet him. So was I.

CHAPTER THREE

Revealed: the secret life of our most successful cyclist (oh yes, she was)

In an Italian restaurant opposite King's Cross station in London, with rush-hour commuters thronging the street outside, Michael Breckon is trying to reassure me that I am not as much of a lost cause as a cyclist as I fear I might be. As I have explained to him via email, despite months of regular riding, I am no closer to becoming the kind of rider I had aspired to be. On the Essex lanes, I have struggled to hold the wheel of men several decades older than I am. At Regent's Park, I cannot stay with the quick group for more than a lap. I grew up believing that I had stamina, having had some success in middle-distance running when I was a teenager, but cycling has changed that.

'That email worried me,' Michael says. 'Why are you worried about getting dropped? You don't know who the other riders are or what their training is. You have to know what you want to do and get on with it and don't bother when you can't keep up with someone.'

This is easier to say when you have Michael's talent. He was once ranked fifteenth among the country's time-trialists. His best achievement came in 1958, aged twenty-one, when he won the team award with Yorkshire Road Club in the British Best All-Rounder (BBAR) competition, which was decided by riders' average speeds in time-trials covering fifty and one hundred miles, and twelve hours. And, at the age of sixty-three, he beat the hour for twenty-five miles.

I could not hope to get close to that even after six months' regular riding. 'Yes, but it takes time to find out what you're capable of,' Michael says. 'It wasn't till 1957 [so late!] that I realised what I might be able to do, and that was after three years of really trying.'

I am in need of training advice. There is so much available in magazines and online that I do not know where to begin. What does he suggest I do differently? 'My own view is that most of the stuff written is codswallop and that there is, absolutely, no substitution for miles, miles and more miles. When I was racing, either in the Sixties or as a vet, I never even entered a race until I had 3,000 miles in my legs that year.'

As I am only a few weeks' cycling short of that figure, I suspect that I might need more than that. Michael insists that I should not give up. I can see how he helped nurture a generation of Canada's best cyclists, having served as their national team manager when he lived there in the 1970s. (It was a good time, apparently, for a Briton interested in fitness to be living in North America. 'I would come into the office on Monday, tell people I'd been for a fifty-mile ride at the weekend, and they would be dead impressed. In Britain, if you had told somebody you'd done that, they would have said you were bloody mad.') 'You're only out to beat yourself. Beating others along the way is a nice bonus but not necessary,' he says.

I have not asked to meet Michael simply for cycling advice. I want also to pick his brains about potential interviewees for this book. He suggests Ken Russell, aka the Lone Wolf, the Yorkshireman who won the 1952 Tour of Britain without the support of a team. Michael is confident that it is the only case of a solo rider claiming victory in a major stage race. Arthur Metcalfe is another possibility. He, too, was from Yorkshire – perhaps there is something in the water – and, in 1966, was the first Briton to win the national road race title and BBAR in the same year. 'It helped to bridge the divide that still existed between the two disciplines,' he says. Michael knew Metcalfe. 'He was a remarkable rider.'

He mentions the 'rebel' grass-track racing scene that is almost as old as the sport itself. Competitors entered under pseudonyms and often raced at secret locations, allowing amateurs to compete for prize money even when it was outlawed. Though nowhere near as popular as it once was, grass-track racing remains a breeding ground for young talent. Victoria Pendleton, for one, learnt her craft there.

We settle on Beryl Burton, the multiple world and national champion and a former friend and neighbour of Michael's – and inevitably from Yorkshire. I wonder, though, if one chapter of his life in cycling is briefly worth retelling, too. It is not about competition but it is almost certainly unique and might just be the most romantic cycling adventure that I have heard of. 'Yes, but it is all so complicated,' Michael says.

The National Byways Project was conceived in 1996 during a conversation that Michael had with Victor Emery, the Canadian businessman and 1964 Olympic bobsleigh gold medallist who had retired to London, and Alan Rushton, a cycling promoter.

At the time, the sport had declined from its brief flirtation with the mainstream that Rushton had inspired with his televised criteriums in the previous decade. Seeking a new idea to reinvigorate the sport, the men settled on drawing maps that would identify the best cycling routes – they had to be quiet, basically – and provide historical background into the places of interest near by. 'We were not trying to provide the quickest cycle route between two points,' says Michael. Sustrans, the cycling charity, did that with its National Cycle Network. 'Sustrans gave you an opportunity to ride, while we give you a reason to.'

Once the £1.3 million funding had been secured, Michael was given the task of drawing up the maps. Thus, he took to his camper van and embarked on the most unlikely adventure. He travelled through south-west Scotland and north-east England. He covered the Midlands and on through the south-west. He rode every potential road to check that it met the criteria: no more than two cars per mile while riding at an average speed of ten miles per hour. Often he would cover the chosen routes twice to ensure the traffic never exceeded the limit. He made contact with local tourist boards, liaised with Sustrans – with whom the byways project shares only about ten per cent of its routes – and swotted up on local history.

His partner Carole visited him but he was happily alone for long periods. He felt 'an atmosphere' as he crossed a Civil War battlefield (from the real 1640s one, rather than the more recent cycling 'civil war'), passing woods from which Royalist cavalry charged, leading to 5,000 deaths. He wondered on the 'ageless beauty' of Romney Marsh in the Kent wetlands. He drew a route that passed the cottage near Dorchester in which

Thomas Hardy grew up and went close to Lawrence of Arabia's home. He had signage erected and the maps printed, with detailed annotations.

I'm not certain if I find his endeavour bonkers or inspired. Perhaps it is both. 'I didn't work all the time,' he says. 'I took evenings off.' Recently retired from a marketing job with Raleigh, he took a modest wage but carried on working long after the money ran out, motivated by the thought of converting people to his sport.

To attract more investment, he persuaded high-profile contacts to become involved. His old friend Phil Liggett, the TV commentator, led corporate rides over parts of the route. Britain's 1992 Olympic gold medallist Chris Boardman, the mountaineer Sir Chris Bonington and the explorer Sir Ranulph Fiennes joined the Byways committee. Lord Foster, the architect and a keen cyclist, agreed to serve as the project's honorary president.

They raised some money but not the £500,000 needed to complete the research and fund the promotional campaign it would have required, leaving the project unfinished, hence Michael's 'it is all so complicated' comment. He mapped 4,500 miles of roads but never had the cash to promote them.

If you are interested, the maps are still for sale on the Byways website, www.thenationalbyway.org, and the signs are still up, with a logo similar to that of Hovis, an original sponsor. Should you see one, it might be worth reflecting on the work that went into them. 'I just ran out of steam,' Michael admits. 'I ended up being owed an awful lot of money, six figures. But it's not because of the money that I'm emotional. It took a chunk of my life.'

*

Beryl Burton is probably the most successful cyclist Briton has ever produced, so good that her palmares is almost difficult to comprehend. In the individual pursuit at the world championships, she won five golds, three silvers and four bronzes; in the world road race championship she scored two victories and one silver; she won a dozen national road race titles, the same number of national individual pursuit crowns, and seventy-one national time-trial championships – yes, seventy-one – over every distance from ten to one hundred miles. Perhaps most incredible of all, she won the British Best All-Rounder competition twenty-five years in a row. She was also a wife and mother, a rhubarb picker and made not a penny from the sport.

When the actress Maxine Peake wrote a radio play about her that transferred to the West Yorkshire Playhouse, she said that Burton had been 'criminally ignored' in popular culture, which was true. After Victoria Pendleton's exploits at London 2012, for example, she was widely and wrongly acclaimed as Britain's greatest ever woman cyclist. My own newspaper, *The Daily Telegraph*, was among the culprits. They made the mistake of judging purely on Olympic medals even though, for decades, female cyclists were not admitted to the Games. Burton was forty-seven by the time they were.

Burton has never been ignored within the cycling community. Geoff Cooke, the former national team manager, told me she was the finest ever cyclist from Britain. Roger St Pierre put her first among cyclists of. Those who knew her were complimentary, too. Michael Breckon recalls her as a 'simple lass, a kind, thoughtful soul; maybe a typical Yorkshire person, which she was through and through'.

When she crops up in conversation, people tend to recall two particular anecdotes from her career. In the first, she hands her fellow long-distance specialist Mike McNamara a liquorice allsort while overtaking him during a twelve-hour time-trial, the discipline for which McNamara held the British record. Burton was en route to surpassing his landmark by almost a mile, eventually covering 277.25 miles. The record still stood for women in 2015, underlining how unique was her talent, though presumably the event still left a sour taste with McNamara.

In the second, Burton refuses to shake her daughter Denise's hand after she defeated her mum in the 1976 national road race championship, a snub so surprising that it propelled domestic cycling into foreign territory then – the back pages of the national press. 'It was very strange,' said John Yates, an old friend of Beryl's from Harrogate, who used to true her wheels. We were introduced at a Yorkshire tea-house while out riding. 'It was very out of character for Beryl; she was a good person, always friendly, always prepared to chat. I never understood it.'

This hinted at something that I had suspected about Burton: that nobody really knew her. Certainly her autobiography does not reveal much about her emotional life, focusing instead on her exhausting catalogue of races. Even Peake's compassionate portrayal of Burton's life left you wanting to know more about its subject. As the *Telegraph* review of the play said: 'The universality of her example was clear, her inner personality less so.' The critic, Dominic Cavendish, added: 'But we don't have to love our sporting champions, do we? We just have to stop to admire – and applaud – them now and again.' It would be nice to know about them, though, especially the most cherished, and especially one with such an awesome record. After all, as a Frenchman is thought to have said: 'If Beryl Burton had been French, Joan of Arc would have to take second place.'

*

I had to negotiate the length of my interview with Denise Burton-Cole. Only when I promised that my visit to her rural home near the Yorkshire town of Ripon would last no longer than an hour did she agree. 'You're lucky,' she says, leading me into the TV room of her tidy bungalow. 'I had stopped doing interviews. We did so many. My dad is getting old and he was finding them quite tiring. It can be hard when you keep digging up the past.'

Denise is fifty-eight, silver-haired and slim; eight stone, yet of medium height. She is frank, expressive and quick to laugh. She soon appears comfortable discussing what feel like difficult subjects, too. The only sign that she is not entirely enthusiastic about the interview is the fact that she settles down without a drink: a sign, I guess, that it is not supposed to last long. I accept a glass of water. 'I was born to get on with stuff,' she says.

Denise recently appeared in the media as a result of Yorkshire hosting the Grand Départ and the simultaneous arrival of Peake's play in Leeds, the script for which included excerpts from an interview that Peake did with Denise and her father, Charlie. It managed to touch on most of the pivotal events in Beryl's life, from the bout of chorea that forced her to miss two years of school, to her teenage romance with Charlie and on to her death, aged fifty-eight. 'I was looking round and people are sobbing, crying, laughing, everything, clapping – the whole audience,' Denise says. 'It was amazing.'

It also took in Denise's arrival in the world in January 1956, when Burton was only eighteen, and married. By then she was already addicted to cycling, having even raised the handlebars on her bike so that she could continue to ride during the early stages of pregnancy.

Shortly after Denise was born, Charlie fixed a sidecar to his bike to take her to events in which Beryl was competing. In time, the sidecar was replaced with a bike trailer, which allowed Denise to pedal too. Beryl was already a rhubarb picker, while Charlie worked as a clerk, but modest wages and frugality meant they did not own a car. Not that their daughter minded. Denise looked on the trips as an adventure, even if she could barely reach the pedals. 'They put blocks on them [the pedals] and the saddle was right down the bottom. I must have been riding miles. Just being sat there was tiring enough, let alone when I pedalled.'

They covered much of the north of England. 'Oh, we went all over,' says Denise. 'They used to ride over to Manchester and places like that. They'd ride over the Pennines, stop at somebody's house probably, race and then ride back again.' They could not afford to pay for accommodation. 'I used to sleep in drawers and everything when I was at places.' (Such thriftiness was a feature of Beryl's career. Even later on in life, they slept in the family car or in a two-man tent before national championships, rather than pay for a hotel.)

Beryl worked on the Yorkshire farm that belonged to Nim Carline, also a successful long-distance cyclist, who was sympathetic to Burton's cycling commitments and proud to employ such a talent. He expected her to work as hard as the men on the farm but, as a fellow member of Morley Cycling Club, he allowed her time off to train and often joined her on rides, pushing Beryl to her limit when, as a young woman, she was still learning what was required of champions.

Quite how much time off Carline permitted was unclear. Denise suspects her mum was often out riding when she was pretending to be at work. 'It was just a feeling I got, looking back.' This seems a little strange. Why did she not just ask? 'We weren't the family that talked a lot. Both my dad and her had quite a Victorian upbringing, quite strict parents. I talk with my children – chat, chat, chat – but not my mum or my dad. He was more chatty, but my mum didn't talk much unless she needed to.'

This might surprise those who remember Beryl as a sociable soul. Vernon Wood, another former club-mate, told the *Morley Observer*, 'she was just a normal Yorkshire lass'. Cycling blogger Terry Wassall, veteran of the 1960s club scene, found her 'friendly, chatty and patient'. Watch *Racing is Life*, Ray Pascoe's film about Beryl, and you see her mixing happily with club-mates of all ages, whether on a club run or after another successful assault on a time-trial record. She even cited her fondness for the club scene as one reason for rejecting all offers to turn professional.

'She was very friendly and helpful with other people,' Denise says. 'She was chatty with other folk, but not with me. You've got like two different kinds of person really. She wasn't horrible, she just wasn't the same [person]. Her personality didn't come out with her immediate family.'

Beryl did once admit to this trait in an interview with *Cycling* magazine. 'It has nothing to do with moods, or with falling out with people,' she said. 'It's just my way, and they all understand this at home. Even with Charlie and Denise, I can go hours without speaking to them. I'll be thinking mostly about the future. I hardly ever think about the past.' As Bernard Thompson observed in that interview, this habit meant that Beryl struggled to recall details even of victories she had claimed recently. Denise suspected her thoughts were focused instead on cycling: about the next race or training ride or how she planned to fit their lives around her schedule.

It made for a stoic household. There was no television and they owned few books. Though Burton enjoyed opera and knitting, she rarely devoted time to pursuits other than cycling and showed little desire to cultivate in Denise any interests that she might have had as a child. 'It was like, "If you can't get there yourself, you don't go",' Denise says. 'They were too busy, too busy cycling and training and doing bikes.' It made Denise determined to bring up her two children differently. 'I actually said I won't bring them up the way I was brought up, meaning I would be there for them. And I've always been, taking them here, there and everywhere.'

In that same interview, Beryl also said that club cycling helped her to overcome her shyness, though much about her character remained a mystery, even to Denise. I am especially surprised to discover that Beryl never once discussed with her daughter her struggle with chorea, which attacked her nervous system so aggressively that she was left paralysed as an eleven year old, unable to speak and stricken with rheumatic fever. It was an experience that Beryl said forged her determination to 'make my mark' on the world.

By doing that through cycling, she gloriously defied the doctors and teachers who insisted she would not amount to much in life. Yet she did not seek to pass on her passion to Denise, leaving her daughter to take up the sport of her own volition, aged eight or nine, when the family moved from Morley to the village of Woodlesford and Denise needed a way to travel the ten miles back to visit her friends and grandmother.

Riding a racing bike that her parents bought for her, she soon found that she enjoyed the sport as much as they did and rode whenever she could. She entered her first competition aged about eleven when Morley CC decided to allow juniors to enter their evening time-trials. She began with five miles, progressed to ten, and was soon competing against her mother as a young adolescent.

Charlie served as mechanic, checking all of the young riders' bikes, though Beryl was too preoccupied to offer much advice during those evening events around the lanes of West Yorkshire. 'It didn't really come across. You know, if I was just born to a regular family, I don't think I would have taken up cycling. It meant everything. And she would say, "Well done" but that's about it. She was the type to give people advice, so she must have given me some somewhere along the line but I don't remember any.'

It must have been difficult, I suggest, for a girl to win the attention of a mother who allowed the sport to consume all her energy. 'Probably, yeah, because children like attention, don't they, and if they're not getting it . . . I remember that I couldn't sit on her knee ever as a young child because I might hurt her legs. I remember being told that quite a few times. I'd go sit on my dad's knee.'

Beryl did eventually teach Denise how to ride the track, slowly leading her around the steep, concrete banking at the velodrome in Leicester when her daughter was fourteen. But mostly it was Charlie who supported their daughter as she rose through the ranks of the sport domestically. Charlie was also Beryl's coach, mentor, emotional brick and chauffeur – they were eventually gifted a car as reward for one of her world-title victories – and his seemed a touchingly selfless existence. He remained with Beryl throughout her life. Unfortunately, he was not strong enough to attend this interview.

'It was a kind of role reversal but it wasn't unusual, not in cycling anyway,' Denise says, 'because a lot of the top women

– it was the same for them, too. The men would do the bikes, they would take them to events, because the women were better than them in their standard.'

Though Denise might not quite have possessed her mother's endurance, and surely nobody has quite matched Beryl's bloody-minded determination, Denise could more than hold her own in the pursuit and possessed a finishing kick that her mother lacked, making her an especially strong proposition in road races.

Aged only sixteen, she finished second to her mother in the road race at the national championships and travelled with her to compete in the worlds. Three years later, in 1975, Denise won a prestigious, six-stage race in France called Les Journées Havro-Cauchoises and claimed bronze in the individual pursuit at the world championships. With such form, it was difficult to pick a favourite from mother and daughter as they prepared to do battle at the next season's national road race championship in Harrogate.

According to Beryl, the event coincided with an especially tense period in their relationship, based on her belief that Denise was not pulling her weight around the house. Denise recalls things differently. 'I had a long list of jobs and, by golly, I made sure I did them!'

What Denise does recall is that her mum fell silent the night before the race. 'Before a major event, she'd be even quieter than usual. And that's how it was then, more than ever. I was a strong contender then so perhaps she was uptight. It appeared like she was going through it all in her mind, what she's going to do. She's rehearsing the whole thing over and over.'

Denise thought little of it and was preparing to leave for the event the next morning when Beryl finally cut through the atmosphere. 'Suddenly, we were on the way out and she just said, "You're not going in the car". Completely out of the blue. It was all a bit strange. I said, "Well, how am I supposed to get there?" They didn't get that bit in the play. We still didn't have a telephone so I couldn't phone anybody.'

Beryl was unmoved. She insisted that her daughter rode the twenty-five miles to Rudding Park, refusing even to allow Charlie to put her daughter's race wheels in the car boot. Instead, Denise hung them from hooks on her frame, and set off alone. 'It's quite a way to Harrogate, I can tell you, and hilly. Straight out of Woodlesford, I'm uphill.'

She did not need to ride all the way, though. On dropping off Beryl, Charlie turned around and picked Denise up about halfway into her trip. By the time she arrived at the venue, Denise insists that she had put the incident out of her mind and had looked on the ride as an enforced warm-up. 'Oh yeah, I was fine. I got changed and my dad put my wheels in and everything like that. I had a cup of tea, then I just tootled up and down and that were it – we were off.'

In her autobiography, Beryl admits that she looked on the duel differently, perhaps partly because Denise had already beaten her in minor events that year. While admitting to being proud that her daughter had emerged as a rival, Beryl wrote: 'I knew I was in for a hard tussle. We were both wearing the colours of Morley CC, but it was to be an all-out, no-holds-barred fight.'

A strong field included five other internationals, among them Carol Barton, a top-ten finisher at the world championship road race; Cathie Swinnerton, who would go on to win the event twice; and Terry Riley, who finished second behind Denise in the French stage race that summer.

On a course with a sharp climb and a long, hard drag, they combined to produce a relentlessly fast pace from the opening lap, creating a seven-strong breakaway group. Fearful of her rivals' finishing speed, especially Denise's, Burton attacked repeatedly in an effort to split the group. By the fourth lap, only five women held her wheel. In the frenzy, Swinnerton and Riley tangled and crashed, ruining their chances. That meant only the Burtons and Barton remained in contention on the final lap. When Beryl attacked again, Barton was broken but, during what Beryl described as a 'savage' sprint over the final 300m, Denise would not be beaten. They finished so close to one another that the judges needed time to settle on a decision before awarding Denise her first national title.

Beryl was upset, not only at the defeat but because she had yet again lost a major road race despite shouldering by far the greatest burden of the work – circumstances that had, by then, denied her several world road race titles. 'It would be nice to record that I felt pleased for her,' Beryl wrote of Denise. 'But this is not a story for some romantic magazine. It is a real-life narrative about ordinary people with jangled nerves and emotions, our bitter conflict played out in almost gladiatorial fashion. Looking at it purely in race terms, I felt that Denise had not done her whack in keeping the breakaway and that again I had "made the race".'

Denise's interpretation of events is more straightforward. 'I was just racing, just racing to win, just as she was racing to win and the other girls were racing to win. She messed the race up.'

Whatever the ethics of the race, even Beryl would admit she was wrong to refuse to shake her daughter's hand on the podium. 'It was not a sporting thing to do. I did our sport a disservice and I can only plead I was not myself at the time.' She added that she was emotionally and physically spent and finally snapped when she could not find Charlie in the throng that surrounded her after the race. 'It was a bit strange,' Denise says. 'I don't know why she did it. I don't think she knew why she did it. Just silly. She just wanted to win and she just got herself completely mixed up.'

In 2010, *Cycling Weekly* said that the pair soon reconciled but the truth was more complicated. Beryl was contrite – 'she didn't direct the apology to that [the podium incident], but it was to do with the whole thing,' Denise says – yet when I ask if her mum ever behaved similarly again, Denise points to an incident the next winter. Her parents suddenly announced that they were moving into a flat that Charlie had been offered with a new job and that Denise had a fortnight to find somewhere else to live. 'I said, "Where am I going to live then?". And she just says, "Well, you'll have to find somewhere". My dad had a word with my auntie and I moved in with her. Well, the new job that my dad had got came with this flat, so I can understand that bit, but the fact that they didn't tell me so that I could prepare for it, that was the shock.'

Though her relatives welcomed Denise, she struggled to fit into their lifestyle. They were not used to the peculiar lifestyle of a devoted athlete. They could not understand her training patterns or fairly strict diet.

A year after moving in with them Denise got married, but the relationship did not work. The inability to share problems with her parents worsened her stress and she eventually spiralled into anorexia. 'It was [down to] everything. I put a lot of stress on myself to do well in cycling. My auntie and my uncle were wonderful but weren't cyclists. Then I suppose not being a close family, I couldn't go to my mum and dad and discuss anything.' Not even anorexia? 'No, we never discussed it. And it was nasty. I went down to six stone. I was really, really tiny.'

Her recovery took several years. While trying to hold down work as a nursery nurse, Denise would make progress only to slip back again. Even when she began to improve, she swung to the opposite extreme and over-ate. 'It's tough. When you're first getting over it, you can't even eat next to people, you just can't. It took me quite a few years to sort it out. It never reoccurred but I had a lot of turmoil. I messed up my twenties. It's a bit of a shame really, isn't it? It's your best years, the twenties into the thirties.'

In the end, being so weak that she could not ride her bike triggered a turnaround. 'I couldn't do what I wanted to do and that was cycle, because I didn't have any strength or energy. Once I'd realised I'd got it, I decided that I've got to get out of this.'

Now Beryl did step up, buying a tandem for the pair of them to ride while Denise regained her strength and confidence in the saddle, a process that did not take long. Soon Denise was fit enough for them to race together, even setting a British tandem record over ten miles. By 1985, after just a winter's training, she was strong enough to regain her place in the British squad, too, and went to the first Tour de l'Aude Cycliste Féminin, a four-day stage race, finishing second overall and winning the King of the Mountains award. The next year she entered the Tour Féminin, the women's version of the Tour de France. She finished down the field but was sufficiently encouraged by her performance to believe that she could challenge for a podium place with another year's training.

That plan progressed well. She went on a six-week training

camp in Majorca and comfortably held her own with a group of leading amateur men. She looked primed to emerge from her mother's shadow. Her plans were derailed when her front spindle snapped while she was climbing a hill on a training ride the day before the national championships, sending Denise flying over the handlebars. 'Nasty, nasty, nasty,' she recalls. 'I broke my back, crushed my vertebrae. I had a lot of trouble with it for years afterwards. I completely smashed my face up. I mean, it's a wonder I look [OK]. I had a lot of work on it.' The problems with her back meant that she did not race again. 'That was my cycling career finished. Gone, just like that.'

Denise does not seem at all sentimental. She says she was brought up to get on with life. 'And that's what I did,' she says. She will admit, however, that her cycling talent went unfulfilled. For, on her comeback, she had been determined to compete in the Olympic and Commonwealth Games, to both of which women cyclists had only just been accepted. Instead her best years were those before she left home and her life fell apart. In the back of her mind, the split with her parents is still a source of frustration.

'It did bother me and I suppose it still bothers me. Sometimes I think, "Well, maybe if that hadn't have happened, this wouldn't have happened and maybe I wouldn't have got ill". You can't blame any one thing but I do wish that some things hadn't happened.'

Before Beryl there was Eileen Sheridan, the first dame of British cycling, who spent years setting British long-distance records only for Beryl to come along and break half of them. Born in Coventry in 1923, Eileen became the quickest British woman at every distance from ten to one hundred miles. She turned professional with Hercules in 1952 and claimed just about every place-to-place record, several of which still stood in 2015. Check out the Road Records Association's website to find her name alongside long neglected routes such as London to Edinburgh, York to Edinburgh, and London to Bath and back. At four foot eleven, she was slight but had huge heart. Eileen hallucinated while riding from Land's End to John O'Groats in 1954 yet still broke the record for it and, for good measure, continued until she had demolished the women's quickest time for 1,000 miles. It took her three days and one hour.

I asked several times if she would be interviewed but was rejected. Eileen insisted that she had had quite enough recent coverage. Her autobiography was reprinted in 2009 and she was the subject of a documentary in 2014. Such overexposure!

She would, however, discuss Beryl, whom she knew quite well. She recalled meeting Beryl at a cycling dinner around 1983 when Beryl, aged forty-seven, was chasing her twenty-fifth consecutive Best British All-Rounder title. 'She looked dreadful, exhausted,' Eileen said. 'I said, "Beryl, why don't you rest on your laurels? You don't need to prove anything any more", but she couldn't rest. She had to keep racing. I suppose she wanted to hold on to the titles for ever.'

What Beryl had not admitted to anyone was that she was suffering from spinal concussion, a condition that made breathing difficult and left her frequently fatigued. She had kept the diagnosis secret from her family because she knew they would try to dissuade her from chasing the landmark. She managed it, narrowly, edging out eighteen-year-old Sue Fenwick, with sterling twenty-five and fifty-mile time-trials on one weekend. It was her last important individual victory and secured an achievement that she must have known would never be surpassed, yet she continued to race on the club scene. Denise says: 'I think she'd just done it for most of her life. She'd pushed her body so much that she'd find it hard not to.'

On 8 May, 1996, Beryl was riding to Denise's home to deliver invitations to her fifty-ninth birthday picnic in four days' time when she suffered coronary failure in the saddle and died, a consequence partly of the heart arrhythmia from which she had always suffered.

Charlie arrived at Denise's house with a policeman to relay the news. 'It was like this big stone falls in your stomach,' she says. 'You're just numb.' By then remarried, Denise was closer to her mum than she had been as a young woman and was looking forward to her children, Mark, aged six, and two-year-old Anna, getting to know their grandmother. Though Denise does not regret anything that went unsaid between them, she is sad that she did not get the chance to impose a little physical affection on her mother. 'You know, my mum and dad were very close and he'd give her a hug and stuff like that, and he'd hug me, but my mum just didn't do it. But I would imagine that, as I've got older, I would have been doing it to her. We all grow up. I'd like to think I would have forced it upon her.'

I suspect Denise would have been happy for the interview to run on beyond its allotted hour, but the story has reached its end. As she shows me to the front door, I realise that I have forgotten to ask an obvious question. For all of Beryl's success, was Britain's most successful cyclist content in the life that she picked? 'I don't know,' Denise says. 'At times, I used to wonder. When she was younger, she probably was. But from the time that I can start remembering, when I was about five, the seriousness crept in – at home it did anyway. She became very determined, very single-minded.'

Beryl often spoke of the affection she felt for Morley CC. Denise was a devoted club cyclist, too, first with Morley and then with Hainault Roads Club when she moved to Essex in the 1980s. Eileen Sheridan said club runs with Coventry CC 'numbered among the happiest moments of my life'. New cyclists tend not to join a club but I need to. I need to know what it feels like to ride in the wonderfully fluent and brisk chain gangs that I have seen on the Essex lanes. I need to learn from its members and I want to experience the camaraderie. I want to hear stories, too.

Hence, I am standing outside a pub in Woodford, Essex, at nine-fifteen on a Sunday morning in October, hoping to keep the wheel of the East London Vélo. They are not the most welcoming bunch, clad in the club-kit black, murmuring a few hellos, a few appearing to be suffering from the previous night.

It has been hard to find out much about the club. They do not provide phone numbers on their website and they have not replied to my emails. I am beginning to wonder if I have broken some etiquette by turning up on spec when a rider in his late twenties introduces himself as Will and calls out for newcomers. I raise a hand, as does a teenager whom, as I soon discover, has turned up on a borrowed bike.

'OK, shouldn't be too tough today,' says Will, the club secretary. 'Most of the guys are coming back after a few weeks' break after the end of the season. Just stick close to the bunch and you should be fine.'

Within half a mile, I am with the teenager, struggling to keep at the back of the group. Within another twenty minutes, they are out of sight. Will has sacrificed his club run to shepherd us through the lanes of Epping Forest. So has a friend of the teenager, who is a member of the club.

'Can be a bit competitive at the start,' Will says. 'There's always a surge of adrenaline.'

I nod, breathlessly, hoping he does not expect me to talk.

'Have you done much riding, then?'

A fair bit, I tell him, in a whisper.

'That's good,' he says. 'A lot of people head out into the lanes a few times, do thirty miles, and think they're fit enough to join us. But it doesn't quite work like that. We don't pootle along on the club run. So, how long do you usually go out for?'

'About thirty miles,' I say, pootling along.

The Vélo, it turns out, are almost purely a racing club. They started life as a sponsored team a decade ago, before losing their backing, but have retained that ethos ever since. Most of their members have climbed at least one category in the racing classifications. Will, a Cambridge graduate who turned to cycling after he missed the competitive buzz of rowing at university, is a third-category rider. There is at least one first-cat, although you will not find him on a club run. 'Gets up at six-thirty, pushes himself hard then returns to spend Sunday with his family.' People live like this?

I confess to Will about my inexperience and he offers to turn the ride into a kind of coaching session for beginners. We practise 'bit and bit', riding two abreast, trying to swap places at the front smoothly. He passes on tips: get closer to the wheel ahead, keep a steady speed when overtaking, look beneath your armpit to judge the distance of the rider behind. So that is why the professionals do it.

Just as I feel like I am being granted access to a secret code, I fail to spot a pothole and blow a puncture as I roll over it. I am embarrassed to report that I have taken all my previous punctures to the bike shop to get them fixed. As I struggle pathetically to repair it, Will takes charge, throwing the dust cap on my tyre valve into the field – an aesthetic thing that all cyclists do, apparently – before rapidly completing the task. 'There are plenty of other clubs around here that you might be better suited to, at least to begin with,' he says. 'I'd be happy to email you a list of them.'

CHAPTER FOUR

At last, the author finds a club who welcome incompetence

With overshoes and mudguards, the five cyclists in the café in Abridge are much better prepared for the gathering storm outside than I am. I got soaked just wheeling my bike from the car through this village in Essex, where Crest CC meet before a club run.

'Vital really,' says Andy, comparing his waterproof overshoes to my sodden footwear. Andy arrived on a tandem with his partner Lorraine. Both are wearing the purple club jerseys. So, too, is John Browning, the club-run captain, who I have spoken to on the phone, and Pete Wragg, aka Flash, a bus driver in his early sixties with long hair and looped ear-ring. John is a taxi driver and of a similar age. Andy and Lorraine are older than me, too.

This is promising. 'Be careful with Flash,' says John, joining me at the back of our small bunch as we head out on the bikes. 'Good rider but he's deaf in one ear.' He is called Flash not because of the speed he showed to win the Essex road race title in the early 1970s but because he once crashed half a dozen times on a club run along a canal. In other words, you could always find him spread on the floor, like the cleaning product, Flash.

John is Twig because, in his racing pomp, he was as thin as the model Twiggy. He is still slim, the product of having cycled a few times a week for five decades. He rides well, too, keeping still and low across the frame. As he gives a potted history of the club, he leans into me closer than any rider has done. I will discover this is normal practice. I am grateful for it now because it is hard to hear him through the wind and rain.

The Crest, he says, was formed in 1935 by an Ilford lamp-lighter who used to ride for his job and decided he wanted to meet other cyclists. In the 1950s it counted among its members Jack Hoobin, the Australian world road race champion who spent summers in Britain. It is still the club for Alan Perkins, winner of the longest ever stage on the Tour of Britain, a 246km slog from Nottingham to Southend in 1961.

Graham Adams, another member not out today, was (possibly) the first Briton to be convicted of doping, in the 1960s. Apparently it was a mix-up and he was innocent but the club still like to remind him of it. Sue Rogers, editor of the club's website, was third in a veterans' world championship.

Twig enjoyed an impressive racing career. Joining the club in the late 1960s, he progressed to first-cat when it was the highest classification before a rider turned semi-professional. (There is an elite category now.) He recalls riding the old Eastway circuit in Hackney, or the Pits as clubs affectionately called it because it was built on the site of what was a rubble dump after the Second World War.

As I push him for more detail, he laughs at the memory of 'bloodbaths', races around a car park in Harlow in the 1960s.

The name of these races came from the fact that only mattresses erected at the side of the makeshift circuit prevented riders from falling into pedestrian tunnels. 'Yeah, I saw a few crashes there,' he says. Twig is wearing only an old-fashioned racing cap for protection these days.

His racing days are over now. Instead he rides socially with the club at home and on occasional trips abroad. With seventy members, there are usually more out on a Sunday than there are today, but a lot of them are on a skiing trip together. Mostly in their forties or older, he says they are careful not to drop newcomers.

I find, then, that the pace is manageable. By the time we reach the village of Matching Green for elevenses, I am thrilled that I have not slowed them down. I am relieved also that Twig has decided to cut the run from four hours to three. My mood turns as we pull into the teahouse and I skid on the wet tarmac, toppling over again. Fortunately nobody knows me well enough to laugh.

'Nope, sorry,' Twig says. 'That has no chance of winning the crash of the season award.' Apparently, the leading contender for this honour was the rider who fell into the New River on the Christmas Eve club run. I suspected it already but, on hearing this, I know that I have found my club. How could I not have done when there is a more inept rider than me in it?

'Oh, I know the Crest very well. It was the first club I ever went out with,' says Roger St Pierre, when I visit this sage of cycling. 'The first time I ever got drunk, I was twelve years of age at the Crest HQ.' This is the Crest club hut near Stansted, which is used for weekend retreats. 'We met these gypsies and they gave us scrumpy cider. We rode down the lane in the pitch dark and went straight down a ditch, about ten of us, killing ourselves laughing.'

I have visited Roger for an insight into what life was like for a cycling journalist during road racing's formative years and to solicit his thoughts on cycling's renaissance. I am hoping he might be able to add to the well-documented reasons for its resurgence: that it is a result of the public's increased desire to keep fit, a heightened sensitivity to the effect of motorised transport on the environment, a means to reduce commuting costs and the knock-on effects of the success of our elite cyclists.

Having spoken to him several times before, and listened as he regaled me with stories and insights from a life in which he has been a racing cyclist, team manager and race organiser, not to mention music promoter, travel writer and book editor, I suspect he will have much to say.

He lives not far from the Crest hut in the Essex village of Wethersfield. A porcelain plaque by the front door announces 'Ici habite un cycliste' ('A cyclist lives here'). The last time I visited it, I was struck by how his home reflected his passions. His outhouse was stocked with about 50,000 LPs, 20,000 singles and stacks of CDs, many acquired while writing for *New Musical Express* and *Record Mirror* or working as a radio DJ and as a promoter with icons such as James Brown, Marvin Gaye, BB King, Jerry Lee Lewis and Bill Haley, but most of the records have been sold to fund his retirement. In the same building, he had enough cycling memorabilia to stock a small museum, though he has sold most of that, too, to the fashion designer and cycling fan Paul Smith, who happily paid a five-figure sum for the collection of books, magazines, race cards and historic photographs among other treasured items. 'That kept me going for a while,' Roger says. There is still plenty of evidence of his lifelong connection to the sport: a book here and there, the racing wheels in the lobby.

Roger has developed Parkinson's since we last met, but he still manages to ride his bike. 'The doctors actually recommend bike riding,' he says. 'It's to do with the way your brain works, the balancing systems. When I'm walking my balance is completely off and I struggle, but when I'm in the saddle I'm fine. It's the same with dancing. I was at a wedding recently and I was able to dance all night.'

Fortunately, his brain is still blade-sharp. Now seventy-three years old, he can recall perfectly how he fell in love with the sport as a child, growing up in Ilford, and could name just about every winner of the Tour de France by the time he fell into that ditch as a drunken twelve year old. He had his first race report published in *The Romford Times* when he was fifteen and, while sixteen and still at school, he was writing for a group of local newspapers, holding down a Saturday job with *Cycle Sport*, the weekly newspaper, and freelancing for the national press. Sometimes he would ride to offices to deliver his copy by hand. Little wonder then that when a vacancy eventually cropped up on *Cycling*'s editorial team on Fleet Street he was a shoo-in for the role at the storied old institution.

In many ways, the history of *Cycling Weekly*, as it is now known, is a history of British cycling as its fortunes have waxed and waned with those of the sport. Established in 1891, it was a journal for the Victorian gent and in its first decade it temporarily changed its name to *Cycling and Moting* to try to cash in on a new pastime that was threatening cycling's popularity: driving a car. Its political allegiance during the sport's civil war meant that it lost readers to other publications such as its spin-off *Sporting Cyclist* and *The Bicycle*. As Roger discovered, it also upset a lot of cyclists.

In 1957 it changed its name again, from *Cycling* to *Cycling and Mopeds* in a misguided attempt to exploit the sudden popularity of scooters that would contribute to the sharp decline in the number of people cycling. Roger remembers the downturn well. 'You can almost name the year it started. In 1959 there were twenty-six clubs in and around Romford. There were twenty-seven races on the Little Waltham circuit round Braintree alone. There were at least nine good bicycle shops within a six-mile radius of Romford. But in 1960 there were only four races on the Little Waltham circuit, there were only three cycling clubs left and two bike shops.'

Perhaps even more damaging than the arrival of the moped was the sudden affordability of small cars such as the Ford Anglia and Mini. 'All of a sudden, that growing-up thing that we all went through where you have a pair of roller-skates, then a bike, then a cheap motorbike, then a car – that whole middle chunk was taken away,' says Roger. 'You had roller-skates, next thing you know you had a motorbike, then a Mini.' The dramatic societal shift turned the bicycle into a no-status symbol. 'By the Sixties it was, "Why are you riding a bike? Can't you afford a car?" If you rode a bike, you were a pleb.'

When Roger got the job with *Cycling* in the early 1960s, the magazine was struggling. Not only was the number of people cycling in decline but the magazine's politics had alienated many of those that remained. It survived, probably, because it had no weekly rival having bought out *The Bicycle*. 'Oh, it was hated,' Roger says. 'The fact that it had sided with time-trialling and had actively campaigned against road racing was like this cross we had to bear.'

Budgetary constraints meant that Roger was part of an editorial team of only three, fulfilling every role from page design to reporting, feature writing and production. The job ran into evenings and weekends, yet still he found time to ride, commuting the fifteen miles to work, riding with chain gangs around the Essex lanes in the winter and competing whenever he could, most often on the tracks at Herne Hill and Paddington and the road circuit at Crystal Palace. As a first-category rider, he was allowed to compete against the best in the country and would often report on events in which he was riding. 'I did the Tour of Ireland twice like that. I was riding 100-mile stages and then going up in the press room until two o'clock in the morning.' His editor was Alan Gayfer, a hard taskmaster but one with an eye for talent. He gave breaks to Phil Liggett, the TV commentator, and Les Woodland, the cycling historian, among others. Gayfer and Roger would fall out frequently. 'He hated me racing,' says Roger. 'He thought my whole life should be that magazine. He once fired me for being five minutes late after I had worked all weekend and then through to three in the morning on the Tuesday. He sacked me five times in total. I just ignored him and turned up again the next morning. It was odd, though. He was a real bastard at work but you could not meet a kinder, more generous person outside the office.'

Eventually, Roger grew sick of this treatment and accepted a music-writing job, but he remained heavily involved in cycling and added team management to his workload. He took squads of British riders all over Europe, yet he never missed an opportunity to race himself, even when accommodation was unaffordable or hard to find. 'I raced in Belgium, France, Spain, Germany, Ireland, Canada, the US, and we were sleeping on school floors, in the crypts of churches, army barracks, even an old German Luftwaffe hangar.'

Roger is a professional storyteller and it is hard not to wonder if occasionally he gilds the truth, but such hardships had been the lot of the amateur British cyclist abroad since the 1950s. While Roger was fortunate to have a job to return to, others crossed the Channel hoping to make a living from the sport. 'Oh, it was terribly under-funded,' he says. 'You'd be sharing beds with complete strangers in real doss-houses.'

The demands of raising three children eventually forced him to give up racing, although he never stopped writing about the sport and is currently producing a series of retrospective pieces for *Cycling Plus* magazine. Living in fine cycling country – the Tour de France passed through his village in 2014 – he encounters scores of cyclists on roads near by, sometimes club runs but more often lone riders, or those in sportives. New cyclists, essentially.

Roger is no reactionary but this is not the sport that he fell in love with. Partly he is annoyed that so much of the equipment is prohibitively expensive for what used to be the working man's pursuit. He also regrets that the old communal spirit that was so special to the sport has been lost. 'People are out, getting healthy and fit and enjoying themselves, which is great, but it's sad that they ride along in isolation. When you get a sportive and there's several thousand people flying past, nobody's talking to each other, and no one's riding in a properly organised bunch. They have these amazing £5,000 bikes but haven't a clue how to ride in the wheels.

'Sadly, we also seem to have lost much of the sociability that used to be one of cycling's major attractions. Why ride in silence? Think of the Tour: even those guys find time to chat whenever the pace eases up. To be honest, that was the thing I liked most in bike racing: being in the middle of the crowd, among all those whirring wheels. I wasn't even interested in forming a breakaway because I loved riding in a huge, great bunch. But you see people now and, even when there's hundreds out there, they're not riding side by side with somebody. Everyone is on their own little island.'

A lot of seasoned club cyclists seem to have reservations about sportives. My experience of them is that they are harmless fun (as long as you turn up on time). They provide motivation to get on the bike and the atmosphere is cheerful. They are occasionally competitive, too, with fast groups forming at the front, although these usually comprise road racers and are too quick for most.

Old-timers, however, think sportives are dangerous because they attract people unused to riding in groups and unable to hold their line, to sit on a wheel or fan out in a cross-wind. There is truth to this, though I suspect some older riders also resent sportives because they offer an alternative to the club run, and thus, they fear, undermine them.

Club riders will often dismiss the sportive as a rebranded and more expensive version of the reliability trial, the massed-start event of decades past in which you were not allowed to finish before a certain time. It was designed as a kind of formal training run, but what usually happened was the hard men went full tilt, turning it into a race in all but name, and then took a sneaky break at the side of the road before the finish to make sure they kept within the time limit.

Roger, however, has an alternative theory, suggesting that sportives have largely replaced time-trials, their predecessor as the bedrock event of the sport in Britain. 'Time-trialling, officially, doesn't have placings,' he explains. 'When we used to do the results in *Cycling*, you just listed them in order of the times but you never put a place in because, officially, it's not a race. You're racing yourself. Well, sportives have filled that role. You don't compete against the other people, you're competing against yourself.' And that, he suggests, is a necessary antidote to modern life. 'People have got too much competition. School, work, everything in life now is down to being number one, lord of the jungle. If you don't push yourself, someone will tread on you. And, deep down, people don't want that pressure. They want to keep fit and they want a personal challenge but they don't want to be rated against others. That's why the sportive has taken off.'

Roger has crammed a lot into his life. While raising three children, he supplemented his day job with freelance journalism. He has written and edited scores of books, too, managing it by skipping a night's sleep twice a week for years. The night before we met, he worked round the clock to meet a deadline. He managed to race for years, too, because he needed only two or three months' training to get fit enough to hang on to the bunch.

I would love to think that it were that easy. If it were, then I could race this year. The problem is that others I have spoken to disagree with him. Alan Norris, the Crest vice-president and general secretary, reckons I need three years' preparation before racing, because it requires as much a technical education as it does raw fitness. Tony Woodcock, a well-known figure on the veterans' scene, reckons it took him the same length of time when he returned to racing after taking early retirement.

A friend of mine, Chris, however, has managed it in about 18 months, and insists that I could emulate him if only I show as much persistence as he has. He has suggested I attend one of his competitions, too, to get an idea of what is involved. Thus I find myself at Redbridge Cycling Centre, affectionately known as Hog Hill, on a Saturday morning in January, marvelling at the scene unfolding before me. There are men pulling up in cars that look like they cost less than the carbon-framed bikes that are tied to the back of them. Outside the new changing rooms, cyclists are warming up on rollers. Small groups of club-mates are clip-clopping up and down the tarmac, preparing for the next race.

It feels serious. A few more riders are stretching hamstrings with the help of a memorial bench. It is dedicated to Dave 'Weapon' Ford, the Crest rider who died in his thirties from septicemia. The bench formerly stood at the Eastway in Hackney, which was cleared to make way for the Olympic site, so was then brought to Hog Hill. Inside the changing rooms, there is a photograph of Eddy Merckx on his one appearance at the Hackney track.

Riders still talk fondly about the Eastway. From 1975 until its closure in 2006, it was the only race track of its kind within striking distance of central London. It was located among chemical factories and allotments. Its first manager, Colin Lewis, rode the Tour de France with Tom Simpson in 1967, the fateful Tour in which Simpson died on Mont Ventoux. Eastway had Clarey Corner's, so called because the first cyclist to crash on it supposedly was John Clarey, the Briton who took the lanterne rouge at the 1968 Tour, awarded to the rider who finishes last.

Its design apparently made for interesting racing, with a challenging climb, technical bends and a finishing straight long enough to produce exciting sprints. Hog Hill is not so well admired, the twelve per cent climb before its finish being considered by some to be a bit too tough. It lacks the urban romance of its predecessor, too, being on the outer reaches of the Central Line and an hour's drive from the City. But it does offer great views of the countryside and the London skyline, as well as a commentator who provides updates on the race in progress.

Right now, it is a fourth-category event. The competitors are lapping the circuit fluently, closely bunched, sweeping expertly around the cornered descent just in front of us, then disappearing from view and re-emerging on the hill.

Chris, a maths teacher who seems to apply himself to training with scientific precision, is nicely positioned about third from the front. In the black and red of Hackney CC, he looks composed, spinning a low gear, pulling hard on the forks as they crest the climb. I realise that his girlfriend, Bea, is here when he hurls a water bottle at her without moving his head.

'Oh, that looked very professional,' I say, walking up to her.

'Was that supposed to be for me?' she says, laughing at the discarded vessel on the ground.

Bea is excited for Chris. She has watched him get fit on rollers in their flat through the winter, cheering him on from the sofa. I have followed his progress, too, on Strava. I have even attempted to emulate a few of his uploaded rides on the stationary bike in my gym. The first time I tried, I almost passed out with the effort and felt too sick to ride for about a fortnight afterwards. Chris generously called it overtraining.

He has never won points before but looks as well placed as anybody as they climb the hill for the final time. As we cheer him on, for a moment it looks as if he might even challenge for victory. Instead he slips back in the short sprint to the finish, and ends up fifth.

'I can't believe it,' he says a few moments later, blowing clouds of air. 'I got points!'

I examine his Garmin and find that he averaged twenty-two miles per hour for the hour-long race. I am impressed.

'It's not about the average,' he says. 'It's the sudden changes in pace that count. You need to be able to withstand them.'

As he catches his breath, Chris provides a quick breakdown of his progress. He first travelled to Hog Hill a year ago and lapped it alone. He was dropped in his first race. Now he reckons he could be third-category by springtime. A senior club-mate, Neil, an artist from Hackney, nods in agreement. I tell them that I feel as though I am years away from being able to emulate him.

'No, it's perfectly possible,' says Neil, who Chris regularly calls on for advice. Neil reckons you need only do intense interval sessions a few times a week for as little as half an hour on rollers or a turbo-trainer to get race fit, assuming you do a long ride at the weekend. 'Then you can get on with the rest of your life.'

This sounds promising. I like cycling but I would like to have a life. I reckon I could manage the programme Neil has outlined. As the cat-one and cat-two riders begin to race, I decide it is best that I leave. I do not want to feel intimidated again. Besides, I have got next winter to catch up with them.

CHAPTER FIVE

Life as Tom Simpson's right-hand man

Spot of trouble at the Crest. *Cycling Weekly* has published a feature on the sale of the club hut, close to which Roger St Pierre first got drunk, and the content doesn't reflect well on the club. It reports that the Crest are cashing in on Stag Hall, their decrepit bungalow near the town of Saffron Walden in Essex, because the club are struggling financially and can't afford to repair the roof. This is true.

What feels harsh is that the situation is portrayed as being a symptom of a club in decline as much as it is a sign of the changed times. This seems especially so when the writer goes on to talk about how Lea Valley CC had such a jolly good time in their nearby hut on the weekend of their open twenty–mile time-trial. Don Keen, Lea Valley's former president, even takes the opportunity to compare his club favourably with ours. 'We're not worried. We'll be running enough events over the year that we can cover anything major. We're quite OK but a lot of clubs would be in difficulty, like the Crest now,' he says, presiding over a generous spread of bacon butties for his riders. Such is Lea Valley's munificence.

Sue Rogers, the Crest website editor who has been working on the sale of Stag Hall, wonders how or if we should respond. Should we defend the club's honour or rise above the perceived slight? We do not want people to think we gave up easily on the building, not when it is part of local cycling history. Crest's is one of several huts on the Northall Road outside the village of Ugley that Essex and East London-based clubs own, as a result of an age-old covenant specifying that accommodation built here was to be used for sporting activity only.

Stag Hall is among the oldest huts, too, with the club having built it in 1964 and used it for years as a weekend retreat, for families, rural club runs and as an overnight stop before a dawn time-trial on the nearby E1 course.

We did not, then, sell it without regret. We offered to loan it to Essex Roads CC, only to be rebuffed. We tried to make the figures work but simply could not justify (possibly even afford) the outlay required for the asbestos roof. Other huts were built using less problematic material, such as timber. And, despite what Don Keen says, the huts are not used nearly as often as they once were. People have more demands on their time. Time-trials have lost their allure. As Sue says, why bed down in premises that smell like 'youth hostels' and are 'infested with mice' when you can drive to the venue in forty-five minutes? It is decided that the club should ignore the perceived provocation. To quote one member, who wished to remain anonymous: 'The *Cycling Weekly* readership is mainly sportive riders and Team Sky followers, who will likely skip over that article, while local club cyclists know about the huts and know the real story.'

Vin Denson's carousing on cycling trips to Essex and beyond

was the stuff of legend among Crest members when he returned from his storied career on the Continent and immersed himself in the local club scene. An outgoing, wine-loving adventure-seeker, he was apparently the first man at the bar on rural tours. He was known to sink pints before a race and was still able to hold his own in the bunch. Perhaps his personality helped him to succeed at a time when so few Britons made a living cycling abroad.

His name first cropped up while out on a Crest club run when, heading past Old Harlow, somebody happened to mention that we were close to the house of a former Tour de France rider. This casual mention of Vin seemed typical of the understated attention that he has always received. For Vin was not merely a regular Tour rider, though that in itself was no mean compliment for a Briton in the 1960s. He was among the most coveted domestiques in the peloton. Tom Simpson viewed him like a brother, Tour de France points classification winner Rik van Looy wanted him for his team and Jacques Anquetil, among the greatest cyclists of all, headhunted Vin. If you want a view of life as a British cyclist in the 1960s, there can be few better to meet.

Vin still looks powerful. As he emerges from the caravan trailer outside his home, you can see in his broad shoulders why slighter men loved to use him to break the wind. He is tanned and healthy-looking for a seventy-eight year old, too. But as he steps down gingerly on to the driveway, he is clearly in some discomfort. 'I was fourteen, fifteen, playing [football] for Chester schoolboys and the whole cartilage popped out,' he says, rubbing his knee. 'Now, they could probably repair it, but I had the whole of the cartilage taken away.' I wince. As a cyclist, did he not suffer as a result? 'Not at all, it was unbelievable. Later, a guy who operated on it said, "So you've just been riding bone on bone but, because you've done so much cycling, you've lubricated the joint and saved your knee".'

Some rehab. Not many cyclists could have covered more miles than Vin in their lifetime. You can see some evidence of that commitment inside his small, slightly cluttered home. In the living room there is a pile of *Cycling Weekly* magazines – there so often is in a cyclist's home – and there are notepads and pens, possibly those with which Vin has started to write his second set of memoirs. The first charted his sporting life. The plan for the second is to talk about the champions he has ridden alongside, not just those mentioned above, but domestic heroes such as Ray Booty, the bespectacled time-trial genius from Nottingham who was the first man to break four hours for 100 miles, and others, including Ken Laidlaw, the first Scot to finish the Tour de France. Near by is a clutch of memorabilia, including photographs and cuttings dating back to Vin's early days as a club cyclist with Chester RC.

Like so many of his generation, Vin was awakened to cycling by watching his father ride to work, in his case an eight-mile trip to an aerodrome where he held down a job as an electrician. Vin thought the world of his old man, a First World War veteran who had survived shootings and a mustard gas attack while laying trench cables, but as a result suffered ill health for the rest of his life, and without complaint. Though he never raced bikes, he always supported Vin, getting up at dawn to watch his son when he began to show his burgeoning talent riding time-trials with Chester RC.

Cycling was always an emotive experience for Vin. He had inherited his first bike from his half-brother when he left for the Second World War, never to return. He died from a brain haemorrhage while flying in the unpressurised cockpit of a Lancaster. 'Far too young,' Vin says, shaking his head, admitting that for years he thought of him while out riding. 'He used to come home on leave. Just a nice guy, a quiet guy, good-looking too.'

As was the way then, Vin had built up his strength without really thinking about it. He enjoyed youth-hostel tours, to the Pennines, Wales and the Lake District. He especially relished overnight 'tourist trials' from Birmingham to Weston-super-Mare and back, say, or from Birmingham to Barmouth, on the west Wales coast, and back. This was people's idea of Saturday-night fun. Little wonder then that when Vin started racing, he found that he was best suited to the fifty-mile time-trial. 'You got fit almost by accident,' he said. 'We might do 180 miles at the weekend, and then maybe ninety to a hundred in the week. That was normal because everybody went everywhere on their bikes.'

His breakthrough season was 1954, when he entered the national championships for the first time, finishing fourth in the fifty-mile time-trial and in the British Best All-Rounder competition. He also launched a memorable assault on the fifty-mile straight-out tandem record. 'Madness, really,' he says, laughing as he recalls the effort. The straight-out time-trial certainly tests the limit of what is reasonable. It is the less commonly contested alternative to the typical out-and-back course, which balances out any benefits from the wind or road gradient. To break the straight-out record, cyclists seek the longest downhill stretch of road they can find, put their head down and hope circumstances prevail in their favour. Road safety takes a back seat.

Vin and his partner, Keith Lawton, picked the Plynlimon Pass in mid-Wales. Vin rode stoker, his head resting on Lawton's back. 'For fifty miles, I saw little else but the blur of trees, lampposts and traffic,' he says. They had friends positioned along the route, setting off traffic lights, standing beside phone boxes so that they could warn each other of the pair's arrival.

Finishing in one hour, forty-six minutes and twenty-three seconds, they shaved a couple of minutes off the British record, though were not credited with it because their designated timekeeper had fallen ill and his replacement had qualified only with the Welsh Cycling Union and not the Road Records Association. Though the record attempt was haphazard, the rules were strict.

Still, the tandem performance and his showing in the individual fifty-miler confirmed Denson as international class. He progressed steadily if unspectacularly: he was shortlisted for the 1956 Olympic Games in Melbourne and he twice almost made a Tour of Britain team, the second time while doing his national service in the Army – where he was stationed with Booty and given much time off to train. The Army took its sports teams' performances seriously.

In 1960 he finally made the national squad, earning a place for successive editions of the Peace Race. He relished the toughness of it: his heavy build limited the bounce on the cobbles; his durability sustained him in the mountains; his preparedness to endure pain meant that he battled on despite several crashes. 'We used to carry a little horsehair scrubbing brush and TCP wrapped in a flannel,' he said. They scrubbed the wound quickly to prevent coal dust infecting it. 'You made it bleed but cleaned it with TCP. You soon forgot the pain.'

By finishing twenty-seventh, he earned himself a place in the British team being put together to contest the 1961 Tour de France.

By then Vin was twenty-six and married to Vi, whom he had met on a club run across Wales: how so many cycling romances were born. By 1961 she was pregnant, and they had just bought their first home, a bungalow in York that Vin had worked hard to deck out, making a breakfast bar in the kitchen from Reynolds 531 tubing. He had a job in construction and was studying to become a quantity surveyor. To tackle the Tour, he would need to give up that lifestyle and turn professional. 'But I had wanted to ride the Tour since I was a kid. Our French teacher had brought all his *cyclisme* books to school, showing me pictures of the Galibier and the snow on it, like a huge glacier. And they were all in colour! We just had *Cycling Weekly* in black and white so I couldn't believe that he'd brought these back. And he talked about the Tour de France and about his big hero, Jean Robic. But I kinda fell in love with Louison Bobet. He looked so relaxed, so full of himself and yet in complete control, and I just thought, "I'd love to be a Bobet".'

A stomach bug ended Vin's Tour prematurely but, in taking the step from amateurism to full-time cycling, the die had been cast. He returned home for a few months but, with Vi's support, he went back to Paris determined to forge a life among the sport's elite.

This was a step that few British cyclists were prepared to take. Brian Robinson had managed it successfully in the 1950s and Stan Brittain, another of Vin's team-mates on the Tour, had spent time in Belgium but most were unwilling to up sticks. Culturally, moving abroad required a much bigger adjustment than it does now. You could also expect to serve an apprenticeship with no guarantee of being paid. As a Briton, you usually had few contacts and had to prove wrong the stereotyped reputation of your compatriot cyclists on the Continent. Five years earlier, British champion Tony Hewson had famously lived in an ambulance and then a caravan with two fellow aspirants, Vic Sutton and Jock Andrews, in a mostly unsuccessful attempt to crack the professional scene.

Vin, though, was undeterred. Such persistence was remarkable given that there were more talented cyclists than him in Britain and that, in lacking a finishing sprint or exceptional climbing ability, he was going to struggle for the wins that would make his name. 'It doesn't bother me to go to a foreign land. It doesn't bother me to speak broken English and try to make myself understood. Some people can adapt to living abroad, some people get homesick, miss people back home. I just thought it was a new challenge. My wife was the same, thankfully.'

He would make up for what he lacked in race-winning ability with doggedness, hard work and formidable stamina. Within a year he had impressed sufficiently to earn a contract serving as a domestique for Pelforth, a Grand Tour team. He earned his money, too, finishing tenth in Milan-San Remo and Paris-Nice, the 'Race to the Sun' that showcased Vin's particular suitability for short stage races. Remarkably, he also had the ability to withstand the demands of such racing when unpaid wages meant he struggled to buy food. 'They'd pay you three months late. They were putting money in their bank, gaining the interest. We couldn't afford meat. It was just fish. We went into the fields and, where they hadn't gone to the edge to do the potatoes and carrots, we used to steal. We used to go with what they call your knocking bag, and you could help yourself.'

He broke into a factory and helped himself to unused timber with which to build a cot, too. He was unwilling to give up.

Often when on a long, lonely breakaway, or when in pain forcing the pace at the front of a bunch, Vin would think of Vi and their son Kevin and how the prize money would provide for them. Other times he thought of his brother. Perhaps most vividly he thought of his father on his two stage victories in the Four Days of Dunkirk. Imagining how his dad suffered on the adjacent fields ensured his pain paled by comparison. 'I remember I just went away on my own,' he says, crouching into imaginary drops. 'I was, like, spitting on my handlebars, thinking of him in the trenches.' He wipes a tear. 'In those circumstances I was as strong as anybody.'

The peloton soon realised this. In frustration Vin – or Vic as the continentals knew him – quit Pelforth for Solo, the team that had as their leader the great Rik van Looy, the 'King of the Classics'. Vin has not a good word to say about Van Looy, claiming that he was tight with his prize money when protocol demanded that he shared it with his henchmen. When Jean Stablinski, Anquetil's domestique, approached Vin about moving again – a great rider was above making such a request himself – Vin did not need to think twice, especially as the team that Anquetil was setting up for Ford-France was the strongest and best financed of all.

The typical sports hack is not easily impressed, not by sportsmen and their feats anyway. But I find it surreal that on the small landing just outside Vin's bathroom, there is a photograph of my host passing a bottle of beer to Anquetil during the Tour. Somehow, as a lowly Essex club cyclist, I expected to be more than one-degree removed from a near-mythical sporting figure, yet here is a near neighbour, a man with whom I share mutual acquaintances in the sport, talking about how one of the most iconic riders once relied on him.

'I always had to ride the closest to Anquetil. My inside leg was slightly longer than his, by about an inch and a quarter. But my bike was designed for him so I had to ride with the saddle almost a quarter [of an inch] lower than it should be. As soon as he got a puncture, he took my bike.'

As well as guiding the Frenchman up mountains, and sheltering him on the flat, he carried a bottle opener and corkscrew for emergency raids on cafés. Anquetil liked a beer during the Tour but occasionally demanded wine. Vin carried a spanner too. Of nervous disposition, the Frenchman demanded that his bike was stripped down every night, yet was never happy with the mechanics' work and invariably demanded that Vin tinkered with it. In a bulging jersey pocket, he also needed a comb to hand as Anquetil liked to slick back his blond hair in front of crowds. Vin even found lodgings for Anquetil's stepchildren in Yorkshire to help them learn English. In an infamously complicated personal life, Anquetil had settled down with the wife and children of his doctor, fathered a daughter with his stepdaughter, and another child by his stepson's wife.

Was it difficult working for such a demanding and eccentric boss? 'Not really, because he was genuine,' says Vin. 'He would always pay you, win or lose, but the others were just robbing bastards. And you knew there was a chance of him winning a Tour de France, winning whatever race, if you worked for him. You'd doubt whether you could win it yourself. And when you're going hard for him, he'd say, "I'm not interested in the Tour of Switzerland, I'm not interested in the Tour of Luxembourg, you've got a chance there." I mean, you had to leave him alone and not tell him what to do, but he was OK.'

What about his personal life? Did the great man not seem a little, well, unorthodox? 'No. I actually never used to think he was that randy. You never really saw him take that much interest in women. Some lads would be, "Whoa, look at the legs on that." But he never came out with anything like that. He was a little stiff. Strange, you know.'

Anquetil was instrumental in Vin claiming the best wins of his career, his overall triumph on the 1965 Tour of Luxembourg and a stage victory at the next year's Giro d'Italia. The latter stood out because he was the first Briton to claim a stage at the Giro. Even when Ford-France withdrew its sponsorship from the team, it did not affect what Vin describes as his golden years because Bic stepped in as a replacement. As a result, he was living the dream when his life suffered a decisive shock at the 1967 Tour.

Tom Simpson was a skinny eighteen year old when he soundly defeated Vin at an Olympic trial in 1956. That was their first meeting and they soon became friends. They had many encounters on the domestic scene, especially grass-track racing around Yorkshire. Simpson tried to persuade Vin to head to France with him rather than take up national service. It didn't work. 'I know it would have killed my dad,' Vin says.

They remained close, though, and after Vin turned pro-fessional Simpson persuaded him to leave France to come and live close to him in Belgium, where their families spent much time together. They had children about the same age. They would also train together in the close season, benefiting from each other's self-discipline. Simpson was among the few men who could match Vin's capacity to suffer. Indeed, history would show that he probably exceeded it, tragically so. 'When we both decided we'd get fit, we could get fit,' Vin says. 'Tom benefited from a lot of miles.'

In competition, though usually on rival teams, they worked together as long as it did not conflict with management orders. 'Tom was a good guy to have in a break. He was never happy just to sit in.'

Only when representing Britain could Vin assist Tom whole-heartedly, though, as he did most successfully when helping to break up the chasing pack to ensure Simpson scored his famous victory at the 1965 world road race championship. As an expression of his gratitude, Simpson gifted Vin a yellow jersey from the Tour de France. In 1962 he had become the first Briton to wear it. (I kicked myself for not asking to see it.) 'He had it for two days. He gave one to his daughter and gave one to me in appreciation of the work I'd done. He became like a brother to me.'

In 1967 they teamed up again when the Tour de France reverted to national rather than trade teams. The switch encouraged Simpson to believe that he could reach the podium in Paris as he knew that the squad would provide him with unequivocal support, unlike his colleagues at Peugeot-BP-Michelin. Though they lost three team-mates in the first week, Simpson was looking strong, placed sixth and ready to launch an assault in the Alps. But he fell ill on the Galibier and dropped like a stone through the general classification.

'He always felt he had to do a ride on the Galibier, although God knows why; that mountain never did him any favours,' Vin wrote in his autobiography. Vin had to help carry his friend up the stairs of the hotel to his bedroom. Later that evening he forced Simpson to eat – all he would accept was a bowl of onion soup – and urged him to give up on trying to finish in the first three. 'He wouldn't listen, though. He was determined.'

Simpson identified Mont Ventoux as the scene for his decisive attack. When he left Vin's wheel to join the first breakaway on the slopes of the iconic climb, Vin offered him a hand-sling and shouted after him, 'Die, die'. 'Christ, I was just trying to encourage him,' he says.

When he next saw Simpson, his team leader was lying by the side of the road with an oxygen mask covering his mouth and his eyes glazed. Vin tried to get to his friend but the British team manager, Alec Taylor, ushered him back into the race, urging him to make up lost time. Always strong on the descent, because his heavier build gave him more momentum than other riders, Vin went down Ventoux 'like a maniac', assuming nothing worse than that Simpson's race was finished and that the responsibility on him had increased as a result. When he arrived at the hotel, Taylor told him that Simpson had died. Vin cried hysterically. He told the BBC he 'felt as if something inside me had died'.

Today, when asked to recall that awful event, he takes a moment to gather his thoughts and looks across at the cuttings on his dining table, as if processing the memory again. Then he says: 'To think that bike riding killed somebody like that was just too much for me.'

He wanted to quit the race but was persuaded to return to the start line the next morning. Quite what was discussed then is the subject of debate. Vin insists that two senior riders, Stablinksi and Rudi Altig, said that the peloton wanted Vin to win the stage in his friend's memory. Vin initially refused, claiming Simpson would rather the race ran competitively.

'They said, "no disrespect Vin, we know you're upset, but this is our choice and this is what everybody voted last night and this is what we want. You've known Tom all your life. He's like a brother to you. We'd just like you to go with twenty kilometres to go, don't get more than two minutes, and win the stage."'

When I spoke to Barry Hoban, Vin's young team-mate and the man who did, in fact, go on to win that day's stage, he insisted that no such agreement was made. Hoban said that he simply took the opportunity to win the stage when it presented itself, racing clear with about forty kilometres left to race. The peloton, he said, wanted only that a Briton should win the race. It was the first of eight stages that the Yorkshireman, a formidable sprinter, would win on the Tour.

Vin recalls what happened rather differently. 'Stablinski comes up, Gimondi comes up: "What's happening? We don't want him to win a stage." And I said, "Look, if I go chasing after another Englishman, even if you lead the way and you take me up there, it's like taking a gold ring off somebody's finger. It looks so bad on television. Leave it as it is. Anyway, I don't really want to stand on a rostrum today."'

Vin soldiered on for another four days but could not shake his grief. He expected to see Simpson ride up alongside him. He grew embittered once the gloomy mood began to lift within the peloton, with riders beginning to chat and laugh again. On the seventeenth stage, in defiance of Taylor and the British team mechanic Harry Hall, Vin slowed to a standstill, ripped off his shirt number and climbed into the back of the team car. 'It really turned me off the Tour. I didn't want to touch it. I thought, "I'll pack in now, go back to England, the children are getting older".'

He pulled out of his contract with Bic and quit cycling to run the bar that he had opened in Ghent with Vi. He grieved long and hard, often breaking out in tears months later. He says that he finally snapped out of it when others began to move on with their lives. Hoban was growing close to Simpson's widow Helen, whom he would eventually marry.

Vin decided to return to the bike for one final season, riding the Giro with the new Italian team Kelvinator, while also competing on the British domestic scene. He signed off his elite career by helping Britain to win a team prize at the Tour for the first time, on the twenty-first stage. It felt like a fitting homage to his friend. 'That helped to ease the upset. I thought, "That's a nice way to finish now".'

The impact of Simpson's death on British cycling was profound. Many within the sport became disillusioned when it emerged that the drugs Simpson had taken contributed to his death. For the same reason, its reputation among people outside the sport suffered, too. As Roger St Pierre, a friend of Simpson, said. 'It set the sport back years.'

Vin notes how the British elite became rudderless as a result, too. Hoban was now the stand-out Briton, but he was not a figurehead and lacked Simpson's authority within the peloton. 'We could all speak to journalists, we could all hold our own if we were in a bunch, we knew we weren't going to let anybody down – we could ride as hard as any of them,' said Vin. 'But Tom was the clear leader. After he went, there was a kind of lapse.'

The tragedy also affected Vin's personal circumstances. For Simpson had secretly negotiated for Vin to join him on the Salvarani team. He had talked to Vin about building chalets on land that Simpson had bought in Corsica. Simpson had also discussed opening a cycling academy in Britain, at which he hoped to employ his most trusted lieutenant. 'He was soon going to retire and he was always saying, "This is what we're going to do. We're not going to have to go back to our jobs. We'll coach and help the next generation."'

Instead, Vin was left to seek more modest employment. Through the cycling journalist Ron White, he arranged to work on the design and construction of a planned cycle track in Harlow, though it was only a temporary position and did not pay enough to support a family. As a result, he fell back into construction work, setting up a company that provided damp-course treatment and preserved timber. He returned to cycling, eventually settling with Redbridge CC. He competed in the local road race leagues and time-trials. He went on club runs and touring holidays and met members of the Crest. He even fulfilled a lifelong ambition by competing in the Mersey twenty-four-hour race, finishing third and helping Redbridge to win the team title. He had finished cycling as he had begun it, at the grass-roots, hence the play on words in the title of his autobiography, *The Full Cycle*.

I ask Vin how long it should take the amateur cyclist, with a job and family, to get competitively fit. 'You can do it in one season, if you put your mind to it and put the miles in over the winter, but it's probably a four-year cycle,' he says. 'You think, "This year I can do that, the next year I can probably get under the hour, get this, get that, then I can ride the championship that I set my mind on winning in four years' time".'

Vin's last great achievement was to beat the hour in a twenty-five-mile TT, aged sixty, after his beloved Vi had succumbed to brain cancer. Training for it provided him with purpose over the lonely year that followed and served as a tribute to the woman who had sacrificed so much to help his cycling career.

Though he scaled back competitions, he continued to ride until his early seventies, until he crashed while trying to avoid a group of schoolchildren on his way to the gym, breaking his pelvis as his hip smashed against the concrete.

The pain was excruciating but he told his companion to help him back on to his bike, as if channelling Tom Simpson's refusal to give up on Mont Ventoux. He reached his destination before accepting that he was in urgent need of medical attention. 'I probably didn't do the right thing but it was just natural to me: I've fallen off; I've got to finish. I was outside Asda but it was almost like falling off in the Tour, thinking, "You've damaged your elbow, you've done something to your collarbone and the side of your hip is killing you", but while you have the adrenaline going, you just keep pumping away. If you're a cyclist, you never lose that spirit.'

As the interview winds up, I offer to give Vin a lift to a leisure centre so that he can enjoy his afternoon swim. En route, we pass an elderly cyclist, whom he recognises. As he twitches in his seat, I wonder how much he misses the pursuit. 'It's OK,' he replies. 'You know why? Every day I can be in the Lake District, I can be in the Pennines, I can be in the Pyrenees, the Alps and be doing what I did many years ago. I've done it all and I've always got that memory.'

CHAPTER SIX

Tea with Alf Engers, maverick, legend and bagel baker

To Abridge in Essex on a Thursday morning to meet Flash and Luca, a Tube driver with the Crest who has exploited the Underground strike to reprise the midweek club run. He insists his support for the protest has nothing to do with the opportunity it offered to get out on the bike, though I'm not convinced. Like me, Luca is playing catch-up in his determination to get race fit. A father-of-two in his early forties, he has returned to cycling only recently, having enjoyed long rides in his youth. It was, it turns out, useful preparation for Tube driving: 'I'm good with monotonous tasks,' he says.

The plan is for us to hold a quicker speed than the leisurely Sunday run. I'm hoping the midweek ride will again become a fixture for the club, as I'm sick of riding in my front room on a recently purchased turbo-trainer and am keen for an alternative.

Coffee is mandatory before any ride, and conversation has turned to famous cyclists seen out on the Essex lanes. Mark Cavendish is mentioned. Until recently he lived in Abridge and apparently now lives near by. So many cyclists claim to have spotted the brilliant Manxman training around these parts that you wonder how he finds time to compete. By most accounts he is quick to buy a round of drinks at tea-house stops and is often seen with Essex boy Alex Dowsett. I wonder in how many other sports does the elite mix with the grass-roots in this way. Dowsett, a stage winner at the Giro in 2013, emerged on the club scene here and still turns up to local time-trials and closed-circuit races, supplementing his training by destroying the fields.

Flash recalls Alf Engers doing something similar in the 1970s on the notoriously competitive Becontree Wheelers midweek club run, which attracted riders from clubs across the region and often mutated into an unofficial road race. 'He'd turn up with holes drilled in his frame,' Flash says, with a rasping laugh. Engers, known as 'the King' because of the extent to which he dominated the domestic time-trial scene, famously did this thinking it would make his bike faster. 'He'd beat everybody out of sight, though the holes didn't do him much good. He thought it would reduce the weight of the bike but, of course, it created pockets of air around the handlebars.'

I am star-struck, again. Of all the great names in British cycling's recent past, few were as fascinating as Engers. Reading about him in old magazines and on forums, I had gained the impression of an enigmatic personality, a rebel who was repeatedly banned by the authorities, who turned up to run-of-the-mill events looking like a rock star and who was so careful to guard his private life that few seemed to know much about him other than that he won races along A-roads again and again and again. This ensured that he was an inspiration to a generation of future champions.

'He was a hero of mine,' Tony Doyle, twice the world pursuit champion in the 1980s, told me. 'At that time, the time-trialling scene was much bigger than road racing and Alf was highly revered, and still is. He was quiet but, in his own way, he had charisma. It was the fact that he was a baker, the fact that they banned him, the fact that he broke competition records and that he was trying to be the first man to break the thirty miles an hour barrier, which was like the cycling equivalent of the four-minute mile, all those things. He had a certain mystique about him.'

I wonder if he is still around. You do not hear much about him: he is not involved with a local club; there are few interviews with him that have been published; contemporaneous reports are limited in what they reveal about Engers the man. Yet I can think of few better ways to portray domestic cycling in that era than through Engers' story.

For all his apparent elusiveness, in the end it was not difficult to track him down. Somebody knew someone who still knew Alf, even though he has not been involved in cycling for almost four decades. I received a call from him while I was at work and explained that I was writing about neglected heroes of the sport. He burst out laughing. 'You flatter me but I think you're forty years too late,' he said. 'I'm not sure any of the cyclists now would want to read about me.'

This is not an uncommon response from the giants of yesteryear. So unused are they to attention that they find the notion laughable. I insist that this cyclist at the very least would like to hear Alf's tale. 'Oh well, in that case, you'd better pop round for tea.'

Alf lives a short ride from Stag Hall in a Hertfordshire village that he has asked remains private. It is prime time-trial country, quiet and flat, close to the E1 route that Alf frequently conquered in his youth. As Alf explains as we settle down in his front room, the village is supposedly a ghostly place. Smoke is often seen rising from fields, emerging from an underground passage that runs up to his church. Folk legend has it that a man once disappeared in the tunnel. It seems an appropriate home for a man who was once a member of the Pagan Federation, especially one with Alf's mystique. 'I'm no longer a member but I would adhere to their beliefs,' he says. 'Basically, it's about respecting the countryside, respecting one another. I don't believe in God, but I believe there's something. It's us and them out there.' He is reluctant to expand on his beliefs. Presumably he is smart enough to know they might be misconstrued in print.

He is a little spectral-like, too, being grey-haired and still wiry thin. Certainly you would recognise Alf now, aged seventy-four, from the photographs of him as a young man, with the aquiline nose and the large, looped ear-ring that was once his signature accessory. 'It's on the acupuncture point for sight, but I didn't think of that at the time,' he explains. 'It was just a fashion thing, long before people were having it done professionally. It was some American bird with two ice cubes on the ear and a needle jabbed through the skin.' He must have stood out in the manly, mostly unreconstructed world of 1970s cycling. 'Oh yeah. I remember meeting these Australians at the Paddington track and I hear, "Is he a poof?"'

Alf was born to a second-generation German baker called Adolf – translation, Alfred – who ran a bakery in Islington, north London. Adolf's father, with whom he shared the Christian name, had worked in the same trade on Roman Road until arsonists vented their hatred of Germans by razing the bakery to the ground during the First World War. Alf's father avoided such enmity by pretending the family was Swiss, but still they were forced to relocate from Islington to Barnet when the Nazis dropped a V2 rocket on their street, destroying the terrace on which the Engers lived and worked.

Alf and his parents were dug out from the rubble. Three bakers were killed. Quite what lasting effect this had on him Alf does not say but it must at least have hardened him. 'It's not something I like to dwell on but, given a key, I can remember everything,' he says, sitting in a large leather armchair in the front room of a house noticeably lacking any trace of his sporting career. The only suggestion that he might be a cyclist is his retro, calf-length cycling shorts.

After the family's move to the suburbs, his father worked every hour to try to rebuild the business, leaving Alf, an only child – though Adolf had children by a previous marriage – to explore the city alone, often when playing truant from school. Travelling to Finsbury Park, he became intrigued with the races that took place within its perimeter fencing. He liked watching Barnet CC on its club runs, too, and eventually summoned the courage to join them. 'It used to fascinate me; the club jerseys, the camaraderie that seemed to exist.' He quickly impressed on the time-trial scene and had begun to wonder how far his natural stamina might take him when, aged fourteen, he crashed on his bike, hitting the concrete so heavily on Highgate Hill in Archway that surgeons had to remove his damaged kneecap. As Alf explains, while rubbing the joint, knee replacement surgery did not exist then. He spent six weeks in hospital and missed so much school that he did not bother to return to it. His disruptive behaviour during lessons meant that he had stopped learning anyway. 'I was trouble,' he admits. 'I was always fighting, with the teachers, with other kids. I just wasn't fitting in.'

Quite what was the root of his volatility as a child is uncertain but his relationship with his father might provide a clue. Alf does not have a good word to say about him. 'He was basically concerned with himself. Horrible thing to say, never speak ill of the dead, but, yeah,' he says, explaining how his dad showed no interest in the exceptional talent his son had already demonstrated. 'Father really could not have cared less. He never helped at all. He never put his hand in his pocket for any cycle equipment, nothing like that.'

While serving as an apprentice in the family business, the fourteen-year-old Alf had lied about his age to acquire the racing licence that the British Cycling Federation issued only to cyclists aged over sixteen.

He was so addicted to competition that he returned to it even before his knee had properly healed, succeeding in regional and then national events. To illustrate the pain he was experiencing at the time, he recalls the night before he first broke the hour mark in a twenty-five-mile time-trial. 'I was sleeping with chicken wire over the bed because I couldn't bear anything touching it [the knee], and [it was] wrapped in a crepe bandage with olive oil on.'

He eventually won the junior road race at the national championships. Then, aged nineteen, he set a new national record for the twenty-five-mile time-trial of fifty-five minutes and eleven seconds, earning sponsorship from a bike shop owner called Ted Gerrard. Based in Archway, and a former national road race champion, Gerrard was popular among cyclists across north London in the 1960s because he sold bikes at a bargain price by selling the handlebars separately, avoiding tax that was levied only on completed bikes.

Rarely did a cyclist step up to semi-professionalism at such a young age but Alf's personal circumstances meant that he couldn't afford to reject the chance to compete for prize money. In the previous year alone, he had got married, become a father and lost his dad without receiving any inheritance because Adolf had not written a will, leaving Alf's half-siblings to fight successfully for ownership of the bakery. 'All of a sudden I went from having prospects to having none, to going out as a pleb worker.' His mother was left penniless, too. 'She was high and dry, no access to money or anything. She had to pawn her wedding ring to live.' It must have been traumatic. 'Yeah, it left a mark. Just made me more determined. What I wanted to do, I was going to do it.'

Not yet, though. The pressure of trying to establish himself as a baker and of bringing up a young family meant that he had little time to race, forcing Alf to give up on his dream of professionalism and reapply for amateur status in 1964. The BCF was having none of it. It cited the rule that said he would need to take a year out before he could return to the non-paid ranks. Three years passed before it finally accepted Alf's request and only then after he produced a doctor's note, wrongly claiming that his old knee injury had rendered him practically infirm.

Clearly, the authorities didn't like Alf, and almost certainly because he constantly challenged the rules of time-trialling to achieve the best result. This maverick streak was inspired by a trip to Biggleswade in Bedfordshire in the early 1950s, during which he watched the Higginson twins, Stan and Bernard, compete in the national time-trial championships for Halesowen CC. Then two of Britain's strongest riders, the Higginsons had upset the old order by adopting a then-unusual riding style in which they kept their upper body perfectly still at a time when almost everyone else was happy to swing sideways across the frame to generate power. 'Down in a crouch, glass of water on the back,' as Alf puts it, adding that the brothers were also innovative for the (blind) courage with which they cut corners, even on single-carriageway roads.

Alf, then, copied their style. He found other ways to shave seconds from his time, too. He made way for cars later than other riders, seemingly regardless of the rule that insisted no cyclist held up traffic. He rode as close as possible to vehicles in front of him before he could be accused of slipstreaming – that, too, was outlawed. He had received his first letter of complaint from the Road Time Trials Council aged sixteen and had several more before he became an independent.

When finally he was allowed to return to amateurism, and thus competition, he was in no mood to start compromising – he needed to make up for lost time. The problem with this attitude in the late 1960s was that the proliferation of affordable small cars had significantly increased the amount of traffic on the roads. Even when riding early on a Sunday morning, you took a significant risk cutting a corner without knowing what you faced coming in the opposite direction.

'I couldn't have cared less,' he says. 'I rode like I rode originally. I wasn't thinking this is ten years on; I was thinking this is how people rode. In fact, the first time-trial I rode when I got reinstated, I got protest letters straight away for cutting corners. I mean, it was all single-carriageway roads. The way I rode was a throwback.'

In the few other interviews he has given, Alf has made a point of paying tribute to a friend of his called Alan Shorter, whom he regarded as a kind of father-figure. He was Alf's mechanic and mentor, driver and adviser.

He was crucial to Alf's success, having worked closely with the budding cyclist ever since he rented a room above the family bakery from which he ran a business repairing wheels. Shorter went on to take over Gerrard's bike shop and provided Alf with the technical support he needed in his ceaseless search for ways to improve the aerodynamics of his bike.

There was hardly a part of the bike that they did not tinker with to see if it could be more efficiently placed or constructed, or even removed. They shortened the cranks and moved the brake levers behind the handlebars. They changed the position of the brake-block stirrups. Alf's wheel clearances were as thin as cigarette paper. He removed the handlebar tape. He rode on silk tyres, known as Clement 'ones' because they were the lightest you could buy. As Flash recalled, he most famously drilled holes in as many parts of his bike as he could, including the frame, saddle and handlebars (though he did eventually realise the mistake in this). Often he would turn up to an early-morning time-trial with an unpainted frame because it had been created only the previous night.

At a time when bicycle manufacturers and cyclists were only just becoming wise to the aerodynamic possibilities of marginal improvements, Alf was similarly radical in the changes that he made to his kit. He wore a plastic skull cap to reduce drag caused by his (fashionably) long hair. To his knowledge, he was the first Briton to wear a skin suit. He turned up to one meeting wrapped in a space blanket because it was impervious to the wind. 'There was lots of interest in it. The pros were coming up and touching it just to see what it was made of.'

Some experiments worked, others didn't. Whatever their success, they rarely impressed the conservative folk who ran the RTTC. Suspicious that such innovations handed Alf an unfair advantage, they tweaked the rules repeatedly to keep up. As for other riders, a few of them made the mistake of trying to ape his developments. 'Someone in Wales was on a club run and says, "Alf's got his stirrups behind here like this",' he recalls. 'Next thing, he's lost two fingers.'

At the time his bakery in Leytonstone, east London, was losing money, but his standing within the domestic cycling community rose rapidly. Within a year of his comeback he had emerged as practically unbeatable in twenty-five-mile time-trials, the discipline's blue riband distance. He twice broke the national record in his first year back and went on to win six national titles in the event, the first in 1969 and then in every season between 1972 and '76. He would probably have won even more titles had he not been banned for familiar reasons in the intervening years.

'He was sensational,' recalls Ian Hallam, a world and Olympic medallist in the pursuit who raced against Alf a few times on the track. 'He was just incredibly talented and really forward thinking. He would turn up with his bike and people would be, "Woah! Look at that thing." People held him in a kind of awe, yet he just did his own thing.'

Alf's image contributed to the aura around him. He turned up to events in a sports car and sheepskin coat. He wore sunglasses, although he claims it was to reduce the effects of hay fever rather than to contribute to his rock-star look. Working evenings, he could not socialise much with other riders, and would turn up at time-trials usually having finished his shift in the bakery in the small hours of the morning. A bit of a loner, he often disappeared quickly after races were finished, too.

Unusually for a competitive rider, he was not especially interested in fraternising with the cycling fraternity, especially the time-trial folk. As he racked up the titles, his overriding ambition was to break the fifty-minute barrier for his event. That meant holding an average speed of 30mph. As Hallam said: 'Nobody thought it could be done.'

Nobody but Alf that is. He had first claimed the twenty-five mile record in 1959 with fifty-five minues and eleven seconds and repeatedly lowered it on his return to the sport. By the time he suffered yet another suspension, in 1979, this time for twelve months and as a result of supposedly dangerous cycling on the A2 in Kent, he had shaved four minutes from that original mark. By now he was almost exhausted by his constant battle with the authorities and reckoned he had the energy for only one more season given over to trying to break through fifty minutes.

'It was about being the first one there that attracted me,' he says. 'It's like climbing Everest, or the four-minute mile. I remember as a kid thinking about Roger Bannister doing it and thinking, "Oh, I can do this. I'll do this if I can." As a kid at school sports, I never, ever got beaten at running. Cycling, people were dropping me. If it wasn't for this knee I probably would have been a runner.'

For this one, final season-long assault on the record, Alf commissioned Alan Rochford, an old friend and by then Shorter's business partner, to build his most ambitious bike yet – one that *Cycling Weekly* anointed the Speed Machine. I have read long threads on cycling forums debating the efficacy of each of its chosen parts. The lugless tubing was Columbus

Pista Leggera but Engers and Rochford used Super Vitus fork blades for their more efficient design. Both the Cinelli fork crown and Campagnolo fork ends were filed down to reduce surface area. The seat pin was hollowed out and they used gear levers from a child's bike.

Working with Rochford's frame builder, Barry Chick, they devoted months of trial and error to perfect the bike. 'I was basically a track man and I wanted a track bike for the road,' Alf says. 'But it just went on and on. The more you did, it seemed to throw up problems. We did away with expander bolts, which led to problems because the bloody handlebars moved. When you took metal out of the seat post, it slid down in the frame. It was all just guesswork. It wasn't like we could go into a wind tunnel and try it all out.' Eventually, Alf got the bike that satisfied his perfectionist streak. 'It's nothing now but, at the time, it was cutting edge.'

He identified a race, on the first Saturday of August, on the A12 into Chelmsford, for the record attempt. It was a fast course, the weather promised to be good and it was relatively accessible from his north London base. Friday nights were the busiest in the bakery but he managed to clock off earlier than usual – at 3am – giving him enough time to return home, eat two cheese rolls and a tin of rice pudding, and then get two hours' sleep before driving with Rochford to the venue. He topped up his energy stores on the way with black coffee and mint cake.

The conditions were damp and windy but Engers felt oddly nerveless as he embarked on his hour-long warm-up. As he told the cycling historian Peter Whitfield, he 'had an incredible and inexplicable feeling of wellbeing', confident in the knowledge that he had left no detail to chance, having even brought tape with which to cover the lace eyelets in his shoes and (hopefully) further reduce the wind resistance.

Crucial to successful time-trials is the art of concentration and by then Engers had learnt to master it. He retained a smooth rhythm and was careful not to push himself even a fraction too much. Or, as he put it, he was 'controlling myself from within, deciding if and when more power should be turned on'. His timing was so precise that, at halfway, he was on schedule to the last second.

Ahead of him now was a solid block of holiday traffic. That was a mixed blessing because, riding beside it, you were partially sheltered from the wind, yet it also threatened to force you to veer from a straight line. What must car passengers unused to being on the road at this hour have thought of these figures racing past their windows?

As the wind dropped, and he engaged top gear, he was forced to drift outside the traffic to avoid colliding with a stack of cycling fans watching him from the side of the road. Experience had taught him that this manoeuvre might return to haunt him but he would not let the prospect of potential complaints distract him as long as he felt so strong. At fifteen miles, he was timed at twenty-five minutes and thirty seconds. Then, with only five miles left and just before a long, nasty incline in the road, Alf's club-mate Jack Lacey held up a sign that read 'It's on!'.

At this point it seems appropriate to ask Alf about his ability to deal with pain, the other essential skill crucial to the successful time-trialist. He bristles at my choice of word. 'It's discomfort, not pain. If you don't want to feel uncomfortable, stay at home and watch TV. How much do you want it? Do you want it enough? Then you're going to put yourself out and make yourself uncomfortable. You're going to have to do things what other people aren't doing. If you don't want to do that, then don't bother.'

As he finally came within sight of the finish, he could see marshals waving their arms in excitement, urging him to keep going. When he entered the finishing straight and a friend shouted 'forty-eight minutes', he admits that his legs felt like lead. If this was not pain, it was very serious discomfort, but still his cadence held steady.

He remembers little about the final seconds of the ride. He recalls only crossing the line, his stomach heaving in exhaustion as people rushed towards him. Rochford was at the head of the throng. He grabbed Alf and planted a kiss on his cheek. 'You've done it,' he said. Alf had hit his deeply coveted target, clocking forty-nine minutes, twenty-four seconds. It was a milestone in cycling history. What was his overwhelming emotion? 'Relief,' he says. 'I just couldn't believe it was over. Ten years of trying, all those disappointments, the bad luck. It was all over.'

The front page of the next edition of *Cycling* celebrated Alf's achievement, but with a familiar caveat. The headline read: 'Engers destroys "25" record but leaves a wake of complaints'. Spectators had written to organisers to complain that Alf had slipstreamed traffic and rode unnecessarily in the middle of the road. Still despairing of the opposition he encountered, Alf says these were 'protests from people who were at home in bed', although that was not true in at least one case. Among the complainants was Crest member John Smith.

For once, the inquiry that was called to examine the legitimacy of Alf's riding ruled in his favour and the landmark stood. The mission that had defined him for so long was completed and he could step away from the sport in peace, albeit exhausted by the sheer pressure he had placed on himself.

'It had stopped becoming fun,' he admits. 'Once you need to win, it stops being fun. In the end I was a night baker and that made it hard. It takes you a long time to wake up before any time-trial so I would make sure I was up at least three hours beforehand, just walking about before anybody else.'

For somebody who did not enjoy himself, nor make a penny from his efforts, that showed incredible determination, I say. I choose not to tell him, though, that I struggle to make it to the nine-thirty a.m. club run. 'Well, if you want to do it, that's what you do,' he says. 'It's the question of, if you're hungry enough to want it, you do it. And if you've done your best and it's not good enough – too bad, but make sure you've done your best. No, I did everything right.'

He was tired, too, with the endless confrontations with the sport's authorities. In fact, the memory of the contempt in which he felt they held him still appears to stir negative emotions in him. 'I know you've got to have rules but you're mixing with people who found the rule book far more important than the sport, and they just took it out of me in the end. I got fed up.'

Several months after our interview, Alf turns up to a screening of a documentary that the cycling film-maker Ray Pascoe has made about him. Dressed with typical flair in a grey three-piece suit, his appearance is enthusiastically received by the old cycling fans who have sold out the venue. Presumably many are delighted just to see him after decades in which he had barely any contact with the sport. After retirement he had taken up triathlon before devoting most of his spare time to fishing, his other great passion.

It is a heartwarming afternoon. The audience chuckles in affectionate recognition when the introduction to the video describes Alf as a 'rebel, mutineer and awkward bastard'. Several greats of the sport, whom Alf either competed against or inspired, offer heartfelt tributes to him. And the audience laps it up during the Q&A afterwards when Alf complains about modern cyclists who jump red lights. Imagine it: cyclists endangering other road users just to save a few seconds.

The discussion understandably does not touch on the fact that Alf has lacked a little purpose since the spring of 2013 when he finally handed in his notice in one of the two adjacent twenty-four-hour bagel shops on Brick Lane and began his well-deserved retirement. (The location of his work might have been the most surprising revelation of our chat. I have visited both of these bakeries for a post-pub snack many times. To think that a sporting legend was toiling out the back.)

With his second wife Judith – fourteen years his junior – still in employment, Alf had time to kill, so he decided recently to investigate whether his knees might be able to cope with cycling again. With arthritis in both joints, his doctor warned him to go gently when he began the comeback, yet Alf soon put paid to that intention when he signed up for a sixty-mile sponsored bike ride beginning in Cambridge that a friend had organised. Finding himself positioned nicely in a fast bunch as they approached a sharp climb just before the finish, he instinctively tuned out the pain – sorry, discomfort – as his companions instinctively turned competitive. 'I thought, "I shouldn't be doing this",' he says. 'These were all new-wave cyclists and one of them had this thing saying you'd done so many miles at however many bloody miles an hour and the group got smaller and smaller. As we started on this hill, one of the group keeled over sideways and collapsed on a parked car.' Respect was due: 'I thought, "Well, he's done his best".'

That Alf made it to the end has ensured that he has continued to ride and he was out for an hour before our interview. I'm not sure, then, that he is entirely joking when he says, 'Oh, I'm doing a bit all right. I have to be careful but, you never know, all these sods racing past me in racing kit at the weekend, maybe their days are numbered.'

CHAPTER SEVEN

'Doping? I just wish I'd done more of it'

On a bitingly cold Sunday morning in early spring, while riding beneath a bright, white sun, John Togher is explaining what life is like as part of possibly the smallest cycling club in Britain. He thinks there are only four members. The website suggests five.

'Well, we can't go out for group rides, for a start. That's why I'm also in the Crest,' says a man known to the club as Grumpy because of his supposedly moody demeanour (an accusation that he insists, albeit stony-faced, is unfair now that he is retired and apparently content).

Quite why the Century Club's membership so rapidly declined is uncertain and unquestionably sad, for it is one of the more interesting institutions of British cycling and one whose history, as Grumpy recalls it, provides a snapshot of what cycling used to be like.

Its beginnings can be traced back to a promotional stunt that *Cycling* magazine ran in 1911 by which, in an attempt to drum up interest in the sport over the winter, it ran a competition offering prizes to riders who completed the most non-competitive 100-mile rides over the next year. Beginning the competition on 1 January, the magazine thought it would appeal to readers who needed motivation to ride in the cold months. It did not expect the project to take off like it did, with 650 riders taking part, each of them submitting entry cards at the end of the twelve months in which a witness signed each completed 'century'. As the Century Club history says: 'This showed outstanding keenness to ride.'

One gold medal, twelve silver and thirty bronze were issued to the most impressive century hauls. These included the sixty hundred-milers that Olive Elliot clocked up as the only female competitor, the 287 that Billy Wells, a fifty-something printer from Salisbury, undertook to earn second place overall and the phenomenal 332 centuries that Marcel Planes, a penniless twenty-one-year-old Londoner, rode on a bike with parts that apparently were held together with string. He won gold and the £5 first prize.

The competition served to draw centurions together for rides. So, when *Cycling* chose not to reprise it, fifty-five of these unusually committed companions met the following January at a hotel on Oxford Circus to form the Century Club. The one criterion for others who wished to join was that they had to satisfy the club committee that they had ridden one hundred miles in ten hours. 'It is still the rule,' Grumpy says.

What was intended as mostly a social enterprise soon turned competitive, with the most determined long-distance riders breaking time-trial records in the Century's name, among them Jack Rossiter, who smashed the Land's End to John O'Groats landmark that had stood for twenty-one years, and Hubert Opperman, the brilliant Australian who was among the most celebrated cyclists of the 1920s and '30s. Grumpy points out that his name is on the club's roll of honour with the tandem records he set, the first of them in 1970 and the most recent twenty-six years on.

Quite by accident, then, I am riding with another living connection to a formative period in the sport, a cyclist in his early sixties, who started out riding time-trials in Hackney's Victoria Park forty-odd years ago and now spends as much of his retirement as he can on the bike. You can see the evidence of his years of practice in the skill and fluency with which he rides, effortlessly leaving me behind on corners and descents through the efficiency of his technique, often taking it upon himself to drop off the bunch to help stragglers get back on it. He passes on welcome tips, too, telling me when I need to drop down a gear, encouraging me to be more assertive when riding near cars. He also offers a solitary compliment. 'You're quite a steady rider,' he says, 'You don't look like a novice.' That this is the first time that a cyclist of his background has said such a thing suggests I have finally made some progress. For this morning at least, then I am also content.

If you join the Crest, you can expect to be renamed. Ron Crawley is Collarbone Ron because the sixty-one year old has broken his clavicle three times while cycling. On each occasion he spent his recovery on the back of a tandem with his arm in a sling.

Dawn McNulty is happy to be called Foghorn Dawn because she soundtracks club rides with her constant, affectionate chatter. Often the only woman on the ride, she looks at it as her way of making up for the imbalance. Alan Shulman, a banker in his late forties who has recently taken up cycling, has had to accept the epithet Wobbly because he cannot hold his line. Graham Adams is Spider. Rather than bend his long legs beneath a dining table, he stretches them out, arachnid-style, just as he does now on a tea-stop while he explains his seminal role in the history of doping.

'Oh, the story has changed so many times over the years,' he says. 'It still comes out and I still find myself having to correct people.'

The story takes place in 1968 when, aged twenty, Spider was summoned to a doping control for the first time, having finished second-last in a twenty-five-mile time-trial outside Braintree. The controls had been tightened on the insistence of the UCI in the aftermath of Tom Simpson's death a year earlier.

Spider had no idea what to expect. 'I was directed to this small marquee about half a mile away from the finish. I thought, "This is a bit odd".' Having performed so badly, especially for a first-category rider, Spider could understand why he was chosen. Perhaps they suspected that he had taken a substance only for it to backfire on him. 'That was the only explanation: that they thought I'd been nobbled. I was just unfit.'

The officials wanted him to provide a urine sample in full view of them, but that was not going to happen. Not only was he too embarrassed to do it but he was dehydrated, having not had a drink during the race. Cyclists then avoided taking water during a time-trial lest the action of lifting the bottle lost them precious seconds. Even when they supplied him with a bottle of Coca-Cola and allowed him twenty minutes' grace, his bladder would not comply. 'And then I just accepted the offer of a lift home. I was just wandering around the results board anyway, thinking they would just leave it because it had taken so long and I had finished almost last anyway.'

Instead, he received his first telegram from the Road Time Trials Council, informing him that he had been suspended from all cycling pending a hearing into his case at a hotel in Liverpool Street, with a potential two-year ban awaiting him as that was the mandatory UCI sanction.

'It shocked me,' says Spider. 'I never doped. I wouldn't have known how to, or where to get it. I didn't even hear of people doing it on the club scene. I was frightened.'

Taking a club-mate for moral support – he realises now he should have hired a lawyer – Spider turned up at the plush City hotel that the RTTC had hired to be confronted by officials who had been summoned from East Anglia, Cornwall and Newcastle, such was the importance of the case. The RTTC told him that he was the first Briton to be tried for doping, though this is not quite true. The road man Ken Hill had been disqualified at the Milk Race three years earlier, downgrading Spider to the first to be sanctioned at a time-trial.

He convinced the officials of his innocence but could not persuade them to let the case drop. Instead, feeling that they needed to make an example of him, they suspended Spider for six months. 'It was a completely arbitrary figure,' he says. 'I was just devastated.'

He tried staying fit during his suspension but struggled for motivation. The incident had turned him off the sport. That he suffered sarcastic, hurtful comments about his fate when he eventually tried to make a comeback, while only half-fit, made him feel worse. Bike racing had been his life and now it had betrayed him. He became so fed up that he decided to start his life afresh, quitting the accountancy studies that he had begun and emigrating with a friend to Spain. They travelled by cycling through France.

He needed several years away before he could feel the incident was behind him, though he admits he still does not know how many people believed him. 'I was at a dinner only the other night and I was described as the guy who got done for doping. It seems to happen all the time.'

Doping, it is accepted, was never as prevalent in Britain as it was on the Continent, though quite to what extent it happened is hard to work out. Most people will tell you of stories they heard of cyclists who picked up products, usually amphetamines, in Belgium and France and experimented with them back home. Almost nobody, however, will admit to taking drugs, certainly not systematically. The usual answer is that they tried it but it did nothing for them, like the politicians who claim that marijuana did nothing for them when they smoked it as a student.

In many cases, at least concerning the cyclists, this is possibly true (though I'm not convinced) and another reason that British riders often give for not dabbling in drugs is believable: they did not know the long-term consequences of it. 'It occurred, even at junior level, but it wasn't scientific,' says Roger St Pierre. 'It was just like having a strong cup of coffee. But nobody put their life at any great risk. It was one of those things where you thought, "What's the point?"'

Occasionally, when pressed, somebody involved in the sport in the 1960s and '70s will admit that, domestically, Britons were not quite as innocent as their reputation suggested. Usually the source will insist on remaining off the record, though not always, as was the case with Tony Woodcock, the Londoner who represented Britain at the Peace Race in 1964, but who quit the sport shortly afterwards having struggled to make any impression on races. 'Ninety per cent of the guys that were winning stuff were on the gear,' Tony said. 'I didn't know at the time. Everyone says this, I suppose, but I was so naive and innocent. I was never offered drugs, I didn't know anybody was on drugs, I just assumed that it was a level playing field and they were better than I was. It wasn't until about five years ago [around 2009], I met a bloke on the scene and he told me what was going on and . . . bloody hell, there's guys I thought were superstars who were on the stuff.' By superstars, he means domestic champions, many of whom could claim that this is just sour grapes. But there is at least one rider who is prepared to talk at length about the drugs he did take, despite never being caught.

Reg Barnett walks gingerly into his local pub in the Kent village of Shoreham, embraces the barman and chef, and then leads us through to a room that he has reserved for the interview. It is not yet lunchtime and the Crown is empty, but Reg expects the conversation to last. 'When I spoke to you last time about my life, I only gave you infinitesimal amounts,' he says, even though what he revealed last time meant that our conversation was among the most entertaining that I have had with any former cyclist.

Interviewing him about Reg Harris, I discovered that Barnett had accepted a pay-off from Harris to help him win the national sprint championship when he made his comeback in middle age. That Harris had cheated his way to the title is a widely accepted truth within the cycling community but one that most others were unwilling to discuss on the record.

During the course of a long lunch in a Victoria hotel, I learnt also that Barnett, a former Olympian and a six-time national sprint champion, had experimented with performance-enhancing drugs, was prepared to talk at length about race-fixing and suspected that cycling had contributed to emotional problems he had suffered since. From a purely professional point of view, then, I am looking forward to catching up with him again. As I explain to him, no other former cyclist that I have encountered would admit to doping. 'Why not?' he says. 'I mean, what's the point, all these years later? Who are you trying to fool?'

Reg is the ideal interviewee: talkative, frank and uninhibited. The only difficulty in reporting on a conversation with him is in trying to keep up while he switches between stories as the memories flood back. Now sixty-nine, he must be a welcome raconteur on his regular evening visits to the Crown, usually while waiting for his lawyer wife to return home from work. He asked that I meet him here rather than in London because two recent knee replacements have made it difficult for him to get around.

The other problem I encounter is in trying to persuade him not to hold too much information back for a book he is planning to write on his life. 'You should see my notes. I've written about 500 bullet points, quarter chapters, half chapters,' he says. 'I remember when I first sat down to write it ten years ago, I was crying while I was writing. I had to stop.'

Born in Anerley, a suburb on the edge of south-east London, Reg's life in cycling began in 1960 when he quit Crystal Palace's football academy aged fifteen because he was sick of the interfering parents on the sidelines. Even though it broke his cab-driver father's heart, he wanted instead to concentrate on the sport he had loved ever since running errands on his bike for a grocery shop. The decision paid off, though, as his finishing sprint was soon impressing onlookers while

representing south London club De Laune CC at Herne Hill
velodrome and at Crystal Palace circuit races. He was deemed
good enough for the British squad before he had turned
nineteen, enabling him to travel to places that a working-class
kid who had never been abroad would previously have only
dreamed about.

He competed on the thriving track scene in Trinidad, where
clouds of marijuana smoke wafted down from the makeshift
terraces and the post-race parties alone made the trip worth-
while. He went to East Germany to race against cyclists
who were among the first to be subject to the communists'
institutionalised doping regimes. Shady employees of the state
trailed him, even offering to train him like an East German in
return for 'speaking highly about the regime' while back in
England. 'My dad would never have let me [do it]. He was a
real royalist, a right-winger. The thought of communism made
him physically sick.'

Reg went to the Low Countries, too, and made contact with
two cyclists who would provide him with the tutelage that would
come to define his cycling career. The first was Ron Baensch,
the brilliant Australian sprinter who had won medals at four
world championships. He lived above a brothel in Antwerp
and invited Reg to visit him again in the winter of 1965, with
a view to making money on the indoor circuit. 'Ronnie had
a room upstairs. He told me, "Don't go wandering about at
night, Reggie, or it'll cost you".'

Reared on the tough track racing scene in Australia, and
by then schooled in the continental scene, Baensch wasted
little time in teaching Reg the difference between amateurism
in Britain and abroad. 'He was hard as nails, one of the best
sprinters this world has ever seen and he was fantastic for me,'

Reg says. 'He taught me tactics and gave me the attitude: win at all costs. Don't matter what it takes, win. It was alien to us because of the British system of fair play.'

They competed together through until February, surviving on their winnings from Belgian kermesses and six-day races – though Reg was amateur and not allowed to make money from the sport, the British Cycling Federation could hardly monitor him so far from home. Meanwhile, he found more conventional accommodation in the family home of a Dutch cyclist called Albert van Midden. Reg also spent a great deal of time with a Belgian, whom he will not name for the simple reason that this was the friend who taught him about doping. 'I had my eyes opened to what cycling was about,' he says. 'By the time I went home, I knew everything you would need to know to win on the road, how to win on the track.'

The plan was for him to wait until he turned professional before he applied this knowledge. He wanted to remain an amateur until after the 1968 Olympic Games in Mexico City – at which he would reach the quarter-finals, reflecting his world ranking of six. The delay also enabled him to win the British amateur sprint title, thus strengthening his hand when it came to negotiating a professional contract.

When the time came, he chose to join Holdsworth, who were among the strongest domestic road teams. The decision prompted much derision from contemporaries, who thought that, with his slight frame and lack of pedigree on the road, Reg was daft to think he could make the step from races that covered a few laps of the track to those that lasted several days.

'Oh, there were people just laughing at me.' He cites the example of John Clarey, who completed the Tour de France (finishing last) in the year that Reg went to Mexico. 'Johnny is a good friend but he was splitting his sides. Loads of them were. I was [to become] "the fallen British sprint champion". No one had ever done it [successfully transferred from track sprinting to the road].'

What the cynics did not realise was that Reg was ready to apply his secret narcotic expertise. 'I had stored it for two years. I knew every product. I knew what it did, quantities, duration, overlaps, controlled release, everything you'd ever want to know to win big bike races. I ain't proud of it. Everyone else was doing it on the Continent. I'm not saying they were doing it here, but I didn't care. I didn't care because I thought a waste of education is a waste of everything. I thought, right, I'm going to go to work.'

Even while working part-time in his brother's steel-erecting business through the winters, he managed to train as hard as anyone over the next eighteen months to build the miles in his legs. 'Even in the freezing cold, training was a pleasure because it was so different from the life I would have had,' he says.

Success duly followed. He won criteriums in Brighton, Bridlington, Warrington, Liverpool, Newcastle and Weston-super-Mare. In the same season he posted fourteen top-ten places in other road races, including a tenth and eleventh place on stages in the Tour of Switzerland, and a tenth-placed finish in the national road race. In a rare double, he was selected to represent Britain in both the sprint and the road race in the same season's world championships. He continued to clean up on the track, too, eventually winning four national sprint titles as a professional and one scratch race title. In one season, Reg reckons he won a third of the races he entered.

Yes, this was mostly only domestic success and perhaps not as impressive as it might be to the modern reader used to Britons winning on the Continent, but only a handful of British cyclists made it as far as the professional scene abroad then. Make no mistake, Reg was exceptional. 'I was trying to prove to myself that everything I learnt worked and it did. It absolutely worked.'

When the race leant itself to a sprint finish, Reg felt almost unbeatable among his compatriots. 'I won the last stage on the Isle of Wight and it was so easy. I don't mean that as disrespect to the super riders who were there: Tony Gowland, Bill Lawrie. But I would come down in the break, a minute or so clear, into the finish and open up with a massive sprint. Nobody [could beat me] until Sid Barras, once he got his act together. He was a better road sprinter.'

Reg has little idea to what extent his domestic rivals doped, if at all. He never discussed it with them. Instead he worked alone, either bringing in the drugs from mainland Europe or using a supplier that he knew in London. 'There used to be a chemist in a place called Bordighera in Italy, just over the border from France. You could pick up whatever you wanted. I took steroids, amphetamines. The designer drug for bike riders at the time was Stenamine, which was Methadrine combined with ephedrine. One to open the lungs, one to drive the heart.'

As Spider discovered to his cost, Reg was operating at a time when the British cycling authorities were attempting to intro-duce a culture of doping controls, but lacked the money to carry them through comprehensively. All you needed to escape detection, it seems, was chutzpah and a little cunning. 'Oh, I got chased around a few hotels,' Reg says. 'I've sat in a room for an hour, busting for a wee, saying to the guy, "Can't go". And I'm telling you, my bladder is like a beach ball, ready to explode. I would have pissed over him and he was seven foot away.'

Reg will admit that he suffered conflicting emotions when he paused to reflect on his behaviour. In a sport that he felt was endemically corrupt, he cared little what his rivals would have thought about his drug-taking, yet he was still prone to feeling ashamed of his methods because he knew that his parents would have disapproved had they only known. He felt especially bad for his dad, an upstanding Army veteran who suffered health problems throughout his life as a result of the bomb that blew up his armoured truck during the Second World War. His mum worked as a maid to wealthy families before bringing up her four children.

Neither of Reg's parents had known much luxury in their lives, making it all the more satisfying for Reg when success helped him to buy them the kind of treats that they had never previously enjoyed. 'We used to go out to restaurants in the West End. I used to send them on holiday. My mum had never stayed in a big hotel and I sent them to the best hotel in Bournemouth. It was beautiful, had an en suite and everything. I'd say to them, "Do what you want".' He had never seen his mum happier. 'She was tough, she had to be, but when I was winning races, you could see the happiness. I did it just to see the smile on her face.'

He was, therefore, caught in the most difficult bind, enjoying great rewards through foul and shameful means. Little wonder that his attitude towards the sport turned increasingly cynical, especially as he discovered in the professional sphere that race-fixing was as endemic as doping had been abroad, and capable of dictating the smallest race as well as the most prestigious of all. 'You could buy and sell a world road championship, or a world sprint championship, if you've got enough money. I've seen it happen: the world sprint championship. I can't say who because he was a dear, dear friend of mine. I'm sat in the hotel. He said, "I couldn't beat him anyway Reg. I might as well have a big suitcase of money. He knew I couldn't beat him but I might have beaten him and that's what makes them nervous." I said, "Yeah, brilliant". It's the fear.'

In Belgium, he watched aghast at the ingenuity with which riders managed to choreograph the chaotic kermesses. 'Water bottles come up with all the odds [written on pieces of paper] at the betting shop. All those riders, big, top men – they undo the bottle and there are the odds. So you then fit the riders to the odds for the benefit of the bookmaker and he gives you your money.'

As a result of this culture, when he accepted an offer from T.I. Raleigh to join a new domestic team in 1973, his motivation had begun to wane. With this move, he had to accept a drop in salary, too. As his results suffered so his mood worsened. 'It may sound like a contradiction but I didn't like what I was in, the whole filthy hypocrisy of it. I just didn't do anything about it. It felt like I was too far into it to get out.' If Reg sounds negative, perhaps even moribund, then his quotes are misleading. He is intense, certainly, and admits that he suffers from mood swings, but when you ask his contemporaries to recall Reg, the memory of him will usually bring a smile to their face. A few will even burst out laughing at the thought of the japes he enjoyed as a cyclist and the engaging force of his personality. Even now he is said to be among the most entertaining characters at veterans' reunions.

He was glad when, in 1975, Falcon returned to him with the offer of a contract that provided a potential route out of the professional scene by setting him up in a bike shop that he would run while also competing as a senior member of their road team. The plan ran aground when he crashed while training and was unable to race again for a year afterwards. He attempted a comeback but his heart was no longer in it.

The bike shop had not worked out either, so he figured that it was time to return to his roots and to devote himself to steel work full-time. 'I was just glad it was all over. I'd had enough. I was among my own people again. It was honest. There was nobody saying, "Don't do that, I'll give you half of this, if you can . . ." We were all in it together.'

When not on building sites, he socialised in pubs and clubs around the Old Kent Road, often alongside people with whom he had grown up and who had similarly gravitated to the city. It was a hedonistic time in his life. No longer worried about his fitness or weight, and free from the strict lifestyle required of a professional athlete, Barnett partied long and hard. Drinking sessions lasted days. He got involved in a different kind of drug. 'I could eat a gram of cocaine and I wouldn't even feel it.'

These drinking dens were especially popular with south London's underworld. 'All those old gangsters loved me. A lot of them were ex-boxers and they loved the fact that I was a British champion. And they knew I was "good" because of the way I am and the way I talk. I had known a lot them personally, for twenty years, since they were kids.'

These men were hardly moral paragons but, for Reg, the honesty he encountered provided a welcome relief from professional cycling. 'I was privileged to be friends with them because they didn't want nothing off you. They wanted you to be part of their life and it was a pleasure because they are so honest in their way. There was none of that fraud, none of that nasty, horrible, back-stabbing crap.'

They never pressurised him to work for them, though

almost inevitably he was tempted, especially with the drink and drugs distorting his good sense. '[The attitude was] you want to be part of it, do you want to earn from it? If you don't, don't matter. We don't ostracise you. You just ain't in the coup.'

Eventually he relented and accepted invitations to work for several south London firms. He involved himself in situations that put his life at risk and threatened the safety of others. He never spilled blood, but the list of jobs that he claims to have undertaken suggests that he was at least a useful employee. 'I couldn't care less at the time about what I was doing,' he says. 'Don't forget, I was off my head. I was off the old Richter scale. And there was no going to the Priory for us.'

Though he didn't realise it at the time, Reg's recklessness was linked to depression that would become so profound that he suffered several psychotic episodes and had to resist efforts to have him committed to a psychiatric hospital. Only when he met his wife Marina in the pub she worked at did he begin to calm down. 'She sorted my life out really,' he says. 'We bought a pub – not good for me to have a pub bought for me but we got one. We had five fantastic years in that pub and then cycling was behind me. I was glad, you know. Then we started living a normal life and I bought this cottage here as our holiday home.' When the pub business began to struggle, Marina retrained as a solicitor and took up work in the city, allowing Reg to retire to the countryside.

He says the quiet lifestyle suits him. As he is careful to take medication to keep his emotions under control and visits a psychiatrist, the dark moods visit him infrequently now.

He has spent time with the psychiatrist trying to identify the root of the depression. The psychiatrist thinks Reg's problems began when he accepted his first professional contract as a cyclist. 'He was convinced. He went back as far as when I was twenty-five, which must be about right. It's when I turned pro on the road and started really going for it.'

Reg is cautious about actually blaming cycling for his problems. Depression, of course, is much too complex for that. But he wonders if the drugs he took affected his serotonin production and if the corruption to which he committed himself damaged his self-esteem. 'I had a time when I didn't even like shaving because I couldn't look at myself in the mirror,' he says. 'I used to think, "The filthy things I've done". Depression can happen to anyone, and I'm stable now, but it was brought on by sport and the drink.'

You can see why Reg was so popular among cyclists. As well as being almost uncomfortably honest, he is smart and funny. However, as somebody who appears to chastise himself more for cheating in bike races than for his criminal activities, he is also complex. Hence, for all his bitterness towards the cycling world that he knew, he is still passionate about the sport. He watches it on TV whenever he can and takes a keen interest in the promising careers of two teenage brothers who live close to him, Ben and Daniel Tulett. He recently travelled to Hog Hill to watch them race and gave them a motivational talk the night before the event that had such emotional force their parents shed a few tears of pride while listening. Reg was fiercely optimistic about Daniel's potential, even before his recent recruitment to British Cycling's Olympic programme. Reg is convinced that his young neighbour could succeed where he was too afraid to tread: on the Continent.

Reg had the opportunity to go abroad on a permanent contract, having received an offer from Guido Costa, the great Italian coach, to join his Filotex team. But he turned

Costa down because he was comfortable with life in England, a decision that remains the one great regret from his cycling career, regardless of the fact that a move to the Continent could have required him to dope more heavily than he did. 'If that's a contradiction, it's a contradiction, but I could have achieved so much more. I wish now I had taken that knowledge abroad and really given it some. I should have gone over there and gone *mano a mano* with them. I'm not proud of it [drug-taking]. What I am sorry about is I didn't do enough of it.'

The next day, I am surprised to receive a telephone call at work from Reg. He wants to talk about the possibility of working with him on the autobiography he wants to write – a fine idea, I tell him – but he also asks me about what I did after we said our goodbyes yesterday. 'I heard you went back to the pub after I left,' he says. This is true. To corroborate his claim about his criminal past, I checked with the landlord if it was true that Eddie Richardson, formerly the leader of south London's most notorious gang, visited Reg in the Crown. And it was. However, I am now worried that I have offended Reg by doubting his sincerity. In retrospect, what I did was a bit sneaky, after all. And though I doubt Reg has enquired for no more sinister reason than out of sheer curiosity, I don't want to offend somebody with his connections.

I explain myself, as humbly as I can. Reg chuckles and says: 'Good idea, Robert. Always best to be thorough.'

CHAPTER EIGHT

Three friends who gave up the rainbow jersey – and regretted it for a lifetime

On the outskirts of Bishop's Stortford, Alan Norris is trying to combine his responsibilities as Crest club-run leader with the task of making me feel less depressed about my bike racing debut during the week. 'It wasn't about fitness – you just needed to be smarter,' he insists, after I explain to him how I was the first competitor to withdraw from the Go-Ride event at the Ford test track in Dunton, near Billericay, which was supposedly for novices. In an event that lasted an hour for almost everybody else, I had collapsed in a heap beside the tarmac within twenty minutes of the start.

'But those twenty minutes are the hardest of the race,' he insists. 'A lot of other riders would have been similar to you but they wouldn't have felt as shocked by that sensation. They would have experienced it before and knew that, once things calmed down, they could recover in the saddle.'

Tactically, my big mistake was apparently to drift to the back to avoid the jostling that took place shortly after the start. It meant that I got cut adrift from the pack with two other back-markers, with no hope of bridging the gap.

'Experience will teach you that,' Alan says. 'You're fit enough to have lasted.'

Now in his late fifties, and once a first-category racer, Alan is confident that his race intelligence would have ensured that he finished the Go-Ride, yet he would not consider entering one because he has long since given up on most massed-start events, whether races or sportives. Like many seasoned cyclists, he considers them unsafe because of the influx of new cyclists who have not learnt how to ride properly in a bunch. He struggles also to understand why anyone would chose a sportive over a club run when essentially they perform the same task.

'The difference with us is that you get to draw on the wealth of experience and knowledge within the club,' he says, 'plus you don't have to pay the entrance fee. But the new-age cyclists don't seem to realise that. A lot of them aren't interested in joining a club.'

Though there are clubs whose membership has increased with the sport's boom, Alan is broadly correct, hence the fact that so many Essex clubs near us seem to be in decline. I have seen club runs with no more than two or three people taking part. Sometimes, lone riders join us because their club cannot get anyone out. The rite of passage in which a novice once learnt his craft with a club seems to be enjoyed now only by the minority of cyclists. Which is a shame, because not only do you benefit from advice and reassurance when you are riding with an established club, but you stumble on a few stories, too.

Ears prick up among the members of Marlow Riders when Willi Moore recalls his career while leading the club run through Buckinghamshire. As part of one of the finest team pursuit line-ups that Britain has ever produced, Willi won world, Olympic and Commonwealth medals in the 1970s, yet it is the story of the outstanding defeat on his palmares that is most likely to enthral listeners. For it represents surely one of the finest acts of sportsmanship British cycling has seen, yet is also one which I hear was regretted by all the team, the core of which comprised his great friends Ian Hallam and Mick Bennett.

'Oh, yes, we all regret it,' Willi says when I meet him in a coffee shop in Marlow to discuss the time in 1973 when he was world champion for all of ten minutes before deciding to give up the title, never to reclaim it. 'It is very prominent, very alive,' he says of the memory. 'I said to my sister once, "I've got no regrets in life", but I have, in reality. It's the one big gap.'

Blimey. I was not quite expecting this depth of feeling, not when almost a lifetime has since passed. 'Yes, but probably on fifty per cent of club rides somebody will bring up my racing background and ask about it. So I'm continuously forced to relive it.'

Willi took up cycling as a teenager in Liverpool in the 1960s after he failed to make the school football team and at last found a pastime in which he could satisfy his innate competitive streak. He progressed quickly, winning the first time-trial that he entered with Merseyside Wheelers, impressing sufficiently at the evening track leagues in Kirkby and Fallowfield, in Manchester, to catch the attention of British team selectors, who asked him to attend an early ergometric test at Liverpool Polytechnic to assess his potential. Long-distance events had emerged as his specialism. They measured his VO_2 max – maximum oxygen intake – and Willi, who as a teenager had shown limited aptitude for sport at school, remembers being told: 'You've got the numbers here to be a potential world champion, unquestionably.' Willi adds: 'It was just so much better than anything they'd seen.'

The ambition, then, was sown in his mind. He packed in an engineering course to concentrate on cycling, preferring to work part-time or live on the dole, as many of the best cyclists of his generation did then. It did not matter to him that his parents had moved to the south-west to retire by the sea, leaving Willi to have to fend for himself. He moved into a cyclists' household, rented accommodation that also served as lodgings for future world champion Gordon Singleton and national record holder Pauline Strong. The spartan lifestyle appealed to him. 'I was on my own in the flat so I had to do everything, maintaining the bike, cleaning the bike, buying tyres, largely did my own mechanics. Entering races, you had to have hard-copy entry forms to post off. It was just the daily grind of living, I suppose. I was on the dole but I never felt as though I had time on my hands.'

He wished his parents could have shown more interest in his endeavours: his mother wondered why he could not follow a more conventional career path and, to his father, organised sport was simply a mystery. A champion baker who seemingly worked almost every waking hour, Willi's father was born with one Achilles tendon shorter than the other, which prevented him from taking part, or nurturing an interest, in sport. 'I remember when my parents retired and I asked them to take me seriously,' Willi says. 'There was a lad at the end of their road who had become a bank manager and my mum said, "Why can't you be like that lovely boy and get a proper job?" Oh dear. Am I glad I didn't go down that road.'

Instead he followed his cycling dream and soon began to compete internationally. To begin with, each competition was chastening. 'We were the poor relations. We turned up at events and the Germans and others would be on these fabulous, fancy bikes made out of titanium or whatever. If there was anything innovative, you could guarantee the other teams would have it before us. We were riding on our own tyres and wheels and we bought our own shorts and everything else.' All that the British federation could afford to give them was the jersey on their backs. It was a world away from what Britain's finest enjoy now. He did not train with an academy but often with other jobless cyclists, albeit those who were out of employment not through choice but circumstance at a time when work was scarce in Liverpool, with its docks and heavy industries in sharp decline.

There was no room for self-pity though. 'The Liverpool Mercury Club used to have chain-gang sessions on a Tuesday and a Thursday and then, because a lot of them were signing on the dole, they'd do a big road ride on a Wednesday,' says Willi. 'And that was largely what my training was based around.'

He was competitive in domestic road races, but most at home in the pursuit, reaching the quarter-finals of the individual event at the 1970 Commonwealth Games. He went to the world championships in the same year as part of a pursuit squad that included the Commonwealth champion Ian Hallam, and was encouraged by their reaching the last eight there, too, with minimal training as a quartet.

Willi is not a boastful man, far from it. He is quietly spoken and thoughtful. You can sense the intelligence that helped him acquire a sports science degree later in life and, in his brief period as a coach, made him among the most respected of his generation. But he will not undersell himself. He will tell you that he had staying power and was the natural choice for the 'man one' position in the team pursuit. Hallam, the best all-round rider in the squad, went second while Bennett was third once he was added to the squad. Though there was little to choose between them, Bennett brought an injection of speed. With Ron Keeble completing the quartet, they dovetailed so well that they went to the 1972 Olympic Games in Munich believing that they could end a run of sixteen years without a medal for British cyclists at the Games.

They managed it, too, claiming bronze and this after Willi had punctured against the eventual winners West Germany in the semi-final. It was an achievement that banished their lingering inferiority complex in international competition and inspired in them the belief that they could defeat the West Germans at the following year's world championships in San Sebastián and win gold.

Their achievement in Munich was overshadowed by the murder of eleven Israeli athletes who were taken hostage by Palestinian militants on the same day that Willi won that bronze medal. The British team were housed in accommodation near by. 'We think we actually heard the shots,' says Willi. 'It wasn't very far from us where the actual shots were fired – and little by little, stuff leaked out. We'd finished competing and first there were shots, then somebody had been killed. "Who's been killed? Where? When? Who? What?" It came out bit by bit. We didn't have tellies in our rooms, and it was largely rumours. When you're at the Olympics, you're so cocooned in your own little bubble that the outside world . . . it sounds really harsh to say it, but it doesn't matter.

'My abiding memory is that it was only when we got back

home to the UK that we realised the extent of the story, the size of it and the exact details of what had happened. To tell you exactly what we knew of it whilst we were actually in the Olympic Village, I couldn't, but I know that it was rumour and counter-rumour.' The elation he felt at creating a small piece of sporting history was, then, thrown into sharp perspective. 'Sadness. That's my overwhelming memory of it.'

Presumably memories get twisted about an event such as this, when you see it replayed time and again. Ian Hallam says they were purposely not told that the hostages had been killed until they returned home. For a while sport seemed irrelevant, he recalls, when I meet him at his dental cosmetic surgery in the Hampshire town of Petersfield and decamp for lunch to a nearby café. In time, though, their sights refocused, their confidence bolstered by the knowledge that they had 'broken the mould' by ending Britain's long run without Olympic success. 'Where there was an inferiority complex, now we truly believed that we could win gold,' he says. 'So it gave us even more motivation to stay together, work together, ride the hardest road races we could.'

It is strange to think that Ian should have suffered from an inferiority complex. This is a man who has spent his life excelling at various pursuits, dominating cycling while studying to be a dental surgeon, switching to windsurfing and becoming a world-class talent at that, before returning to cycling in his fifties and sweeping up almost every available trophy again. 'There's nothing worse than being average at things, being the norm, being mediocre,' he says, seemingly almost bemused that I have asked him to explain his appetite for success.

If his answer makes him sound grandiose, it belies a persona that is quietly spoken, even a touch shy, as he admits when expanding on the topic of his strangely driven character. 'Maybe it stems right back to my childhood, when I was shy. When I started to get involved in cycling and started winning, suddenly people were paying me attention and that built my confidence and my character.'

He started winning almost as soon as he took up competitive cycling in adolescence, having approached a neighbour to ask which club he belonged to. Paul Smith, future fashion icon, told Ian that he was a member of the Beeston Road Club, and that he raced at Harvey Hadden Stadium in nearby Nottingham. Within four years, Ian was national road race champion and had come to the attention of national coach Norman Sheil, with whom he would form a life-changing partnership and one that I had been looking forward to asking Ian about.

It is impossible to know who introduced interval training to cycling, even in Britain. Riders had been employing a version of it unwittingly for decades, sprinting between lampposts or other roadside markers, as part of their training. Sheil had done it in an uncontrolled fashion in the 1950s, and was determined to codify it now as national coach. Working with an academic called Vaughan Thomas, who would go on to set up Britain's first sports science degree at Liverpool Polytechnic, Sheil wanted to measure exactly its biological benefits and had identified Ian as the ideal guinea pig. Thomas was with him when he approached Ian that day and asked if they could take his heart-rate before and after a race. 'It was the last scratch race at an end-of-season meeting,' says Ian, who, it is worth noting, is a good advert for his profession with his toothpaste-commercial smile and a face that is light on worry lines. He is tanned and fit-looking, too, partly a result of his weekly hard cycle ride.

'Norman said to me, "We're setting up some tests at Loughborough University and I want to ask a favour. At the end of the race, we want to measure your pulse rate and see how quickly your pulse returns down to normal. Oh, and I want you to win the race."' Ian complied and produced a set of readings that were promising enough for the two men to invite him to Loughborough for a more detailed examination. It involved taking his pulse and core temperature before, during and after extreme exercise on a static bike and ergonomic rowing machine. 'They were trying to see how they could refine training techniques,' Ian says. 'It was pretty crude by today's standards, but completely new at the time.'

As months passed, Ian had almost forgotten about the intriguing experiment when, in the autumn of 1967, Sheil turned up at Ian's family home and asked if he could personally train him for the following year's Olympic Games. This was a thunderbolt moment. Ian was seventeen and looking no further ahead than his mock A-levels. Certainly he had not dreamt about competing in Mexico City. 'I was blown away. I couldn't believe someone as informed as him would be knocking at my door. And at that point I never really thought I was capable of going to the Olympics.'

He was tempted but concerned that the preparation would conflict with his studies. Back then, all conventional endurance training demanded thousands of miles in the legs. However, Sheil insisted that he would not take Ian away from his textbooks, not when he had devised an interval training plan that would require him to train during the week for no more than half an hour a day.

To Ian, this seemed an ambitious proposal but Sheil was persuasively confident in explaining why it would work. He had studied ideas that were emerging in athletics and pored over scientific textbooks of his own. He had worked closely with Thomas and was certain that he could produce an Olympic athlete in his lunch break, as long as the athlete pushed themselves to the limit. The degree of masochism required makes Sheil chuckle when he recalls his groundbreaking work over the telephone. 'If you threw up, you knew you were doing well,' he says, from his home in Canada. 'I was interval training before interval training had a name. I don't know how I got into it. A lot of people tried it. They would ask, "Can I come training with you?". I'd say yes and I wouldn't see them again. They'd say, "He's an idiot, a madman".' They couldn't push themselves like Sheil did. 'You could do a hundred-mile road race on the back of it [intervals] and not even think about it.'

By this definition, Ian was a madman, too, treating himself to thirty-minute sessions along the residential streets near his home during which he frequently vomited. He would sprint along a 300-metre stretch and recover on an adjacent 50-metre run. His warm-up and recovery was included within the thirty-minute slot on the commute to his improvised training circuit. This does not sound like a teenager's idea of fun. 'I absolutely hated it,' says Ian. 'Other riders who came with me couldn't take it. It was too tough but I was better on my own. I could just push myself to the maximum.' He reached the quarter-finals in Mexico City, a superb achievement for someone so young, yet he also nailed the grades he needed to study dentistry. Sheil had been proven wonderfully correct.

Ian decided he would stick with the regime at university, too, thus while his class-mates put the world to rights in the student bars of Birmingham University, he conquered it on the track, winning gold in the individual pursuit at the Commonwealth Games and silver in the 1970 world championships. Even with a road race at the weekend, he rode less than I do now and I get dropped while lapping Regent's Park.

Maybe I just can't punish myself enough. 'The extent to which you can push yourself is key,' Ian says. 'You've got to get to such a high that, in a race, you're still not as high in intensity as during your training, so you can sustain it. I'd collapse for about half an hour before I could even get showered afterwards.'

Ian and his old team-mates will admit that he was perhaps even stronger in the team event than the individual. He preferred to be racing for others rather than being in the spotlight on his own. As a result, he decided after the hugely promising performance in Munich that he would concentrate on the team pursuit, being determined to win the world champion's rainbow jersey that he had coveted since taking up the sport. 'We truly believed then that we could win gold.'

They replaced the fourth – and weakest – rider in the squad, Ron Keeble, with a youngster from '34 Nomads CC in south London called Rik Evans and began to meet regularly to perfect the vital technical demands of the team pursuit. With Sheil's guidance, they learnt to get into formation quickly and finessed their changes. They attempted countless flying starts until they had as good as nailed it. They did flying kilometres to ensure they could interchange when going even faster than race pace.

'It was working on the principle of minimal gains,' Ian says, 'working on every aspect – by getting our technique as good as it could be, we'd improve our chances of getting the gold medal. When footage is shown now and we look at technique, ours was as good as anyone's. It was as good as the Germans', if not better.'

Soon after the team pursuit event began in San Sebastián, it was quickly evident that the Britons were slicker than most of the field, as they eased through to the semi-finals in front of 5,000 fans at the sold-out Velódromo de Anoeta. There they faced the Dutch, who were strong opposition and came within a second of beating the Brits. The West Germans hammered Poland so easily in the other semi-final that both teams had sat up before the end.

Willi was annoyed about this. He felt the West Germans had colluded with the opposition, striking a deal in which Poland agreed not to exert themselves because they felt victory over the favourites was impossible and would prefer to save themselves for the bronze medal race. Ian is less convinced, noting how team pursuit races often finish up like this once one team has an unassailable lead. Whatever the truth, the West Germans were fresher than the Britons and looked strong as they held a four-second lead going into the final lap. 'We rode a good, smooth race,' Ian says, 'but steadily through the ride they got further and further ahead of us. Clearly we were going to lose. We were going to be silver medallists and, well, you know the story, the whole of the West German team crashed.'

They crashed when the front man struck the shoulder of a Spanish official who had hesitated while replacing one of the sponge blocks that were placed on the track to mark the line that the riders could not cross. Though the blocks do get knocked out of position during a race, it is best not to put them back when four of the world's fastest cyclists are riding towards you at forty miles per hour.

The West Germans were still lying on the boards when the

British team crossed the finish line. 'I remember as if it was yesterday,' says Ian, 'winding down from the ride and shouting to Willi, "We're world champions!" The natural thing that you think when a team crashes is that someone's touched a wheel and it's a technical error – it's down to them, which means you've won, fair and square.'

The Britons' elation did not last long. As the stadium announcer declared them world champions, so a chorus of jeers began to emanate from the opposite side of the track. The West Germans were bloodied, two of them had to go to hospital, and their management was indignant. Though nothing in the rule book provided for what had happened, they lodged an appeal. Sheil approached his men with the news. Ian recalls: 'He said, "If we counter-appeal, we will be world champions." Because they didn't finish, the rules didn't allow them to be awarded the title, so they could not possibly have been gold medallists. Norman said, "I'm leaving it for you guys to decide what to do."'

Quite how the conversation unfolded is disputed. Willi and Ian insist that the decision was unanimous: to give up the gold was the only ethical option. The West Germans had done nothing wrong and would undoubtedly have won had one particular commissaire's brain not turned to sponge. They, it was apparently agreed among the Britons, deserved to be world champions.

Mick Bennett, however, recalls the discussion differently. 'I was outvoted,' he tells me. 'The rule is you stay on your bike and finish. They hit an official. We'd brushed the same official and stayed up.' Mick, the current race director of the Tour of Britain, wanted to keep the title that he had spent his young life dreaming about. That he didn't is still a source of regret.

In fact, it is his only regret. 'I was world champion for half an hour. It's unique. When you sacrifice your life for all those years and that happens . . .'

Mick felt the loss keenly because he had come so far to reach that point, both mentally and physically. As a fifteen year old, he had suffered from a case of Osgood-Schlatter disease that was so severe he had to spend two months with his legs in plaster. With a condition that leaves the patella ligament inflamed and causes acute pain around the knee joint, he had been referred to a physiotherapist uncertain quite how he would recover from it. Certainly he had no sporting ambitions. 'I was crap at sport,' says Mick. 'I was eight stone, sand was kicked in my face on the beach.' Yet when he began to use the static bike in the hospital gym to rebuild the muscles, he was suddenly transformed, quickly clocking times faster than the physio had ever seen. 'He said I ought to take up cycling,' Mick recalls.

Money was scarce at his family home in Sparkbrook, the area of Birmingham where the grim Victorian TV series *Peaky Blinders* is filmed. But, once his knee had healed, Mick received what he has described as a life-changing act of generosity when a neighbour gifted him a second-hand bike built by the Birmingham Small Arms Company, a reputable marque. It was old and rusted but the frame was well made and Mick had no better alternative. He stripped the bike down, repainted the frame and replaced parts. He then rode it to death on the narrow streets around his house and beyond.

'I used to see this guy in this blue tracksuit training, really impressive, always going hard. I eventually found the courage to stop him one day and it was Graham Webb. Turned out he lived two streets from me.' Among the country's strongest road cyclists, Webb would go on to win the world amateur road race

top: A packed crowd watches a race at Herne Hill velodrome, south London, in April 1931.
© *Planet News Archive/SSPL/Getty Images*

bottom: Percy Stallard prepares his bike ahead of the Brighton to Glasgow stage race in August 1945.
© *Keystone/Getty Images*

left: Britain's Tony Hoar (right) rides alongside French rival Henri Sitek on the final stage of the 1955 Tour de France. Sitek is carrying a paper lantern but Hoar was named 'lanterne rouge' when he finished last overall, one place ahead of Sitek.
© Offside/L'Equipe

right: A postage stamp promoting the 1952 Peace Race. The British rider Ian Steel won what was the toughest amateur race in the world, while the British squad claimed the team prize.
© Roger St Pierre

bottom: Tony Hewson takes on food during the 1955 Tour of Britain, which he won. Behind him (from the left) are Dick Bartrop, Ken Mitchell and Des Robinson. © Roger St Pierre

right: Alf Engers receives a starting push from his mentor Alan Shorter at the start of a Herne Hill pursuit race. © *Roger St Pierre*

right: Alf Engers, wearing his national champion's jersey, competes at Herne Hill in April 1963. © *Gerry Cranham/Offside*

left: Beryl Burton with her daughter Denise in March 1963. Denise was seven at the time. Beryl was 25 and at the height of her success, having won her fourth world title the previous year. © *John Pratt/Keystone Features/Getty Images*

right: Vin Denson (left) enjoys an impromptu shower alongside the Italian rider Antonio Bailetti during the ninth stage of the 1966 Giro d'Italia. Denson went on to become the first Briton to win a stage of the Giro that day. *Courtesy of Vin Denson*

bottom: Vin Denson (right) with his British team-mates Tom Simpson (left) and Michael Wright during the first rest day in the 1967 Tour de France. Simpson died five days later after he collapsed while climbing Mont Ventoux. *Courtesy of Vin Denson*

left: Ian Hallam, a formidable British international in the individual and team pursuit, in full flight at a Good Friday meeting at Herne Hill. © *Roger St Pierre*

right: Eddy Merckx competes in the 1977 Glenryck Cup at the Eastway circuit in Hackney Wick, east London. The venue was demolished to make way for the Olympic Park. Britain's Keith Lambert is on his right shoulder.

© *Colorsport/Andrew Cowie*

left: Ian Hallam (left) and Mick Bennett (right) compete at the Eastway in March 1980. The two men were part of the hugely successful British team pursuit quartet in the 1970s, winning world championship silver and two Olympic bronze medals.

© *Colorsport/Andrew Cowie*

left: Britain's Mandy Jones celebrates her victory in the world championship road race at the Goodwood motor racing circuit in September 1982.

© *Colorsport/Stewart Fraser*

right: Tony Doyle (right) shakes hands with Ian Emmerson, the man Doyle succeeded as president of the British Cycling Federation, at Saffron Lane velodrome in Leicester.

© *Roger St Pierre*

right: Beryl Burton at the 1970 track world championships in Leicester, where she won bronze in the individual pursuit in front of her home fans. It was her fourth bronze in the event. She won it five times and claimed silver on three occasions. © *Colorsport*

bottom: Boris Johnson, the Mayor of London, opens Redbridge Cycling Centre in August 2008. It was built to replace Eastway while cyclists awaited the opening of the Lee Valley VeloPark at the site of the London 2012 Olympic Games. © *Cate Gillon/Getty Images*

left: Colin Sturgess celebrates winning the professional road race at the 1990 British championships. © *David Worthy/ EMPICS Sport*

bottom: Nicole Cooke (second right) poses after her victory in the road race at the junior world championships at Plouay, Brittany, in 2000 with her father Tony (right). *Courtesy of the Cooke family*

above: Colin Sturgess during the qualifying rounds for the individual pursuit at the 1988 Olympic Games in Seoul, where he went on to finish fourth. © *Mike Powell/Staff*

title, the first British man to do so since the 1920s. He invited Mick into his home to show him his trophy haul. Inspired, Mick asked what he should do to start racing. 'He said you need to go to Tommy Godwin's Cycles.'

Godwin mentored a generation of Brummie cyclists. The winner of two bronze medals on the track at the 1948 Olympics, he nurtured young talents at Solihull CC and in his capacity as a national team coach. First taught about the importance of self-discipline in sport when he visited boxing gyms while growing up in Connecticut, Godwin insisted that all of his students adhered to a ferocious work ethic. They ate properly, slept fully and covered about 300 miles a week on the bike. Mick flourished under his regime. 'He took me from being a nobody, a snotty-nosed, skinny little kid who had nothing and came from nothing in the back streets of Birmingham, to a bike rider with a future.'

I met Tommy shortly before he died, aged 91, which was shortly after he had carried the Olympic torch through Solihull in 2012 on its way to London. He was a bear of a man, who could talk enthusiastically about cycling all evening. 'He was a nurturer, a gentle giant who could inspire me to do great things on a bike,' says Mick.

Tommy took a special interest in Mick, not only because he was committed and talented and in need of a guiding hand, but also because he was best suited to endurance track racing – just as Godwin had been. Mick was versatile, too, learning road craft on long trips to Holland and impressing in British criteriums as he simultaneously emerged as a pursuit rider of international class. In this context he was not exceptional, but he made up for that with guts, speed and commitment. As Ned Boulting, the cycling TV presenter and journalist, wrote in his book *On the Road Bike,* Mick was 'solid, dependable and valued. He did not tear up the record books.' In 1976, in Montreal, he added a second Olympic bronze medal in the team pursuit to the one he won in Munich, but he never came close to winning the rainbow jersey again.

The quartet's gesture in San Sebastián earned them two prestigious awards that recognised their sportsmanship. First was the International Fair Play Committee's annual award and then the West German cycling federation flew them to the Black Forest to present each of them with a replica world championship gold medal and an Omega Seamaster watch. It represented scant consolation. The gold medal would have been far greater reward for his years of sacrifice. 'I'd rather have a world champ's jersey hanging on my wall,' Mick says. 'They finished with two riders and we finished with three so, effectively, we won. Today, had the same thing happened, it would have been laughed about, yet we gave our medals away.'

Ian is of a similar view now. Experience has taught him that elite sport is ruthless and that you suffer enough instances of misfortune so you must embrace good luck when it comes your way. 'During my career I didn't have any regrets about it at all – it was the right thing to do,' he says, 'but now I see the bigger picture. In sport it's about ability, preparation and dedication and it's about fortune. It was just one occasion where luck went our way and we didn't accept it as a sporting incident – these things happen. And we see it in sport all the time, where rules are bent in order to achieve success.'

It is an intriguing outlook: to be frustrated with a selfless, romantic act taken in your youth. Yet they were not alone in thinking it a mistake. Several rival international teams told them as much immediately afterwards. Ian and Willi wonder if their decision was a result of emerging from an amateur cycling culture that supposedly placed greater emphasis on fair play than the professional scene abroad. (To me, it seems a suspect argument to suggest that Britain is a more sporting nation than others, but I was not there at the time so I'm not inclined to question them.)

At the time they were happy enough with the decision because they assumed they would get a second crack at the rainbow jerseys soon afterwards, but that plan ran aground when Ian punctured during the quarter-final of the following year's world championships and they were eliminated. An amateur career often has a short lifespan, as riders either turn professional or choose to get on with the rest of their lives, and this race was the last in which they would compete together. They all took time out to travel and Ian and Mick eventually returned to the sport, but Willi's competitive days were finished as he took up a coaching role in New Zealand. After a career spent working for GlaxoSmithKline, Willi is now retired, though he does help out at his local bike shop. That customers are unaware of his cycling background seems like a missed opportunity. Hopefully it is not churlish to wonder whether the proprietor would feel differently about promoting his senior employee had he been a world champion. 'There is something quite different about saying, "Oh, we were world championship medallists", to saying, "We were world champions",' Willi admits.

For several years Ian replaced cycling with windsurfing, which he started from scratch yet eventually finished fifth in its world championships. For a man with the ability to excel at whatever the task, this must have been a disappointment. Only fifth? 'I had thought, "Wouldn't it be great to win something in a different sport?",' he says, smiling. 'Eventually, I got a young family and I thought, "Hang on, this is not fair. I need to spend time with my family".'

In time, however, he returned to cycling precisely because the same frustration that has dogged Willi gnawed away at him, too. He wanted not only to race again but to compete in the world masters championships that had become increasingly prominent and bestowed on its aged winners the same rainbow jerseys given to the conventional world champions.

Though inevitably not as competitive, the masters events are still tough. In rising through the categories to become an 'elite' again, Ian was typical of the successful masters athletes. He was also among the most decorated, winning twelve world titles. "Being able to say that I was a world champion – that was the one thing that was driving me in my sporting life, so that was the motivation for going back. It means very little compared to a proper world championship and, in comparison, it isn't really that important within the sport, but personally it was really satisfying.'

CHAPTER NINE

The modest heroine who struggled with fame

On a freezing afternoon in January, in an industrial kitchen beside an athletics track in Dagenham, I have stripped down to my boxer shorts to prepare for an unlikely physical examination. The man conducting it is Tony Harvey, the Crest club coach, whom I have known for all of half an hour, while his two volunteer assistants look on. 'I don't think you need to worry about losing weight,' Tony says, in a tone that does not suggest a man impressed. If there is one aspect of my physique that is to my advantage as an aspiring cyclist, it is my apparent inability to gain weight. I am six foot two and, as Tony discovers, only 70.8 kilograms. This is only 1.8 kilograms more than Bradley Wiggins weighed before he won the Tour but he had spent his winter riding up a volcano, skipping lunch and avoiding alcohol – none of which I am prepared even to consider.

I step on to Tony's electronic scales and allow him to attach a device to my finger, for measuring my pulse. Combined, the technology allows him to read my overall body fat, or adipose tissue as he calls it. I am 9.3 per cent, which apparently means that I sneak into the lower end of what is considered healthy.

Next is visceral body fat, which is the type that lines the organs. On a scale of one to ten per cent, I am one. 'That's the lowest I've seen,' Tony says. He suggests that this is too low but a surgeon friend will guarantee that I need not worry, especially as my skeletal muscle mass is relatively impressive at 43.6 per cent. According to Tony's charts, anything between 39 and 44 per cent is considered high. 'You're a skinny sod,' he says, 'which isn't a bad start if you're going to be cycling up mountains. My first challenge is usually to get people to lose weight.'

I have called on Tony because I have decided to ride the Etape du Tour, the annual sportive that covers the toughest stage of the Tour de France and thus is one of the toughest rides open to an amateur. As I am still not fit enough to race, I figured that I needed a new target, and this was the outstanding option. By riding two iconic Pyrenean cols, the Tourmalet and the Hautacam, climbing in total more than 3,500 metres on an eight-five-mile course, I will learn what it is like truly to suffer in the saddle, a rite of passage for any cyclist.

The Tourmalet promises to be especially difficult. When it was included on the Etape route in 2010, 3,000 of the 10,000 entrants failed to finish. When it returned to the route two years later, only sixty per cent of those taking part reached the end.

Clearly, to stand a hope of completing it, I need to introduce some structure to my training, and Tony seems suited to the task. He teaches young people with learning disabilities how to ride and today, at the Jim Peters Stadium in Dagenham, he has brought with him his CV and evidence of the sports science degree that he is close to completing. He took up full-time coaching only a few years ago, in his early fifties. However, I am more interested in his cycling background. It is more important, I think, than what he will have picked up in a classroom.

He has been riding in Essex since the 1970s and counts his eleventh place in the national twelve-hour time-trial championship as his best achievement. He also held the Bath Road Club 100-mile record with a time of four hours, eight minutes 'and something', having smashed by eight minutes the landmark that had stood for fifteen years. It has begun to feel as though almost every cyclist that I have met of a certain age has impressive achievements to their name. I admit to him that I feel out of my depth. 'I wouldn't,' Tony says. 'A club-mate of mine broke the record seven days later. They never let me forget that.'

He plans to limit my time in the saddle as best he can, with a training plan broken down into six-week blocks – making it easier to tackle mentally – and based around intensive interval training. Alternating bursts of high-intensity effort with periods of recovery, this training method that Norman Sheil pioneered has since been scientifically proven to be a more efficient method of improving fitness than regular exercise. As Tony will explain via email, it works by forcing the fast-twitch muscles to use up all the available oxygen, engaging the body's anaerobic energy system. This, in turn, strengthens muscles, improves the efficiency with which they consume oxygen and increases the body's ability to sustain high levels of power output – all vital qualities when climbing a mountain. It also apparently bestows the fitness benefits of more traditional aerobic exercise.

I have tried doing intervals on my turbo-trainer at home ever since Neil, from Hackney CC, advised it when I met him at Hog Hill. My problem has been that I have not known what intervals to adopt. According to Tony, the one-minute intervals I have tried at Neil's suggestion are too short, being more suited to building up the muscle fibre needed in sprinting and that, as a novice, I should have begun with intervals of three minutes to develop the aerobic capacity I will need for long hours in the saddle. (Later, he will explain that only then will I begin to transform the glucose in my body into energy rather than the creatine phosphate that it uses in shorter intervals. Creatine phosphate, apparently, has no oxidative capacity.)

'I don't want to appear to be dismissing Neil's advice,' Tony says. 'He is actually a friend of mine and a good coach. One-minute intervals have their place and, indeed, we will incorporate them into our sessions. But I prefer to build up from longer intervals for endurance work in the early days of a training regime, and then shorten them later on, once the rider has had a chance to feel the pain involved and learnt how to really hurt himself,' he says, adding with a smile. 'I want you to be feeling sick when you finish one of my sessions.'

I have persuaded four friends – all of them recent converts to cycling – to sign up for the Etape. Only Chris, who I watched at Hog Hill, have I got to know recently. The rest of us have been mates since adolescence. Tom is quietly spoken, six foot five and naturally athletic. He has spent several recent years doing extreme endurance events for reasons that I could never fathom. He has not trained for a while but his powers of self-discipline remain a concern. For years, Andy enjoyed weightlifting but appears to get his adrenaline kicks now by riding unspeakably quickly to work. Fig, to give the other Andy his nickname, recently built a bike from scratch, using an old Bob Jackson steel frame, shortly after his second child was born. In other words, he constructed a means of escape just as he became further tied down. He does not have the time to ride as much as the rest of us but he has natural stamina and, as a veteran of recent triathlons, is formidably determined. Though I will not admit to it, I want to beat all of them and I plan to leave nothing to chance. Hence I am on my way to Cadence, a 'cycling centre' in Crystal Palace, for a professional bike fitting.

Frank Beechinor grew up racing bikes in Cork in the 1980s, when the sport in Ireland enjoyed a mini boom inspired by the success of Stephen Roche and Sean Kelly, the two Irishmen who were among the finest road cyclists of their generation. Returning to the sport in his late forties, he first had the idea for Cadence when he realised that there was nowhere for cyclists who lived in south London to meet before they headed out for their rides into the Kent lanes. He then sold his computer software company for £16 million.

'I remember sitting with my friend Ray, who subsequently founded Cadence with me, and there were about ten cyclists inside Costa there and we were huddling in one corner, everyone else in another corner,' he says. 'And there's about £40,000 worth of bikes outside the window and anyone could have pulled up alongside when we were distracted and ripped off the whole lot. We wanted somewhere that you could go and hang out and not have those worries and not having people look at you like you've got two heads because you're wearing bike gear.'

This was only a couple of years ago and it led to a pop-up cyclists' café that also sold equipment and carried out repairs. It proved popular enough for Frank and Ray to turn the business into a permanent concern that is now almost unrecognisable from those early days. Though still home to a café and workshop, as well as having a range of bikes and equipment on sale, it also offers computer-based bike-fits, watt bikes, blood-lactate tests, personalised coaching and the bike-fitting equipment, among other services. It is all hugely impressive, but looking around Cadence one is tempted to wonder if the industry is, well, turning a little absurd. Sir Dave Brailsford might wax lyrical about the benefits of marginal gains but are there really amateur cyclists out there willing to pay £49 for an oxygen mask and another £35 every time they wish to hook up to the machine that Frank has bought to simulate altitude training?

Apparently, yes, there are, albeit only those of a certain demographic. 'Yes, admittedly club cyclists are really tight with their money – they're like me,' Frank says. 'If I thought I could get something cheaper online, I'd buy it online. But we make money off the affluent, typically new cyclist who has got to spend £7,000 on a bike and money isn't an issue. We know, for example, that sixty per cent of our customers have more than one bike, and that lots of them will have four to five bikes and will spend huge money.'

And yet they're not the only ones spending money on the kind of things offered at Cadence. 'Cycling has produced a new group of riders known as the "frequent enthusiasts",' he explains, 'and they're the ones that people like me are interested in. They're one level down from the banker. They're guys who ride their bike three times a week and do sportives or just go out on the weekend.'

Guys like me, in other words. 'Maybe, yes. LSE did research a couple of years ago. They put that frequent enthusiasts market back then at 650,000 strong and said their average, annual spend on their bike and kit was £2,500. They also spend an average of £700 a year on consumables; gels and maintenance and stuff like that.' I make a few swift calculations and realise that, if you include repairs and cycling trips, I just about fit this description. Christ, I'm spending more on cycling than everything but food and my mortgage. 'You're not alone. Within 10k of here there's about 23,000 frequent enthusiast riders, as well as 800 registered racing cyclists.'

Frank's grand plan is to persuade some of these cyclists to sign up to a subscription-based membership that allows them access to other services within his centre – which could soon include a wind tunnel, given that he has commissioned plans for one. He intends to open other centres, too, and has already viewed a site on the south-western fringe of the city. He thinks that Cadence could become the meeting point for thousands of cyclists. He might just have imagined what the future will look like, assuming that cycling's popularity remains high (and, for the moment, it looks likely only to grow). 'We want to be the first commercial cycling club, but we also want to be a club for clubs,' he says. 'Go back to the 1950s and you had clubs with 1,000 members and all the clubs had a hut at the end of the sports field. By the '80s and '90s those clubs had dropped to twenty members and they were all the hardcore cyclists. Now those clubs are thriving again, but there's nowhere for them to go.'

Certainly this is true of the Crest since Stag Hall was sold, though I'm not sure what they would make of Cadence. I imagine most of them would rely on a bike-fitting by eye and feel, not the Retül technology that cost Frank £10,000, even though he describes it as an 'elaborate Xbox or Wii'.

I head upstairs to the fitting room, hoping that at the very least the experience will make me *look* like a cyclist. For, in about eighteen months of riding a road bike, this is not something I have achieved. In fact, in an attempt to cure the myriad problems I have endured while becoming accustomed to it – perineum pain, lower-back ache, and pins and needles in my hands – I have ended up looking more like a man wishing he was on a sit-up-and-beg bike than an aerodynamic frame. As a result, with my back and arms bolt straight and my saddle as far forward as possible, other cyclists frequently comment on how inefficient I look.

Before I get strapped up to the Xbox, though, the fitter, Alex, insists on performing a quick physiological examination to check for underlying muscular or skeletal problems. His conclusions are predictable. As well as having tight calves and hamstrings, my neck and spine lack the full range of movement, the result of never doing any stretching, ever. He suggests I should think about taking up yoga or pilates, classes in both of which are conveniently available at Cadence. 'I'll think about it,' I nod, stiffly.

Alex then checks my cleats and finds they are several months beyond worn out and promptly replaces them, at a cost. He also checks how much stability they provide in the pedal and decides that they too should be improved, ideally with cycling shoe 'orthotics'. By this he means an insole that provides the increased support that would ease the discomfort I feel in my shoes on longer rides. Here again, Cadence can be of help. 'We provide customised heat-moulded insoles, which includes an hour's service,' he says, noting the cost after I press him for it: £90. Had Frank not kindly offered this fit free of charge, I reckon the muscles in my neck would be even tighter now. (Unless you are also writing a book and can claim to be spreading the word of the cycling revolution, Frank's Retül fit will cost you £150.)

I return to the bike being held in position on a turbo-trainer and wait as Alex places electronic pads on my body so that the Retül software can simulate my position while stationary on the frame, riding slowly and when sprinting. After briefly studying the results, he concurs with what others have said: I need to be lower across the frame, with my back arched and elbows slightly bent. I need also to point my arms straight forward rather than have them splayed. To encourage what overall is admittedly quite a significant change in position, he suggests upgrading several parts. I need narrower handlebars, a more carefully calibrated seat pin and a new stem. I'm not shocked when he suggests purchasing each one right now, and then pops downstairs to find them. I'm fast becoming a not so enthusiastic frequent enthusiast.

I should be grateful really. Retül is cutting-edge technology and Cadence carry out about 100 bike-fittings a month when demand is highest during the summer. Professional teams such as Garmin, RadioShack and Team Sky are just a few of those who have used Retül. Frank has also worked with An Post-Chain Reaction, the Irish team that Sean Kelly co-manages, and conducted personal fittings for professionals including Marco Pinotti and Johnny Hoogerland. They benefited from the 3D software that bases its calculations on medically accepted biomechanical measurements, such as the ideal range of joint flexion and extension.

Often Retül will recommend only fractional changes to the bike that the naked eye will not pick up. In my case, though, the change is so significant that it takes several attempts before I can even hold the position that Alex demanded once he had fitted the new parts. When, finally, I am allowed to watch myself back on the screen, I discover that I do, finally, resemble a proper cyclist, and not one suffering from sciatica. As part of the service, I will also receive an email detailing all the angles to which the parts on my bike should be adjusted in the future, too. All said, it feels like I have made a lot more than a marginal gain this afternoon, but I am still not buying those insoles.

You will not find cutting-edge training technology at Surosa Cycles* in Oldham, but you will be able to call on expertise that money cannot buy. Run by Nigel and Mandy Bishop, it continues a fine British tradition of independent bike shops operated by eminent, retired cycling figures. Traditionally, most of them have declared their ownership in their name. Consider the eponymous shop that Tommy Godwin ran in Birmingham or Swinnerton Cycles in Stoke-on-Trent, which former national track champion Colin owns, having inherited it from his father Roy, a national team mechanic. Harry Hall Cycles, the business that Tom Simpson's mechanic set up, remains a pillar of the Manchester cycling community.

Nigel and Mandy, however, are slower to trade on their achievements, even though he once held the yellow jersey in the Milk Race and Mandy is one of only three British women to win the world road race title. In Mandy's case, this anonymity can lead unenlightened male customers into embarrassing situations. 'It's because there aren't many women in the bike trade,' she says, sitting at the kitchen table of her home near

---

* Surosa Cycles ceased trading in January 2015. Mandy and Nigel continued to run their mail-order business, Fawkes Cycles.

Rochdale. Beside us is Mandy's nineteen-year-old daughter Rebecca, an occasional employee at Surosa, who says men who visit the shop often look right through her when in need of advice. 'I've had it, too,' says Mandy. 'We had one instance, I remember one gentleman was doing that thing where he's looking over your shoulder to see if there's a man in the shop, so I just say, "Oh, Nigel will help you".'

Nigel, Mandy's second husband, could have dealt with the customer but was careful not to let him off the hook. 'My worlds medal was in the cabinet in the shop,' Mandy says. 'The customer asked who it belonged to. Nigel said it was mine and showed it to him. He came into the back of the shop and got on his hands and knees and was saying, "Oh, I'm so sorry".'

Mandy Jones spent a lot of time defying stereotypical views about female cyclists in the late 1970s and 1980s. That is partly why I have visited her, to hear what obstacles she had to overcome to achieve her exceptional victory: she was the only Briton to win a senior world road race title from the time Beryl Burton and Graham Webb did it in 1967 until Nicole Cooke forty-one years later. But, if I am honest, I am here also because I had been told that Mandy's triumph came at some personal cost. I hope it does not sound overly opportunistic, but I suspected there was an untold story to her success.

Life seems to have treated the Bishops well. They live in an idyllic-looking converted barn atop a hill with sweeping views of the West Pennine Moors. The kitchen has a large brick alcove and big wooden table, at which we sit for several hours. Nigel will join us later to discuss his career. Mandy's mum, Judith, will pop through a door that connects this to the adjacent house, the one she shares with her second husband, Bob Porter, a former professional team-mate of Reg Barnett's. There is much cycling history in this building.

Mandy's cycling story began when she joined her local club in Rochdale, West Pennine CC, in the early 1970s and discovered a sport that remained fiercely patriarchal. Quite possibly it may even have regressed in this regard, as cycling was no longer the mainstream family pursuit that it had been in the decades after the Second World War, regardless of Beryl Burton's success. Certainly Mandy's cycling-mad father Barrie had to work hard to transform attitudes within West Pennine to allow his wife and two daughters to enjoy membership. 'It was just full of men,' says Mandy. 'I remember my dad bought us tickets for the club dinner and it was, "Why are you bringing them?". But my dad's attitude was we're part of it, and my mum wouldn't have let him leave us behind anyway!'

Judith and Barrie had met while cycling with East Manchester Clarion in the 1950s, with Judith having turned up to club runs on her father's commuting bike because a girl's one was not fast enough for her. Her daughter had inherited both this single-mindedness and her parents' love of the sport.

Initially, Mandy rode purely because she enjoyed it, joining club runs over the Yorkshire Dales and across the Pennines, heading off on family trips to the Lake District and north Wales. Without intending to, she was building up her strength over some of the country's toughest terrain, becoming the only female rider on West Pennines' A run, a 100-mile trip on a Sunday.

She also began to embarrass a few men in club time-trials. 'I was stood this once at the results board and there was a guy stood in front of me talking to his friend and he says, "So why haven't you ridden today then, George?" And he replies, "What, and get beaten by a bloody woman?" That was the first time it ever came to me. I thought, "Oh, men don't like being beaten." And, well, I just found that hilarious.'

Barrie bought Mandy her first geared bike when she was sixteen, a second-hand, twenty-one-and-a-half-inch Woodrup, which was about two inches too long for her and overgeared. However, money was tight and she put up with it, graduating to the few road races that were available to junior girls at the time. Only when she finished joint winner of the national junior ten-mile time-trial, though, did Mandy show evidence of potentially exceptional talent.

Her boyfriend at the time, Ian Greenhalgh, certainly thought so anyway. A club-mate who was fifteen years older than Mandy, and a domestic professional with the Wightman-Knight team, Ian persuaded her to start training with him in an attempt to exploit her potential. By the time she moved in with him, she was living the life of a full-time athlete.

Surviving on the dole, and Ian's small income from cycling, they rode fifty miles hard each morning and covered eighty to ninety miles with the club's fast group twice a week. Ian's team-mate Jack Kershaw often joined them but neither man made concessions for Mandy. 'Ian was a very determined person,' she says. 'You went out in any weather, didn't make any difference, and he would never let up. He would never go easy on you.'

As far as she knew, no other young women were training with her intensity, which would explain why she graduated to the national road squad within a year and kept her place for the 1980 world championships in the French Alpine town of Sallanches. It was a famously tough course, requiring competitors to scale repeatedly the Côte de Domancy, with a gradient that peaked at sixteen per cent. Still riding her old Woodrup, and without sufficiently low gears, Mandy shocked even herself when she held on for bronze in a sprint finish. 'It was completely unexpected. I knew I had an advantage over a lot of the British girls because they were still working, but I still didn't understand the natural ability that I had. I was too young for that. I was only eighteen.'

For a teenager, her life was formidably stoical. They had hardly any money left after the bills were paid. She had little social life and her father had to drive her to races. She acquired small grants from the Sports Council and a local authority but they went mostly towards her equipment. All that the British Cycling Federation provided was a skin suit and travel expenses. They loaned the women shorts and jerseys that were designed for men. She was prepared to put up with it all because the 1982 world championships were coming to Britain, with the Goodwood motor racing circuit in West Sussex having won the right to stage an event at which Ian was certain she could be competitive in both the pursuit and the road race. 'That was the choice: continue to train full-time, like a professional, just with none of the financial support that a professional gets, with the aim of winning at Goodwood, or to get a part-time job like everyone else.'

With Ian serving as de facto coach, she supplemented her road regime with speed training for the pursuit. Two afternoons a week, she followed Ian's motorbike and alternated between riding in his slipstream and trying to stay beside him while he held a speed of thirty miles per hour.

As Ian's journeyman career began to taper off, so he became more determined that Mandy should do well. If she was reluctant to go out training, he never indulged her. If she was beaten in competition, he took it personally, even once riding off in disgust from a local road race because she had failed to win it. Like the overbearing parent, it seemed he was living out his thwarted ambitions through his girlfriend. 'I felt it was a bit of that,' she said. '[He was thinking,] "I hadn't done it, I couldn't do it and I'd been training you and you've not done it and it reflects badly on me".'

She had only limited opportunities to take part in road races. Women were allowed to compete against junior and third-category men in Britain but she was reluctant to enter those events because the other riders' handling skills were so bad. There was a stronger women's scene on the Continent but foreign promoters did not think to invite British riders and the BCF lacked the money to fund more than the very occasional trip abroad. 'You'd race against these girls at the beginning of the year and you wouldn't see them again. You knew nothing about them until you got to the world championships.'

Nonetheless, she looked in good condition as the Goodwood event approached. She had recovered from two crashes at a recent event in France to finish in the bunch. At the national track championships, she had broken the world record for the five-kilometre pursuit. She had avoided serious injury and kept up her motor-paced training right up until the Wednesday before the weekend of the world championship pursuit. 'Oh, I felt strong. I'm another year older, aren't I? I'm another year fitter, I'm another year stronger and it builds up over the years.'

In that final week, however, she should have cut her work right back or even eliminated it altogether. Instead she was so exhausted come race day that she finished eight seconds down on her usual time and far down the field. It seemed as if two years of preparation and sacrifice had been wasted. 'I was absolutely devastated. I didn't understand what had gone wrong. Whereas now they know all about tapering and resting before an event, it was all basically off the top of our heads about how we do this training.'

With ten days to wait until the worlds road race, she went out only for easy, steady rides to try to recover some motivation. She did not realise that, physically, this recovery period was just what she needed. 'I was so fed up. I didn't feel like talking to anyone. I had to get my head back in gear. Eventually, my attitude was, "I've got nothing to lose". And all I was doing was pottering round so, of course, I was rested.'

The course covered four and a half laps of an eight-mile circuit on the South Downs, taking in the Goodwood racecourse and a ten per cent climb one kilometre from the finish line on the motor racing circuit. (Only in 1991 were women considered capable of courses that were much longer than this.)

Mandy had competed against her four team-mates but had little experience of riding with them. They included the Swinnerton sisters, Margaret and Catherine, who had finished second and third in the nationals, as well as Julie Earnshaw and Pauline Strong, both good riders but not among the favourites to win. There was little hope of them riding a tactical race and working together. Instead, Mandy would need to track every breakaway on her own, just as she did when the first attack came shortly after the start and, again, when it was reeled in by an elite chasing group comprising Maria Canins, future winner of the Tour de Féminin, Gerda Sierens, champion of Belgium, and the German Sandra Schumacher, who would go on to win road race bronze at the 1984 Olympics.

Though each of that trio in turn attempted to break her

rivals, none cracked, enabling Mandy to lead the group as it emerged from a descent with only a lap left. 'I just carried on around Pilly Green corner and I looked back and they'd gone.' This understates the ferocity with which Mandy jumped. As she describes it, her modesty gives way to the old competitive streak that set her apart. 'I'd done it before, where I've got away on a descent just by going round a tricky bend and jumping. It's because everybody's relaxed. They think, "Oh, nobody's going to attack now". It's about taking opportunities.'

What remained, effectively, was an eight-mile time-trial in which she needed to hold off the desperately chasing bunch. Her pursuit training proved invaluable. The cheers of the British fans who watched her lap the motor racing circuit out in front helped to sustain her effort, too, though quite how she managed to hold on to win gold remains something of a mystery to her. 'Even when I watch the race now, it's like watching somebody else,' she told *Cycling Weekly*. 'When everything comes together like it did that day, you don't think about it: you're in the zone. It's what you train for.'

Typically for British cycling at the time, her immediate celebrations were quaintly modest. She spent the evening in the hotel and volunteered to help Ian with his marshalling duties on the circuit the following afternoon, thus swapping the rainbow jersey for dayglo twenty-four hours after winning it. In time, though, the success ensured her life would change markedly. National newspapers wanted to speak to her and she appeared on mainstream TV (*A Question Of Sport* and the children's show *Crackerjack*). She was flooded with invitations to appear at cycling functions and dinners, most of which she felt compelled to accept. This was the grass-roots of the sport through which she had developed, after all.

All of the sudden exposure overwhelmed this twenty-year-old, whose life since school had comprised mostly of riding a bike on the lanes around her home. 'The coverage was good in that I was a girl in a minority sport, but you don't get any training. They do now but we didn't get any training to deal with the media or what it's like. So, yeah, I found it difficult.'

As the time came to return to training, she struggled to summon the motivation for it. In the prolonged build-up to Goodwood, she had not paused to consider what goal she might need to establish beyond it and, as a result, felt purposeless. Mentally, she had also exceeded the amount of pressure that she could withstand from Ian. As she describes it, she broke down. 'I was really, really struggling and it was just because of the way Ian was. He just used to push it and push it and push it. I'd get to the point where I was sometimes at the side of the road and I couldn't breathe and it's like a panic attack and I'd be [she starts gasping] like this and I had to stop. I just cracked in the end.'

She compares their relationship to the troubled one that Victoria Pendleton had with her father. In her autobiography, the double Olympic champion said that her father's impossible demands underpinned her success. 'I remember reading her book, thinking, "Hmm, where have I heard that before?" She's wanting to do it because she wants to show him she can do it. And that's a bit like I was with Ian – "I want to prove to you that I can do this."'

Pendleton has talked often about the positive support she received from Steve Peters, British Cycling's former psychiatrist. Mandy admits that she needed to consult a mental health professional at the time, were only it something that people considered then. Instead she ploughed on, half-heartedly, trying to train alone, while Ian became consumed with the bike shop that they had opened together. Often she would pretend to him that she had been out riding hard when really she had spent the afternoon at Julie Earnshaw's house. 'I didn't do myself any good,' she says, still chastising herself decades later. She made it to the world championships the next year and finished fourth, despite all her difficulties, but knew then it was time to walk away from the sport. 'Basically, in my head, I'd done what I set out to do. And I really, really needed a break. I realise now it wasn't a physical break, it was mental.'

Ian did not respond to my request to interview him about Mandy's success and his role in it. I wanted not only his version of what happened but to hear if he felt it necessary to place that amount of pressure on Mandy to help her fulfil her potential. I hoped also to see whether he still had the charisma Mandy referred to when she was asked what attracted her to him. He could 'charm the birds out of the trees', she said.

'I'd grown up with the cycling club,' she adds. 'I was used to being around cyclists who were a bit older and a bit more mature. I just thought boys my age were stupid at the time, so that was part of the attraction. It was older-man syndrome.'

Not surprisingly, she finds talking about the relationship difficult. We need to stop for a moment so that she can find a tissue to wipe her eyes and compose herself.

The relationship lasted for about another seven years, though Mandy says that 'it had been on the rocks for a long time'. In that time, she had had their son, Sam, and been forced to move back to her dad's house after the bike shop had failed. She had also attempted several comebacks to cycling but struggled to overcome a calf-muscle injury she had suffered while weight training – Ian's idea. Only when she submitted to surgery was it resolved.

Finally, she was able to ride more consistently than she had done for years. She joined her dad's club, Centreville CC, and began to enjoy the sport again. She had returned to her cycling roots and, within about a year, she had regained her place in the British squad for the 1991 world championships. She finished eighth in the team trial and sixteenth in the road race, highly creditable results for somebody who had not even returned to her racing weight. With another solid year of training, she felt she might be able to challenge the elite again.

The national selectors felt similarly confident about her revived potential, placing her on the Olympic programme for the Games in Barcelona. She had looked on enviously since women cyclists had been admitted to the Games in 1984 and now she had a chance to join them.

Life was beginning to look positive again. She had met Nigel while riding with Centreville and that relationship was progressing nicely. For good or bad, his attitude towards Mandy's cycling was the polar opposite of Ian's. Though fiercely committed himself, he never once pushed her when she joined him in the strong group of racing cyclists at Centreville. They trained solidly together through the winter, both off road and on it, for variety. They were following a mountain trail one day when, suddenly, Mandy felt shooting pains through her back whenever she pushed on the pedal. 'It was horrendous. I literally I had to crawl through the front door when I got back.'

No expert could figure out the cause of the problem. The British team management sent her to London for a CAT scan, which revealed no obvious issue apart from a slightly protruding spinal disc that may have been pressing on a nerve. But the pain would not go away. She was sent to the National Sports Centre at Lilleshall for a course of intensive rehabilitation, but that too had little benefit. With the weeks counting down to Barcelona and no sign of improvement, eventually she had to give up on her Olympic dream. 'Talk about major depression. Oh, [I felt] really bad, incredibly bad for the next three months. I was in such a hole. It was not just that I couldn't race. I was thinking I could never ride my bike again.'

She was right. The problem, which was never identified, prevented her from racing competitively again. To replace it, she took up fell running for a while. She progressed from it to mountain marathons, but neither of them replaced her first love. 'I never enjoyed them really, not like riding my bike. I always, always felt there was more [to achieve]. Whether it was going for the Olympic title and maybe for world records, I never felt I had got to my full potential. I could have gone faster.'

Today, the most Mandy can manage is gentle family rides with Nigel and Rebecca, also an accomplished bike rider who spent four years training at the Manchester velodrome and had impressed coaches before simply deciding to give up, as teenagers will do. Mandy's experience with Ian at a similar stage of her life had presumably warned her against trying to persuade Rebecca to change her mind. 'I was nearly destroyed when I came out of that relationship. My confidence was absolutely rock bottom and it took a long time to get it back. If it wasn't for Nigel, it would have taken hold of me.'

Does she regret the relationship, then? 'No, I don't have any regrets about it, I don't see the point. I could say we'll turn the clocks back and [ensure] it never happened but, if it hadn't happened, I might not have won the world championships and I certainly wouldn't have had Sam. You know, we had some very good times together, but it was a very, very explosive relationship. There's just no way it would have lasted.'

CHAPTER TEN

Lunch with a pensioner who conquered
the world, twice

In the deserted Essex hamlet of Navestock, on a sunlit Friday evening when the rest of the world has strangely found more rewarding pursuits, I am preparing with a group of twenty-six other cyclists to ride in a circle, twice. Having arrived late, and cycled the fifteen miles here in a hurry, I am disinclined to join my opponents scaling the third-category hill near by to warm up. Most of them appear to be taking the Becontree Wheelers ten-mile time-trial with utmost seriousness, using tri-bars, wearing aerodynamic helmets. I cycle around the green beside the start line, trying to look purposeful, watching with bemusement as others tighten parts on their bikes that I did not know were adjustable, awaiting my starting slot. Having signed in at the last moment, I have been given the third one from last.

The start is marked by a white line painted on the road, a sneaky act done without council permission, though just such a line has been painted and repainted around here since the circuit was first used for time-trials eight decades ago. Alex Dowsett has held the course record for several years, having repeatedly trimmed it so that it stands now at 'nineteen minutes something', according to the timekeeper, Arthur Harragan. Dowsett claims that a tractor slowed him up when he most recently set the landmark.

I am hoping to beat 'evens', which requires an average of twenty miles per hour and would mean breaking thirty minutes. It is the typical novice's target and, after six weeks following my coach Tony's training plan, I think it is within my capability. Certainly the times I have clocked on the turbo-trainer would suggest as much. The start is touchingly formal, with an official holding me balanced while I clip in, ready to push me off as Harragan counts down from ten. That the owner of my local bike shop is my minute man has provided added motivation. Only the other day I was patronised by him, again confirming my theory that independent bike-shops adopt the philosophy that the customer rarely knows best.

I do not see him for dust. Instead, I am overtaken by both of the two cyclists behind me on the first of the two laps. I am left to battle on alone, gradually lowering my speed so that I stay within eighty-five per cent of my maximum heart-rate, the tempo that I have discovered through riding the turbo is the one I can sustain. This is not ideal. The perfect time-trial involves a steady pace, not gradual decline. By the end of the effort I can hardly breathe yet, oddly, I am not the slowest in the field. With a time of thirty minutes fifty-three seconds, I finish twenty-fourth. Not awful, perhaps, but demoralising nonetheless, especially when I discover that the sixty-six year old whom I meet afterwards, Malcolm Haigh, covered the distance in twenty-seven minutes twenty-eight seconds, which apparently was his personal best over the distance on a single speed.

Presumably he is a lifetime veteran of the sport? 'Actually no,' Malcolm says, tearing open one of the packets of Jaffa Cakes that the organisers have provided. 'I've only been doing it for about five years.'

I have made, it turns out, several mistakes. As Tony explains, having studied the statistics of my ride on Strava, I should not have ridden so far to get to the event in the first place. Nor should I have embarked on a long ride twenty-four hours earlier if I had wanted to record a good time at Navestock. Most importantly, however, I underestimated how important is the art of concentration in the discipline. Apparently, this is not easily learnt. 'Your psychological preparation wasn't there,' Tony says. 'When you do any event, you need to be clear about what you want out of it. If you decide that it is just miles, then enjoy the experience and forget the time. If you want to do the best ride you can, then give yourself a chance. Ride out really easy, in plenty of time, and work on a frame of mind conducive to extreme concentration.' Only then, he says, can you extract every drop of energy from your muscles. 'TTs require the acquisition of a skill that doesn't happen just like that. You need to 'know' your body intimately, understand its strengths and limitations, which only comes from experience. Your HR never went to its extremes so you should have had more to give. Don't be despondent. Understand what affected your performance and address it for the next time.'

Malcolm Haigh's performance would have seemed remarkable had I not heard similar tales of cyclists continuing to improve into middle age and beyond. Read the results from races run by the League of Veteran Racing Cyclists and you will find their speeds compare favourably to cat-three and cat-four races. At Dunton, I was well beaten by men in their fifties.

Hog Hill, a more demanding circuit, attracts cyclists of similar seniority. Cycling seems to challenge popular wisdom that, physically, we peak in our late thirties, and no more so than in the case of a septuagenarian cyclist called Tony Woodcock, tales about whom are legend on the Essex scene. In the past few months alone, I was told that he split the field (and thus broke the rules) by forcing the pace on a local Audax ride. Members of the Crest recall how Tony rode himself into unconsciousness while on a Sussex sportive. I know first-category riders that Tony joins on training rides. They seem awed by the determination with which Tony twice became world masters champion when approaching retirement age and with which he continues to ride. I need to meet the man.

Tony is not easy to track down. He is no longer attached to a club and the few people in regular contact with him were reluctant to pass on his number, saying he likes his privacy. When I do finally acquire an email address for him, he is training in the Pyrenees, though he replies warmly enough and suggests we combine the interview with a ride.

I arrive at his home in the village of Blackmore in Essex in full kit, albeit with the intention of chatting first, then riding. There are two large trophies in the living room cabinet, spoils from world championships, but apparently there is a lot more silverware more discreetly displayed in another room. Tony quickly brushes away his wife Diane's suggestion that I take a look at them. 'He doesn't want to see that,' he says.

Tony is a no-bullshit type of bloke. As we sit down in his back garden, he explains that he is no longer closely involved in a club because he could not bear the endless committee meetings involved. As a man who spent his working life in the logistics department of Procter & Gamble, the American multinational, he had been taught to use all discussions efficiently. 'You go to a meeting with low-skilled participants and it drives you raving mad because they're all chipping in with stuff that's irrelevant. It takes hours and hours, and at the end no decisions are made, nothing's going to change. I just got fed up of it.'

My evening working hours prevent me from attending Crest committee meetings, though I can relate to his point. Cycling clubs are fiercely democratic. Votes have to be taken on every decision, from whether the club name should appear on the back or the front of the shorts to whether a new member should be given a free jersey. (They shouldn't, it turned out, oddly enough.)

So I like him already. I am slightly in awe of his physical condition, too. He is tanned and remarkably strong-looking for a seventy-three-year-old man, with broad shoulders and thick calves. He speaks intensely, too, holding eye contact, thinking through his answers carefully. I figure I need to be especially attentive and try particularly hard not to say anything irrelevant.

To understand why Tony has retained his extreme, competitive edge, you need to know how he started in the sport, as a teenager growing up in Walthamstow, north-east London. He was the son of a proof-reader father, who managed both to enjoy cycling yet show little interest in Tony's aptitude for it. 'He loved the game. He cycled until he dropped dead of cancer. He had done some time-trialling in his youth but he just didn't like racing. He didn't have that ethic in him. You've either got it or you haven't.'

Tony had it. Without any financial or emotional support

from his dad, he became a cat-one racer and eventually an independent, making one appearance for Britain in the 1964 Peace Race. It suited Tony because it was so damn hard and he was bloody-minded, even for a road man. Without any experience of stage racing abroad, he finished as the highest-placed Briton, fortieth in a field of 120 starters. 'The Eastern Europeans were all drugged up to the eyeballs and us lot were just lambs to the slaughter. I loved every minute of it.'

The next year, he accepted an invitation to turn semi-professional, though it proved to be a mistake. With a young family to bring up and a burgeoning career, he could not find time to train or compete and struggled when he did make it to a race. As a result, he quit the sport aged twenty-six and hardly thought about it again until he was out walking, two decades later, when he spotted a discarded bike half-submerged in a river. At the time, he had been wondering how he might spend his free time now that his children were grown up. In retrospect, this seems like divine intervention.

The bike was, inevitably, in bad condition, bent and rusted, and merely an old, steel, commuting-type bike. Tony lacked the money to buy a new one, but reckoned he could make it serviceable. He stripped it back, replaced a few parts and straightened the wheels. He also added drop handlebars then hit the road.

He began by riding the fifteen miles to his mum's house and back but soon found it was good for rides of several hours. Before long he was reacquainting himself with the lanes he had known intimately in his youth.

The thought of racing again had not even occurred to him when he met the Crest's Alan Perkins while out training. Tony remembers him as 'a superstar' locally, thanks in part to that victory in the longest ever stage of the Milk Race, the 246km second stage in 1961. 'He said, "They're all still riding, the guys you used to know. There's this vets' racing thing going on." Admittedly, he also said I needed to get a new bike.'

He took Perkins' advice and embarked on his racing apprenticeship all over again. He joined a local club in Hornchurch, got dropped on the first club run but persevered. He spent £600 on a decent bike, which, in 1987, was a fortune to him. He went down to the Eastway and raced until he could keep in the bunch, regardless that at first the speeds 'terrified' him.

This rite of passage sounds familiar. How long did it take him to get race fit? 'Three years, but it took me five years of suffering like a dog to get back to where I wanted to be. If I was going to race, I was going to race to get wins. I rode everything I could find; I rode 100-mile road races, reliability trials, all sorts. One weekend, I think I rode an eighty-mile race on the Saturday and a 100-mile race on the Sunday. The following weekend we had a three-stage thing. On the second stage, I just ran out of energy. I was so exhausted but I knew that, to get back up, I had to suffer, which I did and it worked in the end.'

Five years? Boxers need about four months to prepare for twelve rounds of unspeakable punishment. Training plans for marathons typically last the same length of time. Is bike racing really that hard? 'It is something else, no doubt about that,' says Tony. 'It's varying your speed. If you run a marathon, you're going to run it at a speed you can sustain. You're going to get into it, get warmed up and achieve a position where you think, "I can hold this". It's nothing like coming to a massive hill about five miles long and some idiot goes haring up it because he's a good climber and you've got to hang in there, and then get down the other side at forty-five mph. The variation is what kills you.'

He gradually moved through the racing categories until eventually he was first-category again, holding his own against the best amateurs of any age. He was consumed by racing. Indirectly, it led to the break-up of his marriage a year after he started racing again. 'It was a tempestuous relationship and it had gone pear-shaped. But I remember I'd been out all day, I'd ridden a race and we sit over the dinner table and I started talking about what happened. She's saying, "Don't talk to me about your bloody sport. I don't want to know." I thought, "That's not good." It was one of those moments.'

His next pivotal moment came aged fifty-five when Procter & Gamble offered him early retirement. Rather than view it as an opportunity for a life of golf and slippers, Tony spied a chance to step up his training regime. He accepted the generous deal and devoted himself to the sport. 'I went to a course they send you on for retirement. All they're trying to do is find you another job. I said, "I don't want another job. I want to ride my bike." I had got back to winning things and I knew that fifty-five to sixty was the time when I could focus on racing. I thought, "Right, I'm going to give it a good innings."'

He allowed himself three intense rides each week, either races or training sessions. He would have cycled more but knew that his age meant that he needed his rest, too. 'As a vet, you are limited. You might have more time on your hands but you can't do loads more training because you won't recover.'

The regime suited him because he prefers to ride intensely, or not at all. And intensely means even harder than many of his opponents in a race. Tony will never simply sit in the bunch, hoping to get a place in the sprint. He aims to make a point as much with his performance as his result. 'I don't want to sit in. I want to get up the road and prove to everyone that I'm stronger than they are. It doesn't often work but that's what I try to do.'

With that attitude and his unusual self-discipline, he continued to improve. Aged fifty-eight, he completed An Post Rás, the eight-stage tour of Ireland, alongside professionals. It was known for its fierce unpredictability, involving far more attacks than a British domestic race. 'A flat-out, madcap event with 150 Irishmen out to ensure you don't get anywhere.'

Two years later he won the world masters road race with a courageous solo attack over a hilly course in Belgium. Another two years on, he regained the title when he joined a two-man break and jumped his rival with three kilometres left. A world masters road race is equivalent to a first-category race in Britain yet Tony destroyed the field.

I can think of no other physically demanding sport in which it is possible to maintain such levels of performance at so advanced an age. For someone who has come to the sport relatively late in life, it is inspiring. 'I was amazed that I could hang in there against top-quality riders. But, in cycling, some guys in their sixties are doing better now than they did in their thirties. As you get older, you learn things about life; about what it takes and what you have to do.

'A lot of those guys, when they were in their twenties or thirties, didn't have a clue. They weren't getting anywhere because they weren't doing it right. They had a strange lifestyle or something, you know, they weren't dieting properly or trying hard enough. But you learn stuff, as you get older, and that knowledge becomes valuable and you can put it to good use.'

How did it feel to win the rainbow jersey? 'It was life-changing. As I was riding I was thinking, "My God, I'm going to win the worlds." You can't get much better than that. You think, "I've done it. However crap I ride after this, I can still say I've done it."' He suffered sceptical comments about the value of winning a competition that is broken down into five-year age categories but the mockery drew a terse response from Tony. 'A local guy said to me – and he wasn't the first – "I've heard it's Mickey Mouse." And I said, "Well, you do it. You get off your arse, enter it and come back and tell me it's Mickey Mouse."'

He declined the invitation, apparently. Perhaps he lacked Tony's focus. Most people do, regardless of their age. Has he ever wondered what made him so addicted to competition? Was there more to it than a love of racing? 'I have wondered. I'm a bit insecure and that helps. I've got this need to sort of prove what I can do, a need for respect from my peers in the game – if they think I'm OK then I feel that I'm OK. I think that comes out of my childhood where I was treated like an idiot and not supported.'

He is talking about his dad. It is the oldest and most potent tale of all: the overachiever driven to spend his or her life proving wrong the difficult or distant parent. Tony is smart enough to know that, at his age, it might be wearing thin as an explanation. 'Don't get me wrong, maturity is where you stop blaming your parents, and mine did what they thought was best for me, but my old man was such a miserable old bastard. I never got any respect or encouragement out of him.'

The fire still burns in him, regardless of the terrible run of injuries that have ruined his hopes for the past five seasons. To begin with, he suffered a huge tear in his quad muscle when he fell down a flight of stairs while drunk on New Year's Eve, curtailing his winter training. He then broke a collarbone when he crashed during a race and was also forced to spend time out after that black-out on the South Downs with the Crest.

That was a terrifying experience, both for him and the riders with him. 'We came to "the wall" that goes straight up for about half a mile and I remember thinking, "I'm giving it everything, I'm bloody knackered but I'll probably be all right" and I woke up looking up at paramedics. I had just collapsed. Hit the deck, no warning, no dizzy spells, no feelings of funniness, just knackered. I took about twenty minutes to come around. They thought I was dead. They couldn't find a pulse to start with. Perhaps I was.' He endured several months of tests. Doctors feared a problem with his brain, then his heart, or, failing that, his lungs, yet found no defect. 'I just rode myself into oblivion.'

His ambitions for this season collapsed when he tripped on concrete while on a cycling holiday in Thailand and suffered a broken kneecap. He admits that he finds it difficult now to keep pace with men a decade younger than him in vets' races, but still his hunger is undiminished. Now back training, he reckons he needs another year free of injury to become competitive again. I am almost glad that the interview has run on for so long that we're unable to go riding, lest I was too slow for him. 'The chances of me beating sixty year olds are slim and getting slimmer,' he says, 'but I just love the game, you know. I still get a buzz from putting a number on. And I can still keep up and compete a bit and help to make a few legs hurt.' Does he dream about reclaiming the rainbow jersey? 'I would love to go there next year and win it again,' he says. 'Oh, yeah, I still want to win races.'

CHAPTER ELEVEN

How a track legend fought back from the brink of death

In the lounge of the Woking Holiday Inn, a two-time world champion is giving me a motivational talk. 'What do you want to do with your cycling?' asks Tony Doyle, about an hour into our interview. As hard as it might be to believe, I hadn't planned to talk about myself, but I'm grateful for the interest: no other interviewee has done this.

I tell him that I have just completed my first fast club run with the Crest and found it exhilarating. Not only did I keep up but I shouldered some of the work at the front and kept a wheel when they raced up the hills – as you always do on training runs, apparently – and I even overheard the club-run leader, Ian 'Rocket' Samuel, suggest that I might make a useful addition to the club team. Which was thrilling.

I tell Tony, then, that I hope simply to keep progressing, to finish the Etape and maybe then to race. I am surprised when such modest ambitions appear to fire his imagination. 'Right, so you want to improve, good,' he says, 'What time do you go to bed before the club run?' About ten minutes after the last glass of red wine, I say. 'Go earlier. Give yourself enough time to relax and not worry about getting to sleep. What time do you arrive at the run?' Bang on time, I lie. 'Get there ten minutes earlier. Same reason. You'll feel in a better frame of mind. When do you pack your food?' And so it goes on: I should prepare grub the night before, always turn up with a clean bike, use race wheels, spend more time on the front of the group during the run, set myself physical targets.

'Every little thing matters, fitness-wise and psychologically,' he says. 'When you come to the race or the club run or the sportive, you'll know that you've done everything you can, and then you'll perform better, too.' It occurs to me that life must be exhausting for the type of personalities who excel at sport.

Not that Tony is tiring company. He has been accommodating, chatty and quick to crack a joke since the first moment I made contact with him via email. He immediately posted a copy of his authorised biography to ensure that I could read about his remarkable career in time for our meeting, he cruelly mocked my allegiance to Tottenham (predictably, for a Chelsea fan) and enquired about my cycling background (the question that every seasoned cyclist asks). He was also, inevitably, early for the interview.

It has gone well, so far, I think. We have covered his introduction to the sport while growing up in Ashford, near Heathrow Airport, as the son of a headmaster and one of five children, then taking in the typically (for a champion) quick impression he made on the club scene, representing the Clarence Wheelers, and the complicated relationship he endured with British Cycling while representing the national team. That reached its nadir at the 1980 Olympics when he was overlooked for the individual pursuit despite beating Sean Yates in a ride-off to decide who should be given the one spot on the team. As he admits over a second pot of tea, the sense of injustice he felt helped to propel him to the world title in the individual pursuit immediately afterwards, having turned professional on his return from the Moscow Games.

Only now, though, have we reached the first of the two aspects of his career that I especially wanted to talk to him about: his time as one of the most successful ever competitors – and by far Britain's most accomplished – on the 'six-day' racing scene. This was the highly lucrative, unspeakably tough, possibly shady and certainly confusing series of races that thrived from the 1940s through to the 1980s and rewarded only the most technically accomplished cyclists in the world. (The second subject I wanted to cover with him concerned his pivotal role in the transformation of British cycling. We'll come to that.)

'I'd been to watch six-day racing when I first got into cycling,' says Tony. 'I was fifteen and I was enthralled by it: going to Wembley and seeing the likes of Patrick Sercu and Danny Clark right on the boards and feeling and sensing the atmosphere. It was just incredible.'

The Belgian Sercu and Clark, from Australia, were two of the best six-day riders in the late 1970s. Doyle's world championship victory earned him contracts to race against both of them late in the following autumn, when the six-day season started. At the age of only twenty-two, it was an exciting opportunity. He had experienced racing in amateur six-day events previously, winning on his debut in Montreal in 1976, but he knew that this represented a far more demanding test. While an amateur six-day comprised a one-hour Madison each day, the professional version involved several daily sessions that, combined, could last up to twelve hours. It was not quite as demanding as six-day races were in their 1930s heyday, when cyclists would race around the clock, surviving on a diet of amphetamines and caffeine and whatever other pulse-quickening substance they could lay their hands on. But it was still physically demanding, with riders competing in pairs and one of them required to be on the track at all times. Speeds exceeded sixty kilometres an hour and competitors were forced to adapt their skills to all manner of track disciplines, from the sprint to the flying lap and the Madison, the blue riband event named after Madison Square Garden, the New York venue that hosted six-day racing during the jazz age. Whichever pair covered the most laps over the six days won.

Living conditions for the cyclists were tough, too, with organisers often providing discarded hospital beds in living quarters at the venues for the riders to sleep on. Or try to sleep on. Ever resourceful, Tony decided to overcome this obstacle by bringing his own bed with him to his first such event, the Skol Six at Wembley. 'I had a Ford Escort at the time,' he says, 'and turned up with the mattress strapped to the roof and the rest of the bed in the boot.'

At the time Tony had also just agreed to ride for a small professional team, KP Crisps-Viscount, which Ian Hallam had set up, though Tony's immediate ambitions lay with the indoor circuit. This was unusual for an emerging cyclist, especially one whose combination of strength and speed made him especially suited to Classics. As Tony explains: 'The fact that no British rider had really ever made it on the winter tracks in Europe was the incentive. They did well when they'd ridden at home, but they'd never really cracked it in Europe.'

He started promisingly enough at Wembley, conquering his first-timer nerves to finish a respectable eighth overall in partnership with the experienced West German Udo Hempel. 'The big dread was to make a mistake and bring Sercu off,' he told his biographer, Geoffrey Nicholson, 'but your strongest instinct is to survive, to get round.'

This was more difficult than it might sound. With riders cycling to the point of exhaustion, and the appearance of special guest competitors who often lacked track craft, crashes were relatively frequent in six-day racing, and the threat of serious injury magnified. Many of the most accomplished men in the sport simply could not handle the intensity of it. Tony, for example, recalls how Francis Castaing, twice the French national road race champion and a stage winner at the Tour de France, quit after fifteen minutes of his first six-day race. Sean Kelly tried to master the dangers and risks of the small indoor wooden tracks only to repeatedly refuse promoters' pleas to actually start a professional six-day. Established names from the road scene were happy simply to finish six-days, much less succeed at them. 'It's hard,' says Tony. 'When you're riding on the road there's things happening, the scenery changes, weather changes, not always for the better but at least it changes. And, at times, you can switch off, you can have a little chat. But on the track things are happening so quick, you've got to concentrate. If you make one mistake, you're down or you've brought someone else down.'

As Tony discovered, in a sport with an unofficial internal hierarchy, new riders had to serve an apprenticeship, too, especially one who had won the world title within weeks of turning professional and earned a clutch of coveted six-day contracts as a result. 'That put a lot of noses out of joint,' he admits. 'It meant the first winter was very, very tough. You're almost counting the days down, but there was the challenge of trying finally to make it and get into that front group of riders.'

He was, then, persistent. For his second six-day he went

to Berlin and found conditions were even worse than at Wembley, with riders crammed into a windowless, airless cabin adjacent to public toilets. He went on to Munich and found that the velodrome there turned into a nightclub once the riding had ceased, as if to ensure that sleep was off-menu. With promoters determined to squeeze as many six-days as possible into road racing's close season, Tony found himself flying or driving overnight between venues, competing everywhere from Copenhagen to Dortmund and Rotterdam. He recalls staying in caravans outside venues, while funfairs organised to coincide with the competition buzzed and twinkled near by. The noise alone was enough to exhaust the cyclists, with live bands, late bars and raucous crowds meaning it hardly ever let up.

'Psychologically and physically, nothing can prepare you for the six-day circuit: the living conditions, how you're treated,' he says. 'I was absolutely shattered when I first started to ride them.' Yet, as he returned for more the following autumn, he found the lifestyle slowly beginning to suit him. Had he risked attempting to crack the road racing scene abroad – and he received offers from teams – he would likely not have been given the time to tailor his training for six-day racing or competed in as many events as he did. With KP Crisps-Viscount, however, he was practically his own boss, allowing him to go abroad for warm-weather training as he wished, or to head down to Herne Hill in deepest winter, sweeping leaves from the track so he could do interval training alone.

He reckons it took three years to establish himself on the six-day circuit, by which he means not only challenging for victories and being paired with the top riders – in his case, this was most often Danny Clark, Tony's teenage hero – but more that he was able to dish out some of the punishment that he had long endured. 'You've got to go through a lot of pain, a lot of suffering, but you finally start to find that you're making other riders' legs ache and you're making it tough for the top riders. And then you become good at masking the fact that you're struggling, and thriving on their suffering. Only then, and all of a sudden, you start to earn their respect.'

It helped that his and Clark's attributes dovetailed. A hard-boiled Tasmanian, Clark claimed that he competed mostly for the financial reward, whereas the romance of the sport also fuelled Tony's ambitions. Clark's sprinting ability complemented Tony's exceptional endurance, while the Briton's calm demeanour balanced the older man's nervy, more brittle personality. Clark's experience also ensured them respect within the Blue Train, the group of elite riders who called the shots and were named after the luxury express train that once ran from Calais to the French Riviera.

Together, they scored some stunning victories. Their triumph in Berlin in October 1983 made Tony the first Briton to win a modern professional six since 1972 and the first to triumph on the Continent since Tom Simpson at Brussels in 1965. A week later, in Dortmund, he became the first Briton ever to register a second victory. And when an injury to Clark interrupted their partnership, his success scarcely slowed. He partnered, among others, Gary Wiggins – Bradley's dad – and the great Francesco Moser, winner of the Giro d'Italia. With his unusually fast, fluid pedalling style and adept handling skills, Tony was often asked to look after greats of the road such as Greg LeMond, Laurent Fignon and Stephen Roche on their guest appearances. When promoters eventually agreed to pair him again with Clark, they became only the third team in the modern history of six-day racing to win five meetings in a season, in the winter of 1988.

By then, Tony was the *seigneur*, the boss of the Blue Train who negotiated with promoters on its behalf and to whom other leading riders deferred. In other words, he had finally achieved what he had set out to do when he tied the roof rack to his Ford Escort eight years earlier. For all the talent he had shown, it had been a triumph of will as much as anything else, requiring him to skip almost a decade's worth of family parties and weddings and baptisms. It had required loyalty and patience from his wife, Anne, too, and years spent forcing himself to adhere to a strict lifestyle.

Sure, other elite athletes have made similar sacrifices, but you can understand why Tony bristles when I bring up the two criticisms that are often levelled against six-day racing, thus undermining its reputation. The first is the one that describes it as a 'circus', as much entertainment as sport, with races that should not be taken seriously because some of them are fixed. 'Ignorance,' Tony says, insisting that it is impossible to choreograph races conducted at such speeds. 'They [the cynics] don't fully understand it and a little bit of knowledge is dangerous. They don't know what's involved and don't appreciate the dangers and the speeds and duration of it. It's easy to be knowledgeable from a distance, but the day-to-day and the actual grind, they've got no idea.' He admits that influential riders might decide not to contest a smaller race to allow, say, a home rider to win or to give someone else a moment in the spotlight, but insists that all his important wins were legitimate.

Either way, it is small cheese: this is a night's entertainment and race-fixing has always happened in cycling. So, too, has doping, which is the second criticism forever thrown at the six-day scene: that it was awash with drugs, amphetamines especially. Tony thinks such reports are exaggerated. 'I was aware that some people had [doped] but the problem has never been as great as everyone likes to think it is,' he says. 'Bike riders are like everybody else. They've got consciences, they've got families to support, families who love and care for them, and the majority of people don't want to do things that are going to damage their family's name. Yeah, there are people who are prepared to take risks, but the vast majority don't.'

I am not here to find out if he doped – he never tested positive – but, as we're on the subject, I feel obliged to ask the question. He looks at me squarely and says: 'The majority of people have pushed things to the line but most of us have got a conscience and we know that if we step over that line, the consequences are very severe; it could be the end of our career and it could be very damaging to our reputation.'

On Sunday, 12 November, 1989, Tony lay second overall in the Munich six-day and was confident of emboldening his reputation further with victory in the most prestigious six of all when he launched an attack from the bunch in an effort to gain a lap's advantage on the rest of the field. As Tony went to overtake Marat Ganeev, a Russian neo-pro who was on the front of the string of riders, the young man veered suddenly, cutting into Tony's path without looking behind or indicating his intention, a mistake that only a novice could commit. In front of 14,000 fans, Tony crashed, slid down the boards and smashed his head against the concrete floor, almost instantly slipping into unconsciousness.

Pandemonium ensued. Even though he had been racing for four hours and his body temperature was in freefall, the medical staff left him uncovered. They also failed to strap him on to the stretcher and dropped him as he was being carried down concrete steps that led out of the velodrome. When they discovered the ambulance was at the opposite end of the venue, they carried Doyle around the outside in the near-freezing cold. A Munich newspaper said afterwards that the accident 'was the worst in the history of the six-day . . . and paralysed spectators'. But that was not quite true: many whistled in disgust as the life-threatening mistakes were played out on the big screen.

When eventually Tony made it to hospital, it was found that he had extensive bruising to the brain, multiple fractures to his shoulder and elbow, and a lung infection, presumably picked up on the walkabout outside the velodrome. Eight days passed before his condition stabilised. Doctors were uncertain if he would survive. His wife and sister flew over from London and requested for the last rites to be read to him. 'When you've got an injury like that, you have no way of knowing how you are going to recover,' he says.

Only after ten days in a coma did he begin to show flickers of responsiveness. As doctors became confident that he had battled through the critical period, Tony's family arranged for him to be flown by air ambulance to RAF Northolt, from where a police escort transferred him to the intensive care unit at Charing Cross Hospital. He would spend two months there, his memory shot, unable to swallow, barely able to move and rapidly losing weight. 'He was just sitting in a darkened room, practically unable to recognise you,' said his friend, Alan Rushton, the race promoter. 'He'd lost I don't know how many stone. He was gaunt, unshaven, yellow and looked at you in a really difficult way, totally vacant. It was awful.'

By this point in his career, Doyle had won his second world pursuit crown and claimed three silvers in the event. He had won bronze at the worlds, too, in the pursuit and a silver medal in the points race, placing him among the most decorated British athletes of any sport in that era. Though cycling was still a minority concern, his status meant that his family had to work hard to play down the gravity of his condition to the press. They wanted not only to avoid sensational coverage but feared that suggestions his life was in danger would ruin any hope of winning future contracts. 'With all the journalists phoning, we decided to clam up,' Rushton said. 'He wasn't speaking to us. He was unconscious best part of the time. If you say an athlete is like that, you're writing him off. And we didn't want to do that because it was his commercial future we were writing off – for the sake of the story.'

He did eventually begin to come round and, after two months, was well enough to be transferred to a rehabilitation unit in Surrey, albeit one whose medical staff were uncertain to what degree he would recover. He had lost nearly all his motor-functioning skills, he could not walk unaided, he could not speak properly nor feed himself. His muscles had wasted. But two things stood in his favour. He had no memory of the crash and little recollection of the time that had passed since, so he was not overly traumatised. He was also unusually single-minded. Cycling had taught him to focus on a goal and pursue it, with no thought for the possibility that he might fail. 'I really didn't appreciate the seriousness of what happened,' he said.

In the rehab centre was a static bike. After being there for only two weeks, Tony insisted on trying it. He lasted just six minutes with no resistance, but returned to it the next day and the one after that until eventually he had devised his own training programme (just as he had always done) and was spending several hours on the bike each day. Two months later he walked out of the centre, with his thoughts turned to competition again. He made his comeback the following spring, in a city centre criterium around wet, narrow Portsmouth streets, finishing halfway down the field. The event was televised but the cameras paid him scant attention. In fact, for years he did not reveal the gravity of his accident for, as Rushton explained, he did not want to scare off potential sponsors. 'It was an incredible experience to have gone through it and come out the other end. I just wasn't sure whether to go back and ride the six-days. Physically and mentally, I didn't know whether I would be able to deal with the pressures.'

He went to Harley Street for a medical to assess his suitability. Coincidentally, the doctor he visited had been on duty in Charing Cross Hospital when Tony was flown in from Munich. 'He was like, "What are you doing here? When I saw you, you were a vegetable. No one could make a recovery like that."' This provided Tony with the confidence he needed to return to the boards. He started modestly, carefully, before finishing fifth in Dortmund, then fourth in Grenoble, until eventually he pitched up in Munich again, twelve months after he had almost died there.

His relationship with the venue was complicated. He had investigated the possibility of claiming compensation for the medical staff's mishaps, only to be told the video tapes showing his crash and the aftermath had mysteriously gone missing. But the velodrome staff greeted him warmly on his return and he was given an enthusiastic welcome by the crowd. The organisers did him a favour by pairing him with Clark again for the first time since his comeback. 'There was a point to prove, to myself rather than anyone else,' says Tony.

With Clark determined for his old comrade to do well, they pushed hard from the start, hovering close to the lead for the first five days, and they only narrowly trailed the leaders, Adriano Baffi and Pierangelo Bincoletto, going into the final Madison. With ten minutes of the racing to go, they gained a lap on the Italian pair and held on to win. Despite all his world championship success, Doyle regards it as the most satisfying result of his career. 'I was so determined to do well that I almost had not an out-of-body experience, but certainly an extra gear of determination. I'd rate it as high as my world titles, perhaps even higher. What it meant and how I overcame the injury . . . I should not have been capable of that.'

CHAPTER TWELVE

The accountant who went to buy a bike and ended up running the sport

In 1995, with the British Cycling Federation losing money, the national team struggling and the ruling body's membership in apparently terminal decline, its president, Ian Emmerson, decided to overhaul the management structure. In an effort to make it more dynamic, he ripped apart the old committee-based system that had governed it and created several directorships instead, giving them overall authority for their department, whether it was elite road racing, the track, the clubs and so on.

Tony Doyle, having just been forced to quit competitive cycling as a result of a broken back he suffered in a crash at the Zurich six-day, spotted an opportunity. With two young children, and no qualifications aside from his achievements in the sport, he needed to begin a new career and this presented a chance to gain experience in coaching and officialdom. Though all the positions were voluntary, it would widen his skill set and complement his side line in promotional work.

In accepting the role of director of track racing, he hoped also that he would be able to put something back into the sport that had served him so well. While most officials were club cyclists and career administrators, he figured that, at the age of thirty-six, he could bring energy and expertise. What he did not anticipate was quite how difficult it would be to institute change. The deckchairs had been rearranged but the same people manned the boat and the hierarchy remained sorely disconnected from the grass roots of the sport.

'It was clear quite quickly,' says Tony, 'that there were two distinct categories: the members – the competitors – and the officials and there was a big divide. The officials were becoming more and more out of touch with the everyday member.'

It was the sport's age-old problem: the volunteers who ran it lacked management skills and athletic expertise. Many cyclists questioned the motivations of the blazer brigade, as they were known, too. 'A lot of officials, they originally get involved because they want to help and encourage more people to take part and spread the benefits of the sport but, once they start having some influence, that power is used in the wrong way. In many cases that power was abused.'

It was felt that the federation had missed several excellent opportunities to attract people to the sport, most notably Chris Boardman's gold at the 1992 Olympics, but also his high-profile battle for the world hour record with Graeme Obree and the construction of the Manchester velodrome in 1994, part of the failed bids to stage the 1996 and 2000 Olympic Games but which would eventually be used for the 2002 Commonwealth Games. A world-class sporting facility, it had turned into a white elephant, often empty and haemorrhaging money.

With Emmerson's presidential term coming to an end shortly afterwards, Tony decided to run for the top job. This was a highly ambitious move. He had minimal administrative or management experience, he was much younger than most of the men within the federation's hierarchy, and had spent most of his career as a professional rider, with limited contact or knowledge of the politics within the BCF.

However, he still had close ties with Clarence Wheelers and knew what would appeal to the clubs, who would be voting for a new president. He promised to lobby hard for improved safety measures on the road. He vowed to increase support for clubs to help them put on races and events. He would refresh coaching schemes, helping club members to become ride leaders or commissaires or coaches. In short, he focused on empowering the average cyclist. 'I wanted to shake up the system, to let people know cyclists had a voice and that it needed to be heard.'

The old guard was furious when he was elected. Presumably most of them knew their positions were under threat after years of climbing the ladder. In response, the existing board appealed against Tony's appointment, claiming it represented a conflict of interests because he had worked for Alan Rushton's company, Sport for Television, which was hoping to profit from the 1996 world championships that were due to be held in Manchester. Tony won a court case to prove the claims were unfounded. Instead, he says, they were motivated by 'total resentment'. Keith Bingham covered the events for *Cycling Weekly* and said the board had broken its own rules with the protest. In Ellis Bacon's book *Great British Cycling*, Bingham was quoted: 'Doyle's ticket was to address those things that the BCF wouldn't. The membership were fed up and wanted change at a time when the membership was in decline. But they [the board] decided they couldn't work with Doyle, for whatever reason, and they rejected him. They were in breach of the BCF's own constitution because he'd been elected by the membership.'

The board called an emergency general meeting and held another presidential vote but Tony won that, too. The board had promised to resign if this happened. Instead it took out a civil case against him, prompting a complex trail of claim and counter-claim, until eventually Tony resigned in frustration at the situation. He had been in office for only five months. 'I was a young man. I was still president but they were taking me to court. I thought, "How can I conduct any meaningful business?" The federation's legal expenses were covered but not mine. I had no option but to resign and fight them on a civil basis.'

He wanted to claim back his legal costs and to expose what he felt was the hypocrisy of the board's opposition to him. Having seen the accounts, and the federation's internal business, he suspected that it was guilty not only of poor management but incompetence. To prove this, he needed to call on the help of a forty-eight-year-old accountant who had just returned to club cycling after a decade away from it. His name was Peter King.

'I'd just had a medical and the doctor said things that can go wrong were going wrong: blood pressure and weight and so on,' Peter says, when I visit him at his office near Dorking in Surrey. 'So I decided that I would get out the one bike I had kept from my cycling days.'

Initially he rode alone, simply to get fit, but was persuaded to step up his training when a friend at his former club, Redhill CC, said they were organising a twenty-five-mile time-trial and wanted old members to take part. Deciding to upgrade his bike for the task, Peter was in a bike shop on Box Hill when its proprietor, Tony Mills, proposed a deal. Mills was a cycling official who knew Tony Doyle and was working with him to expose the federation's shortcomings. 'He said, "You're an accountant, aren't you? We think the BCF has got itself into a mess but we don't fully understand the accounts. I'll sell you this bike at a special discount if you'll look at them and tell us what's going on."'

Peter gladly accepted and drew up an analysis of the accounts that agreed with the suspicion of suggested mismanagement. With his work done he assumed he could then return to his handsome, new, bright yellow bike. Instead, on reading his faxed conclusions, Mills and Doyle asked Peter if, first, he would explain them to the federation's regional division and then to the national council at its next sitting in Rotherham. 'Each division could send a number of national councillors,' says Peter. 'With a bit of rule-bending I ended up as one of them, so that I could stand up at the meeting and ask difficult questions.'

The list of problems he had identified was long and potentially explosive. Though he cannot recall them all now, Jon Trickett, the Labour MP for Hemsworth in West Yorkshire, detailed them in an address to Parliament through which he wanted to express his concerns for the sport – Trickett was a member of Otley CC. He explained that the Manchester velodrome was losing money, that management accounts showed 'a major weakness relating to forecasting income and expenditure', that there was 'inadequate financial accountability and control' and, most damagingly of all, that there were 'potential or perceived conflicts of interest involving some board members'. It had emerged that one director's clothing company supplied the national team, another ran the design house that drew up and printed the federation's artwork and a third was a major shareholder in a company that organised races for the ruling body.

In highlighting these problems at the meeting of the national council, it was hoped that Peter would not only force the removal of the board – through a vote of no-confidence – but allow Tony Doyle to return to the presidency. In effect, they were planning a coup. 'I was working with Tony,' Peter says. 'What he was trying to do was to set up a parallel group of people who could take over if that happened [a no-confidence vote]. I remember sitting up until well past midnight with the group of people that Tony was leading, trying to organise who would do what.' They worked until late in the evening before the meeting. Then Peter carried on on his own. 'I had to sit up for most of the rest of the night writing a CV because you had to have a CV to be elected. So I went to bed about three o'clock and got up at about six to get ready for the meeting.'

The meeting was even more explosive than Peter had envisaged. He had not even finished presenting his case when two prominent delegates, Brian Cookson and Willie Tarran, successfully proposed the vote of no-confidence. The rebels, however, were denied the opportunity to accede to power. Instead, the council insisted that they elected a committee of eleven volunteers from the floor to take charge of the federation.

Peter was the only candidate for the role of treasurer. Tarran and Cookson were elected, too, but Tony wasn't, possibly because there was no obvious job for him without a presidential position. For the time being at least, no one person would hold authority over this hastily assembled group of volunteers now in charge of British cycling. 'We basically had to go away and try to sort out the mess it had got itself into,' Peter says.

The most urgent task was swiftly tackled when the committee convinced the Sports Council that it could end the financial mismanagement of the sport, thus ensuring that it continued to receive at least £300,000 annual funding that was crucial to the BCF's existence. The Sports Council, however, realised that it needed to pay somebody with financial expertise to manage the promised rescue job and thus Peter became a part-time employee of the federation, initially on a two-month contract, and then on a permanent basis six months later when he was appointed chief executive.

Barely a few months after he had innocently visited his local bike shop, with no ambitions other than not to embarrass himself against old club-mates, he was now the most powerful man in the sport. He was employed on a three-day-week basis but the job required him to work more hours than many people manage in a week. Commuting from Surrey to Manchester, he would get up at four o'clock on Wednesdays, catch the first flight north, make it to his desk by nine and still be working in the hotel in the early hours of each morning. For a man who had his own successful accountancy business and no need of the extra work, it was, as Peter admits, 'a lunatic thing to do', especially as he had just seen his children off to university and was preparing to settle down to an easier life.

Although he will acknowledge that he inherited a formidable work ethic from a father who laboured seven days a week as a painter, decorator and gardener, Peter is still unsure as to why he took on such an enormous task. 'I guess I was just trying to help out a lot of people who were trying to do their best for cycling, which was a sport I had enjoyed for some of my life.'

Presumably the power bestowed on him was exhilarating, too. Especially when, with none of the old guard left to undermine him, he was able to overhaul the ruling body as he saw fit.

When I ask him to pick out the pivotal changes he introduced, he names apparently subtle ones. With the federation insolvent to the tune of £100,000, he increased membership fees by twenty-five per cent and asked clubs to pay them in advance – to his disbelief, the announcement of this earned him a round of applause from club delegates, as if delighted that somebody in the ruling body had finally worked out how to balance the books.

Incredibly, he also persuaded clubs to provide the federation with interest-free loans – all repaid – and secured local authority and Sports Council subsidies for the Manchester velodrome. Without it, he says, the professional home for several generations of future world champions would almost certainly have closed down.

Working with Brian Cookson, who had been appointed president when the committee eventually decided it needed a political figurehead, he also instituted a key aspect of Tony Doyle's campaign by uniting the disparate disciplines of the sport: cyclo-cross, mountain bike, BMX and cycle speedway, as well as the road and the track. This expanded body was rebranded as British Cycling.

'The big advantage we had was that cycling was so bad it couldn't get any worse,' Peter says. 'It couldn't have been worse financially or structurally. I was able to do more probably in the first four years than in all previous years added together because things were so bad.'

His successes ensured that British Cycling received National Lottery funding when it was allocated for the first time in 1997 and allowed Peter to recruit a key employee, Peter

Keen, as performance director. A young sports scientist who had worked with Tony Doyle and Chris Boardman, Keen's CV was impressive but he appealed to Peter also because of his ambition. Keen proposed that the ruling body should focus on developing cyclists for the track because it was easier for them to win championship medals than it was for road cyclists, whose events were less controlled and offered fewer medals in relation to the number of competitors. Keen and King also declared that Britain should aim to become the highest-ranked nation in the world. At the same time Peter told his board that the ruling body should target an increase in membership from 13,000 to 100,000, increasing both the profile of the sport and their income from subscriptions.

For decades cycling in Britain had been a marginal concern and, internationally, the country was second-rate. Only individuals with little or no experience of that past could have been so ambitious. 'We had a lot of difficulty in getting people on side. The idea that you could aspire to be the best was something people couldn't grasp. But why would you aim to be anything else? If you actually aimed to do something, you wouldn't aim to be second best, would you?'

The approach worked famously well. Beginning with the gold medal that Jason Queally won in the one-kilometre time-trial at the 2000 Olympics, products of British Cycling's new development programme enjoyed years of success. Most impressively, they won eight golds at both the 2008 and 2012 Olympics, and subsequently transferred their winning touch to road racing through Team Sky.

These achievements, of course, have helped to inspire thousands of people to take up the sport or cycle more frequently. Only recently, British Cycling finally achieved Peter's second ambition of attaining 100,000 members. There have been other reasons, of course, but there is no doubt that Peter and his team of volunteers played a pivotal role in the sport's renaissance.

What does he think might have happened to British cycling without their intervention? 'Firstly, the Sports Council would have withheld the money they'd been giving, and then they would have also withheld the Lottery funding and, without that, the sport wouldn't have developed as it has. What we probably were able to prevent was an even worse financial catastrophe than the one that struck us. Conceivably, it could have gone the same way as athletics; athletics at that time ended up insolvent and they had to create new organisations to take over the running and financing of it. But it's one of those things you don't think about. You do what you have to do and get lucky.'

It is quite a legacy for someone who had no experience in sports management before he struck that deal for a new yellow bike. Did he ever get to ride it? 'Yes, eventually! It ended up behind the sofa there [beside his desk] for two to three years. Even in all the years I was going to Manchester, working in a cramped office under the track, I only ever went on the track once. There was just so much to do.'

Yet never once in his twelve years in charge did Peter call on Tony Doyle's assistance, even though he had been instrumental in the former's appointment. This, I know, upsets Tony. Having clocked up more track time than perhaps any British cyclist, and having had ambitions to be part of the world-class performance plan, he thought that they might have exploited his technical expertise or perhaps considered him for an executive or even ambassadorial role.

Such positions are scarce, of course, but it still seems a little odd. After all, he was arguably the most successful British cyclist of his generation. Peter, for his part, insists that it was not his job to appoint directors and it did not occur to him that Tony might have wanted to be involved. That Tony never applied for a position inevitably counted against him but Peter would agree that Tony nonetheless was the final, significant victim of the old petty-minded factional culture that had afflicted the sport's administration for decades. 'I know Tony feels a bit sore that nobody ever invited him back in. And I can understand that because the truth is, if he hadn't done what he did, that revolution might not have happened. But he has his friends and he has his enemies. And in those days, it really was a political place.'

CHAPTER THIRTEEN

'Cycling in the 1980s? Loners, eccentrics and builders who shaved their legs'

When Tony Doyle was competing abroad, he often kept note of race details and phoned them into the sports desks of national newspapers back home, ensuring improved coverage both of his exploits but also the sport at a time when it was otherwise neglected outside of the cycling press. He is similarly proactive after our interview, keeping in contact with occasional emails and phone calls, suggesting ideas, offering bits of advice, or just chewing the fat like few interviewees do. Today, over the phone, he is pointing out another factor in the sport's resurgence that I had not considered: that the BMX and mountain-bike crazes in the 1980s and early 1990s introduced to the sport many of the men and women who now run it. 'People shouldn't forget the importance of that period,' he says. 'It meant cycling became fun again.'

Like a lot of 1980s kids, I lapped up both activities, graduating rapidly from BMX Boxer to Grifter to, best of all, the Chopper, ensuring a shot of nostalgia whenever I see the most uncomfortable bike designed since the tricycle. I also embraced mountain bikes. I did not bomb down precipitous slopes like the Californian originators of the phenomenon, but then suburban Hertfordshire tended to frown upon maverick behaviour.

Hardly anybody I knew, though, used a road bike, let alone raced on one. At grass-roots level, it seemed popular mostly with kids who could not play football, or loners who needed a sport that would introduce them to other loners, or those children whose hippyish parents preferred touring holidays to getting Tangoed on a package holiday. As one Crest veteran of that scene proudly put it on a recent training run, the sport then was 'mostly for weirdos'.

I put this theory to Nick Hussey when I visit him at the offices of his cycling company, Vulpine, in south-west London. Now in his early forties, Nick started bike racing while growing up near Nottingham. 'That is exactly what it was: a weird, bizarre, unknowable world,' he says, sitting on a stool at a large, high table on a suburban industrial estate. Surrounding us are racks of clothing samples, while upstairs his young team work on his blossoming, commuter brand. We will come to the story of its success – not least because I want to know why decent cycling gear is so damn expensive – but I have come to speak to Nick mainly because I want to hear what it was like to be immersed in the grass roots of the sport as it reached what, arguably, was its nadir. And because, of the few survivors that I know from that period, his story is possibly the most interesting.

Nick had a difficult upbringing. His alcoholic father was mostly absent from his life and he was mercilessly bullied at the type of tough comprehensive where bookish, shy youngsters often struggled to fit in. In search of a community that would accept him, he simply called the British Cycling

Federation and asked them to recommend a club, as you could do back then. They suggested the Trent Valley RC, a racing outfit comprised mostly of unforgiving men from blue-collar backgrounds whom Nick says worked as hard on the bike as they did in their day jobs.

'It was a very, very small world. Everyone knew each other and it was all racing based. You were an old boy who used to race and now you did club runs, or you did club runs to race, which made it aggressive and intimidating, initially at least. A lot of the top racers were big, burly, scary blokes because that was the style of racing then – brickies or mechanics or whatever, hard, hard men – and I just got intimidated into following their rules. It was a sort of indoctrination: "You'd better fucking do what you're supposed to do or you're going to get thrown in that ditch." And I saw people have that done to them.'

Fascinated with the sport since he watched Bernard Hinault and Greg LeMond's glorious battle for the 1986 Tour de France on TV, Nick was desperate to earn the respect of these men. 'It took me a long time, but I was determined to be accepted. And I did that by being able to keep up or contribute and in being able to follow the rules. I pretty much sat there in silence, terrified, and slowly got fitter and I learnt to suffer.'

Being talented, he impressed in time-trials but struggled with the physical intimidation dished out in road races. The men of the club embraced him in a way that other kids rarely did. 'There was this thing: "We are cyclists. We follow these rules and do these things and nobody else understands us."' Like shaving their legs. 'Yes! To be an outsider who shaves their legs at puberty in a shared changing room in a rough school, it's not a good thing. But you're not part of that world until you shave your legs. And that world mattered more to me than the normal world.'

Nick is far from being a geek now. He looks like a typical trendy entrepreneur, with waistcoat, jeans and beard. He is no shrinking violet either: he is the only one of my interviewees who tries to decide the direction of the conversation. But, as I am quite enjoying it, I am happy to sit in his slipstream. 'I was this lonely kid who was suddenly accepted in this closed, tight-knit world, and it was intoxicating. It was like being a mod or a rocker.'

In the early 1990s Nick accepted a place at Liverpool John Moores University to study sports science in the hope that it would lead to a career in cycling. He continued to immerse himself in the sport but found that the resistance to it seemed to be more pronounced. Just as locals did in Nottingham, so here they tried to sabotage the races that he helped to stage.

'It got so much grief. I used to work in a pub on the local East Midlands circuit, and I would overhear locals talking about how they tried to disrupt races because it pissed them off. They'd slam on the brakes and take a few riders down or they spat out the window. This was the sort of atmosphere that we were in. Cycling was this bizarre thing that few people liked or even understood.'

It was around that time that he was forced suddenly to stop cycling because of a congenital back problem. It turned out that his spine had not properly developed, and years of being bent over a racing frame had exacerbated the problem. The thought of pursuing a coaching career while unable to ride was not an appealing one, so he fell into the Madchester nightclub world, working as a promoter and enjoying the kind of hedonistic lifestyle that years of devotion to cycling had denied him. Only when he pitched up at a video production company in Soho in the Noughties did he start riding again seriously, initially to commute but then with his local club after yoga and weight-training had strengthened his back.

I can remember this period, when cycling to work marked you as an outsider, especially in London, where there were no bicycle lanes to help you navigate the roads and few facilities for cyclists in offices. Instead, you lashed the bike to railings and got changed in the gents. 'I was turning up to work in full club kit and being sweaty and stinky because it was just polyester, plastic clothing, so I was employing people who were laughing at me behind my back. There was no shower so I would have to join a gym. I thought, "I'm obsessed by cycling and I find this a pain in the arse. No wonder there are not loads more cyclists."'

When the clothing company Rapha was launched in the early Noughties, introducing stylish cycling gear to the market, Nick quickly overhauled his cycling wardrobe. Now he could ride to work in clothes that wicked away perspiration without looking comical.

I have always struggled to justify buying a Rapha jersey when you could instead purchase, say, a flight to New York, but the clothes transformed the market and remain popular, even if Rapha reportedly struggles to turn a profit. Now cyclists are happy to pay £180 for a merino jersey or £160 for cycling jeans. As Nick discovered when he sold his gear online three years ago before launching Vulpine, Rapha gear *appreciates*, too.

Rapha's success had inspired him to reignite his teenage dream to make a living from cycling. While the Rapha brand is slick, serious, even a bit intimidating, his USP was to introduce a commuter brand that was colourful, irreverent and inclusive, if just as pricey. He has probably come closer to threatening Rapha's dominance of the market than any of the several companies it inspired. Vulpine has been shortlisted for awards, earned almost unanimously positive reviews and recently set up a new clothing line in partnership with Sir Chris Hoy, at the multiple Olympic champion's request. 'That was an interesting phone call,' Nick says.

He has also co-sponsored a women's team that has just signed up Laura Trott and competed in the women's Tour of Britain. Nick travelled in the team car with the directeur sportive, waving at the thousands who had lined the streets, marvelling at just how far his sport had progressed.

'It's bizarre,' he says. 'I don't want to overstate it but cycling saved me as a kid, when it could all have gone tits-up. But the sport was a joke, a nonentity. It was on its knees for so long. For it to be where it is now and for me to be here doing this . . . I can't believe it.'

In a café in the east London suburb of Wanstead, while recovering from a ride with my four friends who are doing the Etape, the conversation has turned to our cycling gear. Tom, it is noted, looks smart in his Rapha gear and has confounded the stereotype relating to fans of the brand by smiling, several times. Fig has revealed that he is not prepared to wear Lycra regardless of the weather conditions or length of ride. A furniture designer, he insists that it is only an aesthetic choice, though I wonder if he has got something to hide. Andy, a corporate accountant and otherwise modest man, appears to have put more thought into his outfit than he ever does his civvies, with a carefully matched black and white ensemble.

I enquire after his Gore-Tex jacket. 'One hundred and

seventy pounds on Wiggle,' he says, proudly, 'which is actually cheap. You'd pay a lot more on the high street.' He is right on this point, Gore-Tex being unusually light, warm and waterproof. There are cheaper alternatives, but you will struggle to find good, inexpensive cycling gear, a fact that Nick Hussey puts down to the overheads involved, though I am not so sure. One retailer told me that Italian factories charge £15 for jerseys that you will find selling for £150 to Britain's new wave of cyclists. I know of a cyclist who runs a sideline buying carbon frames from Far East factories and selling them on for a fraction of the price that big brands charge for the same product.

Frank Beechinor, at Cadence, says, 'Imagine if you and I were in the pub ten years ago and said, "I've got this idea for this business. We're going to sell cycling jerseys for £200." No one would have taken you seriously, but they've pulled it off. It's nuts. There are frames coming out of the factory door in Taiwan at £200 and they've us convinced we need to spend £3,900 on them.'

Together, I would guess that our five bikes stacked outside the café are worth about £10,000. They include a Canyon that Andy imported from Germany and an Orbea with spec that Chris has spent about as much upgrading as he did to buy it.

We are clichéd Mamils and proud of it. Being men, we are also bad at organising our social life and this is our first ride together since we signed up to the Etape six months ago. As a result, nobody is certain quite how much training anyone else has been doing.

Chris is still racing and has clocked many more miles than anyone else. For several months, I followed my coach Tony's plan, which more or less comprised a weekly schedule of two to three interval sessions, a long ride and commuting. The plan was to build up gradually, introducing a second long ride and shortening my intervals from three minutes to one once I had established a fitness base. A six-week bout of man flu derailed that plan and I am now playing catch-up. I cycled intermittently during it but not nearly enough. After a couple of weeks back, and with only a month to the Etape, I am hoping at least to reach my fitness level before the lurgy struck.

Everybody else claims to have done little to no training. Andy insists he got bored of the rollers within about a fortnight of buying them and has merely commuted. Fig says family ties have limited him to commuting and a few thirty-mile rides. His Strava account backs this up. I follow it closely. Tom has done a couple of sportives but, aside from that, cycled only to work. I tell them that I do not know whether to believe them. I am uncertain whether they are as secretly competitive as I am. Tom smiles, again, saying: 'You had better hope not or else you won't look good in the book.'

CHAPTER FOURTEEN

How Chris Boardman's teenage nemesis ended up homeless

Over the telephone from the athletics track in Dagenham, where she is coaching alongside Tony Harvey, Nikki Juniper is trying to explain why she gave up a good job in the City about a year ago, aged thirty-one, to pursue an unlikely dream of becoming a professional cyclist. 'Look, I'm realistic,' she says. 'I know that British Cycling are only interested in sixteen or seventeen year olds, especially when there's so much talent coming through, but I've had my power figures measured and I know they're as good as the top elite riders, so I still believe I could get a contract, if not here, in America.'

I had called Tony for a final pep talk before the Etape but he thought I might want to speak to Nikki instead, given that she is currently leading the Women's Road Race Series, a domestic competition that features many of Britain's best professionals as well as amateurs and semi-pros such as her.

It is a formidable achievement. Previously a keen triathlete, she concentrated on cycling in her late twenties when injury forced her to quit running, yet now she holds her own against world-class riders such as Katie Archibald, Laura Trott and Sarah Storey.

She has had to move back in with her parents and has hired a coach but otherwise operates alone, with little of the support of her rivals. She gets up in the early hours to drive herself to races all over the country and has to fit thirty hours of training in a week around her coaching work.

She is proof that, though elite British cycling is enjoying a boom, there are superb cyclists on the fringes of that scene enduring many of the hardships that their predecessors of past decades did in pursuit of their dream. Nikki's determination is even more impressive because life on the women's professional scene is poorly paid and precarious, with sponsors frequently pulling out and the number of big races decreasing. 'Oh, I know what's like,' she says, laughing. 'I went on the Tour of Holland and we stayed in cheap hotels with bed bugs. I'm sure a lot of people must think I'm mad but it had been my dream to give cycling a real go for a while, and I figured at my age this would be my last chance.'

But why do it? 'Well, cycling is like a drug, isn't it?' she says. 'It's almost something you can't properly explain. It's just . . . nothing else matters when on the bike. That feeling of freedom, whether you're just heading down a country lane, in a peloton, or climbing a mountain in the Pyrenees.'

What key advice, then, does she have for my trip to the Pyrenees? 'You have done a few centuries, right?' No, but I was thinking of attempting two in the week ahead. 'Don't, it's too late. Anything you do now won't make any difference and you'll just risk using energy unnecessarily.'

She turns to the most important tasks to remember during the ride. 'Take hairpins around the outside, it's the safest route; get in and out on the saddle to give your bum a rest, and bring two 500-millilitre bottles, one filled with water and the other with a powdered mix of carbohydrates and electrolytes.' She adds that I should eat every forty minutes and drink every twenty minutes, and refuel ten to fifteen minutes before the mountain – any sooner and I would risk feeling sick. She also suggests that I upgrade the wheels that came with my bike for a lighter pair worth at least about £200.

I agree that I will. If I cannot do anything about my fitness at this stage, I will pay whatever it costs to buy a marginal gain.

Like any sport, cycling is awash with stories of lost talent. Some, like Nikki, came to the sport too late to exploit properly their potential – though we should not write her off just yet. Others such as, say, Alf Engers, fell foul of the authorities and found that political resentment undermined them. Though Alf achieved much, he never transferred his talent abroad. As an amateur, that would have required him to be selected for the national team. A few other riders showed flashes of exceptional ability but lacked the ingredients required for sustained success. Mentally, they were too brittle, perhaps, or quite often too outspoken.

In 1985 Darryl Webster won every national time-trial title on the road, and also triumphed in the individual and team pursuit. He seemed destined for greatness – Alf Engers calls him the finest talent he has seen on a bike – yet he quit the sport within four years after a disastrous spell with Spanish professional team Teka. When I spoke to him, Darryl agreed that his divisive personality counted against him: he spoke his mind regardless of whom he offended, a ruinous trait at a time when professional contracts were so difficult to win and when only superstar cyclists could get away with not submitting themselves wholly to the will of the management. Darryl also believes his refusal ever to dope counted against him, at a time when it was endemic within the sport, though even he can point to a yet more gifted British cyclist who never went close to fulfilling the awesome potential he displayed as a young man.

He is not alone in citing Colin Sturgess as the great lost talent of that era, either. Tony Doyle described him similarly. Tony Cooke, father of the former Olympic champion Nicole, agreed that the gap between what could have been achieved and what happened was never greater than in Colin's case. They both thought that his story deserved to be told. What follows, then, is an account of how the greatest talent of his generation went from world champion to destitution and then produced an unlikely twist in the tale.

Colin lives with his parents in a small terraced house in Leicester. For a forty-six-year-old man, the situation is far from ideal but it is still a significant improvement on his previous accommodation and his parents, Ann and Alan, do their best to look after him, allowing Colin to store his time-trial bike in the small living room, for example. They prepare for us a generous lunch of cold meats, cheeses and salads.

Possibly they went to such effort because I have known Ann for a couple of years. A former cyclist herself, who once competed alongside Beryl Burton in the world road race championship, she helped to track down former greats of the sport for the British Olympic Association in the build-up to London 2012 and helped to put me in contact with a few of them, too. But I suspect her and Alan are keen also for what could potentially be a difficult afternoon to pass as smoothly as possible. That at least would explain their apparent nervousness and the touching way in which Alan frequently places a hand on Ann's to stop her from interrupting her son. Clearly, they do not want to say anything to upset Colin.

Apart from the occasional outburst of frustration at his mum – which you could understand – Colin, for his part, is apparently relaxed, even when discussing the most painful subjects. He is also articulate, succinct and a careful listener. You can see why boredom, as he admits, has been getting the better of him now that he is jobless.

Though the East Midlands has been the family home for three decades, their story begins in apartheid South Africa, to which they had relocated from Yorkshire after Alan was offered a job there as a telephone engineer. As an exceptional former club cyclist himself, who won the national team pursuit title among other accolades, Alan was keen for the family to maintain their cycling connection and agreed to assist in setting up the first organised races for schoolchildren in his new country. He also helped to break down a few racial barriers among the younger generation by encouraging kids from different ethnicities to race against one another.

Colin remembers his schooling in the sport fondly. 'Cycling was segregated in the '70s but, by the time we were there, things had opened up a lot,' he says. 'There were black and Indian riders and some really, really good cyclists. How on earth they ever managed it is phenomenal. They were living in bloody holes and shacks. How on earth would you afford to keep a bike running?'

Initially, Colin was an enthusiastic but unexceptional participant in the junior races. He would win occasionally but he did not take the pastime seriously. As Ann recalls, he was a 'bugger, because he was always freewheeling', though something in his attitude towards the sport changed when, aged thirteen, the family returned to England to watch the 1982 world track championships at the Saffron Lane velodrome in Leicester.

Usually, an impressionable kid would be taken in with the unpredictable drama of the sprint, but the pursuit transfixed Colin. 'I always liked more the endurance side of the sport. Sprinting was very exciting but there was just something about seeing the German funny bikes of the day and all this aerodynamic kit. Sprinters were just big powerful guys riding track bikes; there wasn't that bling factor to it. And, while you can flick through old cycling magazines as a kid, it's all black and white and it doesn't capture the imagination like seeing it physically. So that sort of drew me in: "Wow, I'd love to give this a go."'

Being so young, he began to train by riding with cyclists who were older and stronger than him, though not long afterwards Alan assisted in his development by suggesting that he paced Colin on his motorbike. For the pursuit rider, motor-paced training is especially efficient (and Colin would use it for years to come) because it allows you to travel at a higher speed for longer than you would doing interval training alone. Compared to using a training partner on a bike, the increased time in the slipstream also allows you to ride in a lower gear, encouraging a smoother pedalling style.

There were not many (if any) fourteen and fifteen year olds putting such thought into cycling in 1980s South Africa. As a result, and also because he clearly had an aptitude for endurance cycling, he emerged as the outstanding talent in his age group, claiming a clean sweep of his three events in the national junior championships as a sixteen year old: the kilo, the pursuit and points race. Ann and Alan had thought that they might want Colin to study for his A levels in Britain anyway but his cycling achievements persuaded them to relocate from Johannesburg.

With South Africa banned from international sporting competition, and training resources even more limited than in England, they knew that Colin could hope to fulfil his potential only within the British cycling set-up. That it meant giving up their comfortable expat existence didn't matter to them. 'Yeah, the lifestyle was a bit of a downturn but . . .' Alan says. 'We have survived,' Ann says, completing his sentence.

They returned to Leicester because Ann's sister lived there. That the national velodrome, the one at which the British team trained, was only walking distance from their home added to the city's appeal.

Colin's first significant event on his return was the national junior championships, in which he entered the three events that he had won in the equivalent competition in South Africa. This new contest would pitch him against the most promising young talent in British cycling, Chris Boardman, the prodigy from Merseyside who had smashed national schoolboy time-trial records and was on the fringes of the national senior team.

Boardman was confident and outgoing, whereas Colin was reserved. He had impressed with his race results on joining local club Zenith but few thought him capable of beating British cycling's bright young hope in the individual pursuit, Boardman's specialist event. Yet Colin managed that and also won the kilo, breaking the national junior record in both events. He finished third in the points race, too.

Not only did the performances suddenly place him among the elite of the sport but it triggered a tense rivalry with Boardman – who was only four months older than Colin – that would continue through their teenage years. Never once did Colin lose a pursuit to the future Olympic and world champion. 'Chris was always going to be good,' Colin says. 'As a schoolboy he'd won umpteen races and done all these fantastic times in time-trials. So I knew that this guy was supposed to be something super special and I think – well, I know – it put his nose out of joint when I came along and scuppered his ambitions.'

Colin defeated Boardman in the pursuit at the following year's nationals and, again, at the 1986 Commonwealth Games, claiming silver while his team-mate came eighth. At the next season's world championships, Colin broke his own national record and showed such promise against the best in the sport that he decided to postpone third-level education to concentrate on the 1988 Olympics in Seoul.

Once he had left school, then, the family began to operate like a small team, with Alan serving as Colin's coach – they followed an old East German training manual that Alan owned – and Ann taking care of his administrative needs. As had always been the case for Britain's best cyclists, particularly amateurs, he survived on a shoe-string budget. He was supplied with equipment and about £500 funding but otherwise, financially, he relied on his parents.

He could have made much more use of the coaching that the British Cycling Federation offered at the Saffron Lane velodrome but experience had taught him that the motor-paced work with his dad was more beneficial. It meant he was pushed much harder than his team-mates on the track.

'I didn't see the point in going down to the velodrome to ride maybe twenty 'k' a day of pursuit training when I could be out on the road smashing myself behind a motorbike for 100k. Plus, you can't ride an outdoor velodrome in the rain, so you would lose days' training.' In effectively opting out of the national squad's training programme, he cast himself as an outsider. This did not endear him to the management or to his team-mates. Arguably, it would count against him years later, as we shall discover. 'Yeah, I was always an outsider. No disrespect to the boys I was racing with but I was definitely not one of the clique.'

However hard he trained, though, he knew that the Olympics would present him with a formidable task. There, he faced supposedly amateur opponents from behind the Iron Curtain who lived and trained (and doped) like professionals, as well as the first graduates of Australia's Institute of Sport, which would turn it into the world's most successful track cycling nation.

In finishing fourth, then, he exceeded expectations. Had his semi-final not pitched him against by far the outstanding rider in the field and eventual winner, the Soviet Lithuanian Gintautas Umaras, he might have fared even better. 'It's mind-boggling to think what we were up against, the "State", the Russians, East Germans . . .'

Colin was far from disheartened. Aged nineteen, he knew that he had much room for improvement. Moreover, he could look forward to the prospect of turning professional with the Belgium-based team ADR, having signed a 'pre-contract' deal with them before the Games. This was one of the strongest teams in the peloton and had arranged for Greg LeMond to join them, too, as team leader, the 1986 Tour de France champion having recovered from a freak shooting accident that had forced him to miss the past two seasons.

For many riders, the first season in the professional road ranks is the hardest. Not only are you unused to the physical demands of the racing but many of the seasoned cyclists will endeavour to ensure that you serve a tough apprenticeship. By way of example, Colin recalls how even team-mates would occasionally leave him exposed until he had earned their respect. 'One of the old riders kept telling me to attack and I would, again and again, until this old pro rode up to me and said, "What are you doing? Don't listen to your team-mates. Use your head, man."'

Colin could hold his own in a sprint but he did not possess an exceptional kick, while his relatively broad physique meant that he could not compete against the best climbers. But his endurance ensured that he could shoulder more than his share of the work in a bunch. He was also determined and prepared to suffer, so he earned his contemporaries' respect in that first season. He even managed to claim a couple of kermesse victories and placed well in several other races.

The main event of his season, however, was the world championships in Lyon. The professional pursuit was often easier than the amateur because only road teams offered professional contracts then, limiting the amount of tailored preparation that its riders could undertake for the track. In 1989, however, this was not the case as the two strongest amateurs in previous seasons had graduated to the paid ranks with Colin. Umaras had joined the crack Soviet team Alfa Lum, while Australia's Dean Woods had signed for the German outfit Stuttgart.

Two years older than Colin, Woods had caught him in the Commonwealth final – with riders starting on opposite sides of the track in the pursuit, this eventuality secures victory – but Colin knew that he had since bridged the gap to him. Fitter than perhaps he had ever been after a season's hard toil as a professional, he felt he could challenge Umaras now too, only for the Lithuanian to withdraw mysteriously while in the velodrome. This left Woods and Colin to justify their seedings by reaching the gold-medal ride. Colin and Alan prepared assiduously. They correctly predicted that Woods would ride steadily until three kilometres were left and would then attack, hoping to build up an unassailable lead. In response, Colin decided to bide his time, ensuring that he remained within striking distance of his opponent heading into the final lap. Then he planned to kick for home.

It was a bold tactical plan and risked gifting Woods too much of a lead. Even the British TV commentator Hugh Porter, himself a former world pursuit champion who judged a race as well as anybody, said that he suspected Woods had 'timed his effort to perfection' as he triggered the bell with a lead of more than a second. However, though Colin had frequently demonstrated his ability to summon unexpected speed towards the end of a race, Porter had underestimated him and here too he began to strip back the deficit with astonishing ease.

Pursuit riders usually are among the most fluent and elegant of cyclists but, as Colin chased Woods down, he rocked across the saddle like a sprinter, shoulders swaying, head bobbing. Poor Porter said he could not believe it when Colin sat up before the end and still won by 1.66 seconds. Colin told the website Velo Veritas that 'I still get people saying it's one of the best pursuits they've ever seen'. Today, when I ask him if I was right in thinking that he looked across at Woods at the bell as if to let him know what was about to happen, he agrees, with a smile. 'I just knew I had Deano. I was just backing off, having a breather, knowing that he would have to be a second and a half ahead of me in the last kilo, and he wasn't.'

The tactic was chosen not only because it would earn him victory but also to entertain the crowd. In fact, Colin always tried to adhere to this even if it jeopardised his chances of success. 'It backfired a couple of times but nine out of ten, it just led to people enjoying watching me riding a bike because I had this electrifying finish. And it put the fear of God into many opponents, because they just . . . it almost psyched them out, even if I was having a really bad day.'

Even now Colin feels 'a buzz' when he watches this performance again. For Alan, whom you can see on the inside of the track, waving his arms, shouting out time-checks as Colin surges past him, it served as wonderful vindication of their homespun philosophies. Probably, it helped to earn Colin a new contract with the strong Dutch team Tulip when ADR collapsed as a result of its sponsor's withdrawal from the sport a year later, leaving Colin owed wages and prize money.

Unfortunately, with Tulip, his performances were solid if unremarkable. Perhaps most disappointingly, though he broke the five-kilometre world pursuit record, he could not repeat his heroics of Lyon on the track, but he insists that he probably would have won more than bronze at the world championships two years later had he accepted the offer of a shot of EPO from a prominent soigneur.

History has taught us to be sceptical about the legitimacy of any cyclist's achievements in that era. All we have to go on is anecdotal evidence. Some riders were 'known' to have doped and others were thought not to have done. Colin, from my experience, is one of the few that falls into the latter category. Nobody has ever accused him of it and several have said he was clean. Darryl Webster, for example, with whom Colin used to train in Leicester, will identify as dopers several former British team-mates who have gone on to hold prominent positions within the sport but he 'believes' Colin was clean. Tony Cooke says likewise, and the Cookes have been among the most vociferous critics of drug use in the sport.

Colin, for his part, suspects that his refusal to become involved in the drug-taking culture contributed to his career rapidly unravelling: when Tulip decided not to renew his contract, he could not find another employer on the Continent and, instead, joined a South African team. When they began to miss wage payments and failed to pay negotiated bonuses, he quit the sport and embarked on an English literature degree at Loughborough University.

It might be surprising to hear that he is not bitter about his treatment within cycling then. If anything, he is even more confident that he took the correct stance towards doping now that we know to what extent EPO and blood-boosting would infect the sport shortly after he departed it. To illustrate the point, he recalls an encounter in the late Nineties with his former Tulip team-mate, Brian Holm, the Dane who admitted to doping. 'I hadn't seen Brian for ages. And he said to me, "Oh man, you got out at the right time. Things got really ugly." So no, I'm not bitter. I chose one way – I chose not to – they chose to dope. I can look at myself in the mirror and say, "I would have made a shitload more money, I would have got more contracts, I would have won more", but I didn't, so I'm happy with that. I can look back on my career and go "I was clean, fine." Other people . . . they chose their own path.'

In the condemnation of drug use in cycling, the guilt that unmasked dopers must carry with them tends not to be mentioned. Yet while those who have been exposed generally are given the opportunity to repent, hundreds more are not. 'Exactly, and that guilt can destroy you,' Colin says. 'It can destroy your mind and your spirit. I know that because I've got enough guilt in my personal life through choices I've made.'

Many journalists will recognise the rookie mistakes that Colin made when he turned up to the 1997 world track championships in Perth with a commission to cover the event for an Australian magazine, his first big job in the industry since graduating from university and then emigrating Down Under with his Australian wife. He borrowed a laptop only to forget to ask for its password. He left his dictaphone in the office. All that he prepared for properly was his downtime, with full cycling kit packed.

At the time, he had been cycling only for fun, most often across off-road trails near his home in Sydney. Watching the competitors in his old event, however, stirred his competitive spirit and he felt the urge to ride the boards again. He borrowed a bike, got a friend to time him and was shocked when he clocked four minutes, forty seconds for four kilometres. That was quicker than some of the entrants who had not made it through qualifying at the pursuit. 'I thought, "Jeez, I wouldn't mind being here again".'

On his return to Sydney, he began training at the New South Wales Institute of Sport under the tutelage of Garry Sutton, brother to Shane, the future British Cycling technical director, and was thrilled to be selected for the Australian national squad. However, he could not imagine competing against

Britain and switched allegiance in time for the following season's Commonwealth Games. This was the first season in which British Cycling had benefited from National Lottery funding and the set-up was already far more professional than when Colin had previously competed.

As part of a quartet that included the young Bradley Wiggins, he won silver in the team pursuit in Kuala Lumpur, earning him a place in the Olympic development squad.

Suddenly Colin was motivated again. 'It was like I had the opportunity to right a few wrongs,' he admits. 'There was a feeling that I hadn't done what I could do and now I had a chance to put that right.'

Success did not come quite so easily to him this time, however. Perhaps years out from the sport had put him back physically. The standard among his domestic rivals had improved as well. However, he suspects his career did not take off quite as he hoped also for political reasons. Nicole Cooke's memory of Manchester-based riders teaming up against him in a race at the city's velodrome supports this interpretation. For his part, Colin admits that he did not fit easily into the new clique that had formed. There were some within the ruling body who remembered how he had snubbed the national set-up in years past. He was being paid less than riders who had spent more time in the system, too, and struggled to contain his frustration with the situation. As he says: 'There was a lot of politics at work behind the scenes and I didn't think it fair.' He walked out on the Olympic progamme. 'It was the hardest decision of my life and one that I still regret.'

Such impetuosity was not unfamiliar to Colin. Although it had not yet been diagnosed, he suffers from bipolar disorder, which makes it difficult for him to keep his emotions balanced.

Like all sufferers, he is vulnerable to enormous highs and crippling lows. On walking out on his Olympic dream, for example, he sought solace in the Sydney party scene and threw himself into it like he once did cycling, living the life that the sport had denied him as a young man, while earning just enough money to survive by working in a friend's bike shop. 'All I wanted to do was have a good time. I wouldn't even have smoked a cigarette as a twenty year old, yet now, alcohol, drugs, coke, pills and whatever, going out to nightclubs for days in a row.'

When eventually he tired of that lifestyle, he embarked on a new career in the wine industry and developed that, too, with the obsessive dedication that helped to make him a world champion. He managed both to produce his own wine and work as a sommelier, drawing up wine lists that won national awards and were short-listed for international honours. He revelled in the combination of the creative and technical skills that the work involved. 'This is a thing about the bipolar aspect of me. You change focus very quickly but you also want to be the best that you can be so, when I turned to the wine industry, I wanted to be so good.'

The problem with his choice of profession was that it also allowed him to indulge his addictive streak. He drank so heavily for so long that, in 2005, his wife of nine years walked out on him and took their six-month-old son with her. 'She came home one day from work, packed up all his goodies, packed up her goodies and left. We never really got to the crux of the matter, but I dare say my lifestyle wasn't what she wanted from a new father, so I don't blame her.'

The split was traumatic but he got through it. He held down his job and started taking medication, having finally received a proper diagnosis. Eventually he established another relationship and got married, only for his demons to contribute to its demise, too. This time he could not cope. He fell off the wagon, lost his job and ended up with nowhere to live. 'I don't mind saying it, I'd lost the plot entirely. It was a mess. We'd moved out of our own house back into her parents' house to try to save for a new place. So it was completely terrible for me to stay there.'

He moved into a backpackers' hostel. This was no place for a man in such a vulnerable state. 'My mental health went south, even worse than it had been. Drinking just went to shit, too, and I ended up sleeping in my car, sleeping in a tent. I had to break into an old run-down house one night because my tent was leaking and there was an abandoned house. I had to break in and sleep in a bloody spare room of the house just to save myself from getting torrentially wet.'

Colin talks about this period in his life without hesitation, even apparently without emotion, but beside him his parents clearly find it difficult, Ann especially. She has let slip a few tears and is unable to answer when I ask what this was like for them. To know that your son has repeatedly considered suicide is unspeakably hard. 'Oh I did, loads of times,' he says. The occasion that springs to his mind followed a row with his parents at around this time. 'I drove off to the top of a look-out on a dirt road with a bottle of vodka with suicidal thoughts. [I drove] 100k an hour down this dirt road.' The car tumbled down a twenty-foot embankment. 'Landed on its roof. Luckily, I wasn't wearing a seatbelt. As it landed, it shot me out. Broken ribs, all sorts of crap.'

Colin prefers not to think what would have become of him had his parents not intervened when word reached them that he had ended up destitute. They bought him a ticket back to England and arranged for a friend in Sydney to get him on the plane. He had nowhere else to go. 'I just left my life. It was devastating.'

This is how Colin ended up here, living back at home, trying to piece his life together again. The process has not run easy. Now on improved medication, he has not suffered another manic episode, though he struggles still with depression. The problem with the pills is that they dull Colin's creative streak. Recently he quit a job in a local cycling shop because he was so bored.

Instead, cycling now provides structure to his days. He tries to get out most days on a training run. Recently, at the age of forty-five, he won the League of Veteran Racing Cyclists' nineteen-mile national time-trial title by almost a minute. He has examined the times clocked at world masters championships and is confident that next year he could challenge for them, even though his medication makes him put on weight. He hopes by then to have found work as a cycling coach, too. More than anything else, he wants money to enable him to visit his son in Australia.

'My spirits have lifted since I've left work but the flip-side is you have more time on your hands and you think more and you almost dig yourself into depression, even though you have more time to ride your bike – which is fantastic because it releases the endorphins.'

The chemical benefits of exercise must be tremendously addictive for the full-time athlete. So, too, the frequent thrill of victory that the most talented of them enjoy. With hindsight, Colin realises now that his inclination towards such emotional extremes helped him to scale such extraordinary heights as a young man. 'It's like, when you've had a peak and you can't hold it, what comes next? The drop. I remember Mum and Dad pinpointing something early in my career – saying that if I had won a race on Saturday or Sunday, I was down by Tuesday, and if I had been away racing and had all these good results, I would always have a bit of a dip. I just kept thinking, "Gotta win, gotta win".'

There is much affection for Sturgess within the cycling community. Unusually among the elite of the sport, which like any close-knit community suffers as much backbiting as it does shared compliments, no one seems to have a bad word to offer about him. Dean Downing, the recently retired professional, calls him his 'mentor and a legend'. Tony Doyle writes by email: 'Colin was a real class act on the bike and he is a really nice guy. He needed to be protected, nurtured and guided. He never really found someone who could help direct him through the rough world of cycling.' Tony Cooke writes: 'Colin is a sincere guy. His life has taken some very difficult turns, with roots going back into his time in cycling. I think he probably didn't make the smartest choices in whom to trust and rely on. The dishonest in this sport rely on the fact that there are a lot of individuals who can be hoodwinked.' By that, Tony means the lies told by those involved in doping and the exaggerated promises that cycling management make to lure riders into a squad and then to keep them sweet. It did not help Colin that, in being so young when he turned professional and in being British, he lacked natural allies within the peloton.

For his part, Colin refuses to seek excuses for the problems he suffered. He knows that he must shoulder some of the blame, too. He will admit, for example, that he should have bitten his tongue more frequently when he disagreed with authority.

I wonder if he has ever looked at Chris Boardman and wondered what might have been. In the year that Colin slipped into his first premature retirement, his old rival won Olympic gold and became a household name. Famously, he went on to hold down a prominent management role within the all-conquering British cycling team, too, and set up an eponymous bike brand that he recently sold for £20 million.

'Yeah, there's been times I think, "Shit, if only. Why couldn't that have been me?" If I had won the Olympics, where would my life have gone? Would I have stayed on the track? Would I have gone for the hour record? Would I have just drawn a line under it and retired? "I'm probably going to make a million pounds in the next year, why bother working? Why bother with a bike any more?" There's all these thoughts, but the decisions were made and you live with them.'

A few months later I email Colin to congratulate him on what seems remarkable news. Not only has he landed a coaching job with a high-end company offering personalised tuition and international training camps, but he has signed up to ride with SportGrub Kuota, the British semi-professional team who compete in the Premier Calendar and selected UCI events among other competitions. According to the cycling press, team manager Andy Swain recruited Colin to add experience to his squad, having been impressed both by recent perfor-mances and his commitment. He has been riding almost 700 kilometres a week.

It seems like the closest thing to a Hollywood-style comeback that he could have hoped for. Unfortunately, his progress has not run as smoothly as fiction and he has suffered a back injury that has so far defied all treatment. 'I damaged a disc while sprinting,' he writes. 'I've been to chiropractors, physios, an acupuncturist, the sports medicine dept of Leicester General, all to no avail. I'm in the queue for another MRI, and then the wait for treatment. It's frustrating to get so close, but the comeback is on hold, for now . . .'

CHAPTER FIFTEEN

Why a military hero inspired
Nicole Cooke and her dad

Of the dozen times that Rick Grogan has completed the Etape, the most memorable one almost killed him. 'It was the day after my first Etape,' he says, over lunch at a restaurant in Victoria. 'We had a summit finish in Les Deux Alpes. I left and drove into Burgundy and the next day I took my bike out for a twenty-mile spin. Not more than a mile from the end, I was on a descent doing thirty miles an hour, and I went head-first into a car going forty miles an hour. I don't remember much of that.'

According to his medical reports, this London-based American businessman suffered twenty-eight fractures, required 500 stitches, survived two brain haemorrhages, had bleeding on the cerebellum and broke nine teeth. 'I basically took a bite out of the windshield,' he says.

He was resuscitated on the road and airlifted to hospital in Dijon, where he spent six days in a coma and a month interned. He required months to recover his basic motor-functioning skills and waited even longer for his memory to return fully. Tony Doyle, a friend of Rick's, helped to nurse him through his recovery, drawing on his experience from his similarly horrific head injury to provide advice and inspiration.

It was through Tony that I heard about Rick. I have asked to meet him because he has more experience of the Etape than anyone of my acquaintance and I am hoping that he might be able to offer practical advice. Before we discuss the event, however, I want to find out more about the cycling trips that he organises for a group of men called Hazbins, who might just be the most powerful collection of amateur cyclists in the world. He has previously refused to disclose their identities despite the attempts of business journalists. He has also declined to reveal what is involved in the trips, which started two decades ago, but seems ready now to change his mind.

I am grateful for this because, from what I have been told, the Hazbins might just exemplify cycling's modern transformation from a working-class pursuit to the preferred passion of the high-rolling businessmen and their ilk better than any other institution about which I have heard. 'I am reluctant to do this,' he says, having tied his folding bike to a nearby tree, 'but seeing as you've got some of the details, I figured I had better make sure you got it right.'

A Harvard graduate and once an elite rower, who won world championship gold with the American lightweight eight in 1974, Rick took up cycling while working in London in the 1980s as an alternative way to satisfy his competitive streak. At the same time, he was developing a formidable career in business and, in 1987, carried out Britain's first major, leveraged buy-out when he took over a packaging company called Cope Allman in a deal worth about £260 million. Although he will not give it a name, this remains his profession: buying and improving companies.

In time, he discovered that several of his old university friends had also taken up cycling, so in 1992 he arranged for a small group of them to embark on a week-long holiday ride from Geneva to Nice. The itinerary involved 100-mile days in the saddle and required them to climb Alpe d'Huez. As most of his companions were also former rowing champions, they relished the challenge and the competition between them. As the trips continued and word of them spread among his connections in London and America, they grew in ambition and size.

As Rick explains, once he has finished catching up with the restaurant owner – Rick used to live near by and came here often – his destinations are carefully chosen for their landscape and sites of cultural interest. Last year they visited American civil war battlefields. They travel with a support car and ask Tony Doyle to travel as ride leader, setting the pace, telling people when they need to accept their limitations and quit for their broom wagon. On their most recent trip, they hired the coach used on President Obama's campaign trail.

Rick calls on the most distinguished after-dinner speakers, usually experts relevant to the destination. On the battlefields tour, the esteemed writer and biographer Walter Isaacson spoke to the group. Supreme Court Justice Stephen Breyer has also addressed them. On a trip to Switzerland, they stopped off at the UCI headquarters in Aigle and Pat McQuaid, former president of the sport's ruling body, closed down its track so that the group could ride on it. They often use their connections to arrange for tourist destinations to be closed so that they can clip-clop through them alone in their cleats. If you are not envious by now, you must be cold-blooded. Or rich.

So, who are the Hazbins? I might be wrong but I've been

told they include a few of the most influential men in Britain and America. Is it true, for example, that Lord Foster attends? 'Oh yes,' says Rick. 'Norman first heard about us when we were about to ride the pilgrimage route to Santiago de Compostela.' The celebrated British architect was borrowing Rick's helicopter at the time. In his late seventies, he has become among the most committed of the Hazbins. 'He is also probably the most determined person I've ever met. He comes every year, he prepares for it, he rides well and he never, ever gives up. His wife has said I've changed his life.' Sir Rocco Forte, the British hotelier worth £250 million, is another name I have heard mentioned. 'Yes, Rocco has been a few times, though he has been injured recently, and is more of a triathlete than a cyclist.'

For all his reluctance about name-dropping, Rick admits he is uncertain whether some would be more upset at being omitted than identified. Thus he adds a few more names: Michael Gollner, once head of Citigroup's private equity business, who trains with Rick in Richmond Park; Tony Mallin, the former vice-chairman of Hambros Bank, who rowed for Britain. You imagine these trips do not want for testosterone.

I'm also interested in the American contingent. They include Dick Cashin, the banker who founded the private equity arm of JPMorgan Chase. 'Tom Foley comes, too. He could be the Governor of Connecticut in a month.' This Republican was previously the US ambassador to Ireland. Rick Haythornthwaite, chairman of the Southbank Centre in London, also attends. 'I've been trying to get John Kerry to come but he's just not been able to so far,' Rick adds, as if it were strange that the US Secretary of State could not find room in his schedule for a good cycling trip. Actually, thinking about it, it does seem a little odd. I mean, we are all busy, right?

'There's another guy. I was told about him eight, nine years ago. I was in Boston and I was asked to confer with him on something. He told me that he rode every day from his home to MIT, I told him I had an idea.' The idea was the Hazbins. 'It took years, though, to get him to come, but he comes every year now.' Apparently, Tim Berners-Lee, the English inventor of the internet, is much more confident in the saddle now, too.

If ever there was proof that cycling has replaced golf, or at the very least joined it, as the corporate activity of choice then the Hazbins is it. Rick claims that you have only to request to join the group to join it (unless you invented the internet or run America, presumably). Before you think of dropping him an email, though, beware that this group of overachievers remain fiercely competitive, holding twenty-two miles an hour in the bunch. Tony Doyle says: 'If you get a puncture, Rick pretends he hasn't seen you. If you're a few minutes late to start, he's out the gate and down the road.'

Rick once invested in cycling, too, becoming a co-sponsor of the US Postal team built around Lance Armstrong, though that experience warned him against putting money into the sport. Asked about Armstrong, he sighs in exasperation. 'He was always difficult, very self-absorbed. He would come to meals with his cap pulled down over his face, wouldn't talk. But we never thought . . . I remember one year, watching the time-trial, outside of Paris. I was sitting there with Lance's mother and a sponsor at the finish, watching a TV. We were so caught up in the emotion of the moment: the triumph over adversity, the story. We all looked back with perfect hindsight and realised these things were impossible but, at the time . . .'

Now he keeps business and pleasure distinct, cycling most mornings around Richmond Park, marvelling at the many more cyclists he encounters than he did a decade ago, ensuring his fitness for the Hazbins trips and occasional organised events such as the Etape or next year's Paris-Roubaix.

When I ask him what advice he would give an Etape debutant, he suggests a reconnaissance (too late) and to resist the temptation to be drawn into a competition with the aggressive riders who will inevitably be taking part. He also suggests that I am careful to drink at least twenty bottles of water during the ride. He once bonked when he consumed only about half that amount. Just before we finish up, he remembers one final piece of advice, though I suspect he might not be serious about it. 'Listen, don't go on a recovery ride, OK?' he says, with a half-smile.

Outside the press tent at the Cheltenham Literature Festival, having just finished a question-and-answer session in which she was typically forthright and composed, Nicole Cooke, the former Olympic and world road race champion, is laughing as she recalls how she had to rewrite her recently published autobiography to make it less depressing. 'There was one – probably the second version of the book – where I thought, "Cor, this is getting a bit sad and heavy" and I asked myself, "How *did* I keep going when all these things were falling apart?",' she recalls, looking relaxed and appearing to enjoy the positive reception that the book has received on its release.

The compliments were all the more satisfying because Nicole, who has just finished her MBA, wrote it herself. Aged only thirty-one, she was a loss to cycling but you suspect she will be a welcome addition to whichever field of work she enters next.

That first draft of her book, *The Breakaway*, became heavy when it reflected on the persistent knee injury that threatened to rule her out of the 2008 Olympics. On reading the auto-biography in its entirety, however, you wonder how she could summon the determination to carry on at many points in her career.

For Nicole, who has agreed to chat before I sit down to interview her father to discuss his unusually pivotal (and largely unheralded) role in her success, spent the best part of two decades overcoming the most demoralising obstacles as a cyclist, from the time she struggled to find road races for teenage girls to the years she spent on the European professional scene – where wages often went unpaid and races disappeared through lost sponsorship.

As she detailed in the explosive statement that she delivered on her retirement in 2013, she encountered carefully imposed, barely concealed doping regimes, too. There were riders who discussed their preferred substances on training runs, and team-mates whom she discovered injecting substances into one another in her bedroom.

She repeatedly had to tackle problems at management level, too, specifically with British Cycling in its nascent years. For as Nicole explained earlier to the TV broadcaster Jill Douglas, who was hosting the Q&A session at Cheltenham, the list of issues she had with the ruling body was long and damning. Perhaps the most hurtful incident involved the team plan for the Olympic road race at those 2008 Games, in which she was made a decoy rider to help her team-mate Emma Pooley target gold even though Nicole was the No.1-ranked rider in the world. Unlike Nicole, Pooley trained within the British Cycling system.

For years, all that kept her going was the ambition to conquer the sport that she had taken up as a girl riding the hills around her home in Wick in the Vale of Glamorgan. 'I just had this dream that was still burning,' she says now.

The dream was quite specific. As a ten year old, Nicole had watched on TV as Robert Millar attacked on Mont Ventoux at the 1993 Tour de France. Two years later she decided that she wanted to win the women's version of the Tour, the Grande Boucle (which until 1998 was known as the Tour de Féminin), and Olympic gold in the road race. She fulfilled both, the former after a Millar-esque solo attack on Mont Ventoux – hence the book's title – and the latter after that decoy-rider plan backfired and Nicole won with a sprint finish.

Both, effectively, were solo victories in a career that was littered with them. For as you read her book, and marvel at the number of confrontations with authorities, you realise that she never had the support that many of her contemporaries did. You also discover that she was a throwback to a different age in that she emerged through the club scene and climbed the ranks of the sport because she loved it, not as a result of being hot-housed by a British Cycling system that often identified its best young talents by going into schools and subjecting pupils to physiological tests, regardless of whether they had even ridden a bike before.

You also realise on enjoying *The Breakaway* that, without her father's input and support, none of Nicole's success would have been possible. Hence the interview I have arranged with Tony. I want to hear what compelled him to fight so hard for his daughter, soliciting the most powerful figures in the sport, challenging national coaches and officials, generally making himself a nuisance because he knew that he knew better. Many parents might have had the desire but few would have had the knowledge, confidence and sheer bloody-mindedness.

It is, of course, a story that I have not examined in this book. I have encountered a wonderful range of heroes, spoken to their partners, coaches and training companions, but I have yet to meet a mentor, someone who made a champion the person they were and there can be few better examples in cycling of a wise old guiding hand than Tony Cooke.

As we queue for coffee, and Tony quizzes me about the book I wrote on Reg Harris, it is clear quite quickly that his knowledge of the sport is excellent. He can describe the domestic racing scene in the 1970s in detail and knows all of the names that crop up. He raced with Coventry CC, too, although he didn't achieve as much as his brother, who competed at national level.

Tony transferred that knowledge and passion to Nicole when he introduced her to cycling, though he was never a pushy parent. Nicole has said that, if anything, the opposite was true.

'No, she was always very self-motivated,' Tony says, recalling how she would push him and her brother Craig to ride faster when she felt they were slacking on the commute to school. Tony is a science teacher.

'She's still the same. Whilst Nicole's been doing her MBA she has ridden in with me, but she goes on into Cardiff. It's an hour and a half one way, an hour and forty-five minutes the other and she's done that every day. She finished her MBA and, last week, she says, "No, I'm not coming into school with you, Dad, I want a longer ride."'

He might not have needed to push Nicole but he jockeyed those in charge whenever he felt the entrenched sexism of the sport was holding his daughter back. This happened often in her teenage years, when they discovered that there were no races over the distance that she wished to compete, or that arcane rules prevented a youth from racing against seniors, even though she was quicker than them. She proved her point perhaps most dramatically when, aged fourteen, British Cycling informed her by letter that she was not allowed to enter the 800 metres event at the national championships and she responded by defeating its winner in an open age-group omnium at the same event.

At other times, Tony was forced to address what he felt were grave shortcomings with the ruling body's treatment of his daughter. He wanted to know why national squad training camps clashed with crucial exam periods, for example. He could not understand why its coaches did not reconnoitre host cities and courses, forcing him often to book accommodation for his daughter because he did not trust them to get it right. He admits that British Cycling's focus on the track in its nascent years contributed to what he perceived as his daughter's inadequate treatment. Another factor was the management's inexperience in running a professional, elite sport. The problems they faced still get him worked up now, sitting beside a children's play area years later on this sunny afternoon.

Reflecting on those formative years in Nicole's career, he is relieved that she was not hot-housed in the manner of so many – often successful – products of the BC academy. 'I actually wrote to BC about that very point and said: "Look, your coaching staff are just not seeing the wider picture of the development of these young adults. They are not mature enough to make whole life decisions, they need guidance and the pressure your staff are putting on them is inappropriate." I got a response saying: "We offer training facilities and opportunities. It's up to the riders and their parents to decide whether they wish to use them."'

He felt also that BC did not prepare Nicole or other riders properly for what they would face on the Continent when she turned professional, especially the doping that was endemic then and would have been familiar to at least some of the former professionals employed to coach the next generation (many of whom, Tony felt, should not have been given work because of this very 'familiarity'). This led to heartbreaking telephone calls with Nicole while she was abroad. She would tell her dad that she felt much of her dedication was pointless when she knew some of her rivals were doping.

Nicole and Tony also had to contend with being sidelined by BC even though she was her generation's outstanding talent. Being picked as a decoy rider at the 2008 Olympic Games was far from an isolated incident. She was overlooked for the Sydney Olympics as a seventeen year old despite having spent the best part of a season defeating BC academy cyclists. In 2001 she was refused a place in the British squad after a disagreement over the extent of the coaches' authority.

Tony strongly suspects they suffered because they did not toe the authority's line. 'At many times it was tough. There were tears on the end of the phone, there were tears when she came back from Manchester from that team meeting for the Olympics in 2008. There were so many times I saw my daughter's efforts thwarted. She banged her head against brick walls so many times and got a bloody forehead and I shared that with her . . . all the letters I wrote on her behalf.

'I used to think, "How could these guys [at BC] have

so few morals?" I think it's so wrong to be so unfair and so prejudiced in the way they distributed public funds. Did they not understand what being a public employee is? I'm a teacher. I know that, regardless of who is in front of me and how they got there, the colour of their skin or what they do, I'm going to do my best for every one of those children in front of me.'

This sense of civic duty is, it seems, key to Tony's character and should help to explain the fiercely principled streak in Nicole that has made her such an outspoken critic of doping and sexism in cycling. In her retirement statement she rounded on those exposed dopers such as Tyler Hamilton who had profited from describing their experiences. In her Q&A at Cheltenham earlier, she criticised the UCI president, Brian Cookson, for reneging on his manifesto promise to introduce a minimum wage for professional female cyclists. 'Well, we wouldn't want to be a generation that would let down others,' Tony says, when I bring up this conscientiousness that has marked out the Cookes.

Tony has always been careful to uphold the precedent set by his antecedents, especially those who were involved in the military. Tony, for example, served in the Territorial Army for sixteen years. During the Cold War, he was in charge of 100 men supporting a Royal Artillery regiment defending 'assets' on the border with Eastern Europe. It was an uncertain period but the thought of shirking it never occurred to him. 'We were right there, not far from the curtain,' he says. 'We never saw any action but we knew that, if it did come to the trigger, we were going to come out second best against the much larger forces massed across the border.'

More recently he and his wife Denise attended a memorial service in France for a relative who served as an aircraft navigator during the Second World War and died when his plane was shot down. 'Nicole wasn't able to come, she was finishing her MBA, but we wanted to represent his side of the family. Our whole family is very proud of military tradition – we cut all that out of the book.'

The tradition stretches back to Denise's grandfather, who, shortly after D-Day, rescued a German pilot from his crashed and burning Messerschmitt. For saving his life, the pilot presented Denise's grandfather with a Luftwaffe watch. That has been passed on and Nicole's brother, also a pilot, now has care of it. Tony's father was a teenage scout during the Second World War and was on watch and first-aid duty during the Nazi bombing of Coventry, while the public sought refuge in air-raid shelters.

As these stories flow from Tony, I point out the irony in such a scrupulous family producing a daughter who was exceptionally talented in such an unscrupulous sport. 'Indeed. As I say, you don't want to be in a generation that lets down all the good work of the others. You'd rather walk away from the sport.'

Is he glad, then, that Nicole has retired, even though, conceivably, she had several more years left at her physical peak, knee injury notwithstanding? 'Yes I am. I think Nicole has done enough fighting.'

From several perspectives, Nicole was the most recent in a long line of 'outsiders' in British cycling, from Percy Stallard to Ian Steel and from Mandy Jones to Tony Doyle, to others not covered in detail in this book such as Reg Harris, Chris Boardman and Graeme Obree, all of whom achieved through intuition, persistence and often in spite of the system rather than because of it.

When I ask Peter King about his relationship with Nicole, the most successful British road cyclist during his reign in charge of the sport, he admits that it was fraught and did not dovetail with his vision for the British elite. 'It was difficult because they were always so dogmatic. My first real encounter with Tony was having to drive down to the services on the M4 – somewhere near Swindon – to meet him driving from Wales, to discuss whether she could go to an event or how she would go – would she go with a team or separately. And there were lots of incidents like that, and I was always prepared to meet them or talk to them, but if you've got rules and you've set up the system to do things in a certain way, you can't just change them for individuals.'

In other words, there was no longer a place for the maverick, visionary rider. 'It's true that in the past the people who succeeded were those who did their own thing in their own way,' says Peter. 'The difference is, once you bring in Lottery funding, you have to have a structure, a set of rules that work for everybody. British Cycling now is the ultimate no-compromise, win-at-all-costs medal factory and, to be that, you have to have certain parameters from which you're not going to stray.

'I don't know. It's a shame that Nicole's retired from the sport as young as she has, but these things happen . . .'

CHAPTER SIXTEEN

The Etape or, in other words,
the worst experience of everyone's lives

In a cramped triple room in a cheap hotel in Lourdes, above a bar in which a group of drunk-sounding German pilgrims have chosen to celebrate their visit with an unholy and almost unbroken singsong, I am trying unsuccessfully to fall asleep. Also in the room, on adjacent, single beds, sated after an evening carb-loading on beer and pasta, Andy and Chris have long since nodded off. Andy is snoring more loudly than a church organ, while Chris is murmuring in his sleep.

Possibly he is apprehensive about what awaits us in the morning. I know I am. We made the mistake this afternoon of parking up and looking at the lower slopes of the Pyrenean mountain range that we will attempt to cross tomorrow. Having just left the excited atmosphere of the Etape 'village', where we had signed in, I initially found the sight of the mountains awesome, even inspiring, but the reality of the task ahead has begun to sink in.

Perhaps I have been naive but only now has the thought struck that this challenge might prove beyond me. Certainly, I have no real idea what is required to complete it. How could

I have done when the closest task to it that I have undertaken is repeatedly scaling one hill in Essex? Not only that but the organisers have issued a weather warning, urging riders to bring with them clothes that will help them to survive near-freezing temperatures on the Tourmalet. Though conditions are known to be changeable up there, such an announcement is apparently highly unusual. I spoke to a veteran of ten Etapes who had never previously known of one. This could be the most difficult Etape yet.

I re-read my coach's last-minute, emailed instruction on my iPad. 'Most important is that you remember to ride at your own pace,' Tony says, 'regardless of the pressure to follow others, especially at the start when there will be a massive adrenaline rush.' He expects many riders to be swept along by the celebratory mood of the event. 'You have to keep in mind what it is you are trying to achieve,' he continues. 'You're there to experience participating in and completing an Etape. Don't let those early moments fool you. There is a long way to go, especially with the two mountains coming towards the end of the route. Always take advantage of the shelter of the bunch and concentrate on being helped along at an easy pace.'

Jens Voigt, the forty-two-year-old veteran of the Tour, coined the phrase 'shut up legs', but Tony insists it is better to listen to them, especially on the flat, 'feeling the sinews, the tendons' so that they only ever feel light and rhythmic. Only on the mountains should they feel heavy and tired. 'A good gauge is whether you are able to hold a conversation,' he adds. 'At no point on the flat should you be too tired to talk to people around you.'

He offers key points to remember at the worst moments on the climbs, urging me to bear in mind how often I have pushed myself to the point of exhaustion when interval training but still been able to recover in the saddle. It occurs to me that my longest interval has been three minutes, whereas it could take as long as two hours to conquer the Tourmalet, but I take his point: you can ride long after you want to give up. To ensure I use the descents for recovery, he says that I should use a low gear, pedal quickly and never ride so quickly that I do not feel in control of the bike. 'As long as you determine the pace and intensity of your ride at all points,' he writes, 'then you will decide how much you enjoy the experience from the occasion and how good will be your memory of it.'

It is a salutary point: I am here to enjoy myself. Unfortunately, dawn is but three hours away. I log off, bury my head beneath the duvet and pray that the faithful will soon stop singing and go to bed.

The scenes inside the ski shop in the village of Barèges resemble more a panicked January sales rush than a sleepy Pyrenean commune. One man is desperately trying to swap his sunglasses for a beanie hat. 'They're Oakley, worth 200 euros. Oh mate, please.' Another cyclist has called his wife at home in Britain on the shop phone so that she can pass on his credit card details. A woman walks in, shivering, and breaks down in tears, such is the physical torment that she has just suffered on the Tourmalet.

Nobody, it seems, was prepared for it. On the climb, the wind was icy cold and the rain relentless. The summit resembled a misty, lunar landscape. I passed cyclists wrapped in foil at the side of the road to prevent them from descending into hypothermia.

The descent was even worse. I had not envisaged that my

temperature would plummet because my body was not required to work. I suffer from Raynaud's syndrome, making it difficult for blood to reach my extremities. My fingers turned so cold that I spent fifteen minutes in a cattle shed trying to warm up. There were about twenty of Europe's keenest amateur cyclists doing likewise.

Now, in the settlement about halfway down the western side of the Tourmalet, I am sitting on the floor, wrapped in a ski jacket provided by staff. Beside me is a man in his twenties who looks even colder than I feel. Unlike him, I at least have a long-sleeved top and leg warmers. His skin looks translucent. 'I've never known anything like it,' he says, sipping on piping hot coffee, his hands shaking.

Nor have I. The experience has been so traumatic that I have begun to do what no athlete – amateur or professional – should while attempting an endurance event. I am pondering the meaning of it and I am not sure that there is one.

The Etape provided me with motivation to ride over the past six months or so. It helped to get me fit and ensured that I improved my technical knowledge of the sport. It also meant that I spent a little more time with my closest friends than I might otherwise have done. But now I cannot summon one good reason for subjecting myself to further punishment. I could quit now happy in the knowledge that I had scaled one of cycling's greatest peaks in the most formidable circumstances. In the fifty miles leading up to the Tourmalet, I had experienced the thrill of riding on closed roads, too, with riders forming impressively disciplined groups and locals cheering you on.

It is not as if my quitting will affect anyone else. I do not know where my friends are. Andy split us up by attacking when

I suffered a mechanical. In trying to catch him up I left the others behind, but they have probably overtaken me now. I have been in the shop for half an hour.

'Is there a train station in the village?' I ask my shivering companion.

'No. The only way out is to ride,' he says, his eyes vacant. 'Besides, you can't quit. Either you get pulled out or you keep going.'

Cyclists who fail to keep within given time limits are thrown into the 'broom wagon', the coach that follows the race. Rumours have been circulating the shop that it is within about forty-five minutes of the village.

I am tempted to wait and hitch a lift but my companion is right. I cannot give up, not after all the heroic cycling tales I've listened to in the past year or so. For any cyclist a moral imperative insists that he or she should never give up, regardless of however perverse it may seem to continue.

I stamp myself slightly less cold and join the other cyclists swiftly removing the shop of its stock. I buy mittens, an oversized fleece, thermal socks and balaclava. The beanies are sold out. As I step out into the village, I look like a burglar in winter.

It is much quieter now. The storm has passed and the waves of cyclists have reduced to a trickle of lone riders. In the bar on the opposite side of the road, a group are huddled around a small radiator by its entrance, taking turns to stand beside it. I resist the temptation to join them and return to the saddle, eventually returning to blessedly flat or gently inclined roads.

While initially the ride was collegiate, then competitive, now it is reflective. The thoughts that float to the surface of your mind at such moments probably say something important about your character. If so I might need therapy, for all I can do is castigate myself. Could I really be so bad to be this far behind the vast majority of entrants? Why did I not find the time to put in more preparation? How daft must my ski outfit look?

Intermittently, spasms of pain in my calf muscle provide an unwelcome distraction. This first happened while climbing the Tourmalet when the convulsions were so violent that I struggled to retain control of the bike. I assume that it is cramp, the ailment of the unfit, and try to ride it out. Months later, I will discover that I have ripped the muscle and, with each pedal stroke, probably widened the tear.

I can do nothing about my aching thigh muscles. As I discover when I stop at the final food station before the Hautacam, I find it harder to walk now than to ride. Fig and Tom are here, too, eagerly refuelling.

'Worst experience of my life,' says Fig, munching on a baguette.

'Me too,' Tom says, filling his pockets with energy bars. 'Where have you been?'

'I stopped,' I say. 'I was cold. I almost packed it in. But then I went shopping.'

I hold my arms out so that my hands disappear into the cuffs of the fleece.

'I'm boiling,' I admit.

'Get rid of it then.'

'No chance. This cost sixty euros. Plus it might be cold on the Hautacam.'

When the Hautacam was last included on the Tour route, in 2008, the Italian cyclist Leonardo Piepoli won a race that featured attacks and counter-attacks right up until the finish at the summit – as ours is today. Piepoli and his closest rivals Frank Schleck and Juan José Cobo attacked the mountain with childlike enthusiasm, and to a backdrop of lush vegetation and clear skies. It did not look *that* hard.

It *is* hard. Within about ten minutes of beginning the climb I feel as though I am in a world devoid of oxygen. Half an hour on, I have endured pain more prolonged and uncomfortable than I thought I was capable of. At the same time I have suffered the sight of Andy and Chris descending on the opposite side of the road, chatting and joking, apparently carefree. They even waved.

Of the three of us, Tom breaks first, fifty yards ahead, and is now bent over his frame. I am the next to dismount, about a kilometre from the summit. Fig, who has been riding my wheel, wants to stay with me. But, like some fatally wounded soldier, I urge him to go on alone. 'I'll only hold you back,' I say, a touch melodramatically.

As I join the queue of walkers and push my bike up the twelve per cent slope, I can see Fig scaling the remaining hairpins staircased on the mountain, with Tom behind him. Both seem liberated by the sight of the finish. They also seem hours ahead. Cycling lore says you can never beat a mountain but you can suffer defeat on one. Even though I summon the energy to ride the last three kilometres, I cross the finish line unhappy. Not only have I lost to the mountain but, worse than that, I have lost to all of my friends.

'It's over,' Fig says, striding towards me, clearly ecstatic. As we take it in turns to snap photographs of one another, I try to stifle my disappointment. Fig and Tom do their best not to notice, even allowing me a moment alone to reflect on the stunning sweep of the Pyrenees visible beneath the gathering grey clouds.

'Best get moving,' Fig says eventually. 'Don't want to get caught in another storm.'

'Yeah, I guess not,' I reply. 'But at least I'm dressed for it.'

Over the telephone from Vancouver Island, in an accent that betrays the five decades he has spent living in Canada, Tony Hoar is describing what it felt like to suffer worse pain than he had ever known on his first mountainous cycle race. It was during the 1955 Tour de France and Tony was one of only two members of the ten-man British team still left in the race.

'I had the lines of this poem going through my head,' he says. He is referring to 'The Gladiator' by Lord Byron, which he had learnt at school. '*He leans upon his hand; – his manly brow/Consents to death, but conquers agony . . . And through his side the last drops, ebbing slow*, and the final line: *Butchered to make a Roman holiday*. And that's what used to come to my mind, that we're being butchered for other people's entertainment. Everybody is watching you climb these mountains and they're all fine, relaxed and we're killing ourselves.'

Tony became only the second Briton to finish the Tour when he came in last, behind his team-mate Brian Robinson, in 1955. Robinson, the Yorkshireman who went on to become the first Briton to win a stage on the Tour and enjoyed a storied career, is the more celebrated rider. When it was announced that the 2014 Grand Départ would be staged in his home county, he was interviewed more often, it seemed, than any former British rider. But Tony's story is worth retelling, too. Arguably, he overcame greater odds than Robinson to finish the Tour that year. His experience is also more likely to resonate with the typical amateur. It should certainly provide them with inspiration.

Born in the Hampshire town of Emsworth, on the south coast, he learnt his craft riding grass tracks and on hard tracks at Brighton, Southampton and Portsmouth, making his name as a powerful sprinter. 'I won tons of races on grass. I found I could win on grass long before the hard tracks.'

He also possessed impressive stamina, having finished third overall in the eight-stage An Post Rás in Ireland and having won two stages of the 1955 thirteen-day Tour of Egypt. At that time, he was working as a plumber for his brother but he did not have to think twice about giving it up when he was offered a place on the Hercules team shortly afterwards. It gave him a weekly salary of £10, which then was about double the average wage.

Hercules was an ambitious sponsor. In the belief that it could capitalise on the growing interest in road racing, it made sure the team enjoyed more privileges than British riders had been accustomed to. At the training camp they had a villa, servants and unlimited food. All that they lacked was any tactical direction. 'There was no routine, say, "OK, we'll do 100 miles a day, do some sprint training", nothing,' says Tony, who is now eighty-two. 'We never really focused on the Tour, nothing of the sort.'

Perhaps because he was known predominantly as a track rider, Tony was not one of what *Bicycle* magazine called the five automatic choices for Britain's Tour team. The five were Robinson, who by then was Britain's most prominent rider, Ian Steel, Dave Bedwell, a.k.a. the Iron Man of Romford, Bob Maitland, the former national road race champion, and Fred Krebs, runner-up in the national road race. They were all included in the final squad.

That only Robinson had much experience of racing abroad was evident within the first couple of days of the Tour when all of the other Britons repeatedly suffered punctures. Robinson had brought his own tyres, but the others had agreed to use what Dunlop had supplied. 'It was a grass-track tyre and they put a road tread on it, God knows why,' Tony recalls. 'We had said, "Well, make sure that they're mature" because tubulars in those days usually had to mature for six to eight months so the rubber got hard.

'Anyway, we had nothing but punctures. We were waiting for team-mates day after day and, finally, we cut one open and they'd only just made them before the race so they were too soft. So we switched to Pirelli tyres and didn't have any more problems. The good thing was we still got our sponsorship money from Dunlop. I think it was 200 quid!'

Only two Britons had previously entered the Tour, Charles Holland and Bill Burl, and both of them failed to finish in 1937. By the twelfth stage of the 1955 Tour, with Mont Ventoux behind them, only Robinson and Tony remained of the British team. 'Some of the guys probably shouldn't have started,' Tony says. 'They just weren't up to it.' Team morale was not what it could have been, with the members of the domestic Hercules team dominating the squad, leading to internal rivalries. 'It's not a good way to have a team. Mixed teams like that.'

Robinson performed commendably, reaching as high as eleventh in the general classification, before finishing nineteenth. Tony, however, endured a very different Tour. As riders behind him in the classification gradually dropped out, he became one of the two main contenders for the lanterne rouge, or 'red lantern', given to the last-placed rider overall. (It was named after the red lantern that used to hang from the back of trains to illuminate them.) The French press loved this. It provided them with a novel story: the plucky Brit who was trying to finish last because it would bestow on him unlikely fame. The winner of the lanterne rouge then won contracts for post-Tour races not given to other riders who finished ahead of him.

Except that Tony was not trying to finish last. 'I didn't even know such a thing existed,' he says. 'I didn't know they had a name for it until I was there. When the press were making a fuss [I thought], "They're pissing around here. They've nothing better to do."'

When only five stages were left, it had become almost certain that either Tony or Henri Sitek, a Frenchman riding for the Mercier team, would scoop the questionable honour. Each day, newspaper men would ask them to drop off the back of the bunch and pretend they were fighting a private duel. 'It was bullshit,' says Tony. 'I don't think I ever saw him in the race unless they came and got him.' Sometimes they asked Tony to pose with a red lantern, a patronising request that only worsened an already onerous task. As none of the bunch waited for them they were fortunate that the commissaires would at least turn a blind eye as they drafted team and press cars to get back on.

Tony admits that he rode in the knowledge that the 'broom wagon was out there, somewhere', but insists that he finished inside the time limit on every stage. Official results, however, say otherwise. On the second day in the Alps he crashed in a tunnel and finished more than four minutes outside the cut-off mark, but was allowed to continue for reasons unclear. Perhaps the organisers showed leniency to the Briton – who was heavier than most other Tour riders – who had never previously ridden across mountains and who spoke only a little French, the language of the peloton.

'On the climbs sometimes I'd be on my own, other times you'd team up with a few domestiques. I ended up with a guy from the French team, Bernard Gauthier, a sprinter who was on the national team. He would get spectators to push him and people would push me, too. It would nearly kill them, pushing you for twenty to thirty yards.' What motivated him to carry on? 'Well, I was getting paid to ride and I wanted to finish the Tour. That was quite a thing and I knew I was capable of it.'

At one stage, he witnessed a scene that presaged a notorious chapter in the Tour's history. On Mont Ventoux, he recalls passing Jean Malléjac and several of his companions on the France team. Tony was struck by their deathly, goggle-eyed countenance. Moments later Malléjac would be on the ground, still turning his pedals, apparently hysterical. Later he would claim that his water bottle had been spiked with drugs.

When Tom Simpson died twelve years later on the same mountain, some would regret that the lessons from what happened to Malléjac that day had not been learnt. 'I never took dope,' Tony says. 'I knew that if I wanted to win races [I would have to]. You're going to get the odd win. Later that year I had a stage win in the Tour of Holland and I was second on the last day, but you're not going to be consistent because you don't take that stuff they're all taking, but I just thought that was the most stupid thing anybody could do to their bodies.'

By the time the peloton reached Paris, Tony was assured of last place. Well positioned in the bunch, he is confident that he could have beaten Robinson to the line in Parc des Princes to become the first Briton literally to finish the race. But that felt unfair on his team-mate. 'Brian was not renowned as a sprinter and, although I had never contested a sprint with him, I felt I could have beaten him into Paris. It was a hard day but I'm sure I could have done it because I was up there with the bunch. He was above me in the classification but I would have been the first to finish the Tour. But he'd done the better ride.'

Tony says that he has not previously admitted to this quietly selfless act. I wonder if he regrets it.

'I think letting Brian through was a silly thing to do,' he says, laughing. 'I should have fucking sprinted it.'

Tony retired a year later, abandoning the Vuelta a España because he was frustrated with the chaotic organisation of his combined Swiss-British team. At a time when the life of a professional cyclist was never less than precarious, to walk out on the sport in such circumstances was perfectly understandable. Soon afterwards he emigrated to Canada, having fallen in love with its landscape and lifestyle when he competed in the 1954 Empire Games in Vancouver. He has lived there since but retained strong connections to cycling. He helped set up the International BMX Federation and ran four world championships, until the UCI scented an opportunity and muscled in on them. He organised and raced in veterans' competitions. He still rides several times a week.

In the workshop attached to his home he builds wheeled trailers and transport for people with physical disabilities. We speak late until the evening his time, but he says he will then return to his latest commission and continue on it until about midnight. 'I get orders from all over the world. There's no end to it really. I'm always up at about seven. I take the dogs out or go for a ride and I start working by nine and I'm in there most nights until twelve. It's just me. I do it all, the design, the cutting and welding.'

I balk at his work ethic but then realise that the same attitude helped him to get through that seminal Tour, ensuring that he set a vital precedent for any young, emerging and relatively inexperienced British cyclist who was uncertain whether he could tackle the toughest race of all.

EPILOGUE

On a cold Sunday morning in March, with everybody else in the Essex village of Debden apparently asleep, I am holding a flag out the back window of Twig's car while a pack of about sixty racing cyclists follow us through the high street. Twig is driving and his daughter, Marie-Cait, is on the walkie-talkie beside him. 'Drop it!' she says, as the rows of pretty houses give way to countryside. I withdraw the flag, signalling the end of the neutralised section of the Crest road race, and Twig presses on the accelerator to allow the riders to increase their pace. To judge by his speedometer, the bunch is travelling at about twenty-five miles an hour. 'That's about what you would expect for a race like this,' he says. 'It will be interesting to see if they can hold it, it being so early in the season.'

The course is seventy miles, which is long for a spring race but the added distance means extra points, which attracts entrants. The course is a new one for the Crest. It cuts a loop around the town of Saffron Walden and traverses one steep 100-metre hill. In three and a half hours, we lap it eight times.

Just looking through the back window, at the four-man

breakaway that eventually decides the race, is tiring. I had to spend three months off the saddle to allow my calf muscle to heal. I hardly cycled for several months after that while I was writing this book. I fear that the benefits of the miles I covered in preparation for the Etape have been lost. Cycling, like any endurance sport, is cruel like that.

I have, however, learnt to feel satisfied about what I achieved at the Etape. After all, about 3,000 cyclists did not finish it. And, while I resisted the urge to wait for the broom wagon, I learnt that many others actively sought it out. Apparently, there was a party atmosphere on board.

I also realised the benefits in what I had endured. I demanded more of myself physically than I had ever done and I found I was more determined than I had imagined. Everyday physical annoyances – tiredness, hunger, for example – now seem to bother me a bit less than before.

I earned the respect of the Crest and gained a greater appreciation of the challenges faced by elite cyclists. It has been said before but I relate to them a little differently, especially those from decades past, the amateurs with little support and experience, and sometimes a day job to work around.

I also experienced the sweet, surprising satisfaction of getting through something so difficult in the company of friends. As Rick Grogan said: 'No one enjoys pain. You have to be sick to enjoy pain, but there is something enduring, something intense, in suffering with friends that your average person might not understand.' For that reason, three of us have already signed up for the next Etape. Time to begin training again.

ROLL OF HONOUR

Selected palmares for cyclists interviewed in this book.

Ian Steel
Date of birth: 28 December, 1928
Born: Glasgow

1951
Winner, Tour of Britain
Winner, road race, Scottish championships

1952
Winner, Peace Race
Winner, road race, national championships
Winner, Wolverhampton-Llangollen-Wolverhampton
road race

1953
2nd, road race, national championships

Tony Hoar
Date of birth: 10 February, 1932
Born: Hampshire

1954
3rd, An Post Rás (Tour of Ireland)

1955
69th, Tour de France

Vin Denson
Date of birth: 24 November, 1935
Born: Chester

1964
72nd, Tour de France

1965
Winner, Tour of Luxembourg
87th, Tour de France

1966
Winner, Stage 9, Giro d'Italia

1968
62nd Tour de France

Beryl Burton
Date of birth: 12 May, 1937
Born: Leeds

1959
Winner, individual pursuit, world championships
Winner, road race, national championships

1960
Winner, individual pursuit, national championships
Winner, road race, national championships
Winner, individual pursuit, world championships
Winner, road race, world championships

1961
Winner, individual pursuit, national championships
2nd, road race, national championships
2nd, individual pursuit, world championships
2nd, road race, world championships

1962
Winner, individual pursuit, national championships

1963
Winner, individual pursuit, national championships
Winner, road race, national championships
Winner, individual pursuit, world championships

1964
2nd, individual pursuit, world championships

1965
Winner, individual pursuit, world championships
Winner, road race, national championships

1966
Winner, individual pursuit, national championships
Winner, road race, national championships
Winner, individual pursuit, world championships

1967
Winner, road race, national championships
Winner, road race, world championships
3rd, individual pursuit, world championships

1968
Winner, individual pursuit, national championships
Winner, road race, national championships
2nd, individual pursuit, world championships

1970
Winner, individual pursuit, national championships
Winner, road race, national championships
3rd, individual pursuit, world championships

1971
Winner, individual pursuit, national championships
Winner, road race, national championships

1972
Winner, individual pursuit, national championships
Winner, road race, national championships

1973
Winner, individual pursuit, national championships
Winner, road race, national championships
3rd, individual pursuit, world championships

1974
Winner, individual pursuit, national championships
Winner, road race, national championships

1975
3rd, individual pursuit, world championships
Burton also won 71 national time-trial titles. She won the
British Best All-Rounder competition 25 years in a row.

Denise Burton-Cole
Date of birth: 24 January, 1956
Born: Yorkshire

1973
2nd, road race, national championships

1975
2nd, road race, national championships
3rd, individual pursuit, world championships

1976
Winner, road race, national championships

1978
2nd, road race, national championships

1985
2nd, Tour Féminin

Alf Engers
Date of birth: 1 June, 1940
Born: London

1969
Winner, individual time-trial (amateur), national
championships

1972
Winner, individual time-trial (amateur), national
championships

1973

Winner, individual time-trial (amateur), national championships

1974

Winner, individual time-trial (amateur), national championships

1975

Winner, individual time-trial (amateur), national championships

1976

Winner, individual time-trial (amateur), national championships

British time-trial competition records:

1959
25 miles: 55min 11sec

1969
25 miles: 51min 59sec
25 miles: 51min

1975
30 miles: 1hr 2min 27sec

1978
25 miles: 49min 24sec

Reg Barnett
Date of birth: 15 October, 1945
Born: London

1967
Winner, sprint (amateur), national championships

1968
Winner, sprint (amateur), national championships

1969
Winner, sprint (professional), national championships

1970
Winner, sprint (professional), national championships

1971
Winner, scratch race (professional), national championships
2nd, sprint (professional), national championships

1972
Winner, sprint (professional), national championships

1973
Winner, sprint (professional), national championships

Ian Hallam
Date of birth: 24 November, 1948
Born: Nottingham

1970
Winner, individual pursuit, Commonwealth Games
2nd, individual pursuit (amateur), world championships

1972

3rd, team pursuit, Olympic Games

1973

2nd, team pursuit (amateur), world championships

1974

Winner, individual pursuit, Commonwealth Games
Winner, team pursuit, Commonwealth Games
3rd, 1km time-trial, Commonwealth Games
3rd, scratch race, Commonwealth Games
3rd, road race (amateur), national championships

1976

3rd, team pursuit, Olympic Games

Willi Moore
Date of birth: 2 April, 1947
Born: Liverpool

1972

3rd, team pursuit, Olympic Games

1973

2nd, team pursuit (amateur), world championships

1974

Winner, team pursuit, Commonwealth Games
2nd, individual pursuit, Commonwealth Games
2nd, road race (amateur), national championships

Mick Bennett
Date of birth: 8 June, 1949
Born: Birmingham

1972
3rd, team pursuit, Olympic Games

1973
2nd, team pursuit (amateur), world championships

1974
Winner, team pursuit, Commonwealth Games

1976
3rd, team pursuit, Olympic Games

1977
Winner, sprint (professional), national championships

Tony Doyle
Date of birth: 19 May, 1958
Born: Middlesex

1978
3rd, individual pursuit, Commonwealth Games
3rd, team pursuit, Commonwealth Games

1980
Winner, individual pursuit (professional), world
championships

1983
Winner, Berlin six-day
Winner, Dortmund six-day

1984
2nd, individual pursuit (professional), world championships

1985
2nd, individual pursuit (professional), world championships
Winner, Bremen six-day
Winner, Maastricht six-day

1986
Winner, individual pursuit (professional), world
championships
Winner, Copenhagen six-day
Winner, Launceston six-day
Winner, Berlin six-day
Winner, Dortmund six-day
Winner, Grenoble six-day
Winner, Ghent six-day

1987
2nd, points race (professional), world championships
3rd, individual pursuit (professional), world championships
Winner, Copenhagen six-day
Winner, Veneto six-day
Winner, Maastricht six-day

1988
2nd, individual pursuit (professional), world championships
Winner, Bremen six-day
Winner, Rotterdam six-day
Winner, Paris six-day
Winner, Munster six-day

Winner, Berlin six-day
Winner, Dortmund six-day
Winner, Munich six-day

1989
Winner, Cologne six-day

1990
Winner, Munich six-day

1991
Winner, Ghent six-day

Colin Sturgess
Date of birth: 15 December, 1968
Born: Wakefield

1986
2nd, individual pursuit, Commonwealth Games

1989
Winner, individual pursuit (professional), world
championships

1990
Winner, road race (professional), national championships

1991
3rd, individual pursuit (professional), world championships

1998
2nd, team pursuit, Commonwealth Games

Nicole Cooke
Date of birth: 13 April, 1983
Born: Swansea

1999
Winner, road race, national championships

2000
Winner, road race, junior world championships

2001
Winner, road race, national championships
Winner, individual time-trial, junior world championships
Winner, road race, junior world championships

2002
Winner, road race, national championships
Winner, road race, Commonwealth Games

2003
Winner, road race, national championships
3rd, road race, world championships

2004
Winner, Giro d'Italia Femminile
Winner, road race, national championships

2005
Winner, points race, national championships
Winner, road race, national championships
2nd, road race, world championships

2006
Winner, Grand Boucle Féminine
3rd, road race, world championships
3rd, road race, Commonwealth Games
Winner, road race, national championships

2007
Winner, road race, national championships
Winner, Grand Boucle Féminine

2008
Winner, road race, national championships
Winner, road race, Olympic Games
Winner, road race, world championships

2009
Winner, road race, national championships

2010
3rd, road race, national championships

2011
2nd, road race, national
championships

INDEX

ACKNOWLEDGEMENTS

There are several people I need to thank for playing an important role in making this book happen. Humfrey Hunter, my agent, came up with the idea on which it was based and provided expert support during the writing of it. Iain MacGregor was kind enough to commission it and provided just the right encouragement when I needed it. Richard Green and Melissa Smith took up the baton at Aurum when Iain moved to pastures new. Melissa, especially, managed its production smoothly and skilfully.

David Edwards did a superb job of editing the book. Roger St Pierre played a vital role in that too, calling on his remarkable knowledge of British cycling to ensure (hopefully) the book's accuracy. Michael Breckon and John Browning, of the Crest, were more helpful than I could have rightly expected. In fact, I am grateful to all the members of the Crest for being such a welcoming bunch.

Tony Harvey went beyond the call of his duty as a coach. (Any novice cyclist in Essex or east London should hire him. If he can turn me into a half-decent rider, he will do the same for you.) I am grateful, too, that my good friends agreed to join me on the Etape at considerable expense. Most of all, though, I am indebted to the brilliant cyclists who agreed to open up and tell their stories in such detail. Without their co-operation, the book would have quickly run aground.